Combining a detailed ethnography of women home [care workers] of Britain with a precise and thorough examination [of doc-] trine and statutes regulating their work, *Stories of Care* [is] an important contribution to socio-legal research on care work and labour law. Hayes deftly uses character narratives to bring the challenges that home care workers face to life, and she deploys sophisticated social theoretical lenses to show how existing labour law doctrines devalue this emblematic form of women's work.

Judy Fudge, Professor of Labour Law, Kent University, UK

This is an outstanding contribution to the growing field of feminist labour law scholarship: imaginatively conceived and crafted, this is a boundary-breaking critique which uses the voices and experiences of homecare workers to trouble doctrinal categories and challenge received understandings of how law and labour interact.

Joanne Conaghan, Professor of Law, University of Bristol, UK

A rare and valuable insight into the lives and views of women who work in the little-known world of homecare for rates of pay and conditions that shame our society. That there is a correspondence between the predominant gender of the workforce and its low profile and meagre reward is inescapable.

David Brindle, Public Services Editor, The *Guardian*, UK

An utterly compelling account of public sector abuse and labour law failure, but with informed and positive ways forward. Perhaps the best ever example in modern labour scholarship of research-led recommendations. I am unable to think of any as good.

Keith Ewing, Professor of Public Law, Kings College London

We are nothing without the care and support of others. We are most when we understand and truly value the work our carers do to hold our society together. Lydia Hayes has shown through her deep analysis of the stories of a range of care workers how badly undervalued their work is. So, given their increasing importance to our society, her excellent analysis and call for the full recognition of the true importance of their work, could not be more timely.

Robin Allen QC, Cloisters Chambers, UK

An innovative and meticulous combination of ethnography and legal analysis. *Stories of Care* lays bare that homecare provision is built on multiple and deep-seated injustices towards working class women. It makes a compelling case for the state to re-craft labour law and merits a very wide readership.

Lizzie Barmes, Professor of Labour Law and Co-Director of the Centre for Research on Law, Equality and Diversity at Queen Mary University of London, UK

Lydia Hayes illuminates vividly the gendered injustices embedded in home care work in the UK, tracing their origins in discriminatory labour laws and the privatization of social care; firmly grounded in the seldom tapped knowledge of front-line workers themselves, her analysis will be of interest to Canadian, US and wider audiences striving similarly to resist the market-driven degradation of home care work and care in the community.

Jane Aronson, Professor of Social Work, McMasters University, Toronto, Canada

Stories of Care:
A Labour of Law

Gender and Class at Work

LJB Hayes
Lecturer in law and holder of the Law and Society Research Fellowship, Cardiff University

© LJB Hayes 2017

All rights reserved. No reproduction, copy or transmission of this publication may be made without written permission.

No portion of this publication may be reproduced, copied or transmitted save with written permission or in accordance with the provisions of the Copyright, Designs and Patents Act 1988, or under the terms of any licence permitting limited copying issued by the Copyright Licensing Agency, Saffron House, 6–10 Kirby Street, London EC1N 8TS.

Any person who does any unauthorized act in relation to this publication may be liable to criminal prosecution and civil claims for damages.

The author has asserted their right to be identified as the author of this work in accordance with the Copyright, Designs and Patents Act 1988.

First published 2017 by
PALGRAVE

Palgrave in the UK is an imprint of Macmillan Publishers Limited, registered in England, company number 785998, of 4 Crinan Street, London, N1 9XW.

Palgrave® and Macmillan® are registered trademarks in the United States, the United Kingdom, Europe and other countries.

ISBN 978–1–137–61115–4 hardback
ISBN 978–1–137–49259–3 paperback

This book is printed on paper suitable for recycling and made from fully managed and sustained forest sources. Logging, pulping and manufacturing processes are expected to conform to the environmental regulations of the country of origin.

A catalogue record for this book is available from the British Library.

A catalog record for this book is available from the Library of Congress.

To my darling Alun

Palgrave Socio-Legal Studies

Series Editor
David Cowan, Professor of Law and Policy, University of Bristol, UK

Editorial Board

Dame Hazel Genn, Professor of Socio-Legal Studies, University College London, UK

Fiona Haines, Associate Professor, School of Social and Political Science, University of Melbourne, Australia

Herbert Kritzer, Professor of Law and Public Policy, University of Minnesota, USA

Linda Mulcahy, Professor of Law, London School of Economics and Political Science, UK

Carl Stychin, Dean and Professor, The City Law School, City University London, UK

Mariana Valverde, Professor of Criminology, University of Toronto, Canada

Sally Wheeler, Professor of Law, Queen's University Belfast, UK

Contents

	Introduction	1
1	Cheap Nurse (and equal pay law)	30
2	Two-a-Penny (and the protection of employment)	72
3	Mother Superior (and the national minimum wage)	114
4	Choosy Suzy (and the Care Act)	153
	Conclusion	194
References		205
Index		220

Stories of Care:
A Labour of Law

This book was made possible by the generosity of Phil Thomas and board members of the Journal of Law and Society editorial board who agreed to fund my three year research fellowship at Cardiff Law School. I am immensely grateful to all the women who participated in my research, as well as to everyone who has commented on the work in progress, engaged with conference papers and helped me to develop ideas. Special thanks for their advice and inspiration are due to Emily Grabham, Lucy Series, Tonia Novitz, Nicky Priaulx, Angela Devereux, and Ambreena Manji.

Introduction

As the final credits rolled, film director Ken Loach made his way to the front of the cinema to respond to audience questions. His film, *The Spirit of '45*, had captured the public determination and political will that had built Britain's welfare state. Someone sitting near me asked Ken about his motivation for film-making. I fumbled in my handbag, grabbed a pen and immediately copied down his answer on the inside cover of a notebook:

> I see it as my job to make pictures of the world, to share them with other people, hoping they might better understand their own lives, and our place within the world that little bit better.

Here was a very simple explanation for the book I wanted to write. I was inspired to follow my methodological instinct and to paint pictures of the world, not with moving images but with words, the words of homecare workers.

In this book, I create word pictures (which I call character narratives) as points of departure from which to explore how hierarchies of class and gender structure the everyday experiences of homecare workers. To see the world through the eyes of homecare workers means viewing homes as workplaces, seeing physical dependency and mental impairment as a source of employment, and understanding acts of caring as paid work. This perspective challenges many conventional assumptions about caregiving. It also offers distinct insights into law at work.

For homecare workers, legal protections *at* work and legal protection *of* their work are frequently problematic, inaccessible or unenforced. By drawing together techniques of doctrinal analysis with richly detailed descriptions of caring for a living (assembled in the sociological tradition of 'ethnography'), this book offers a critique of law from the perspective of an occupational group who are systematically denied protections or privileges that are routinely available to others. It assembles the first extensive portrayal of UK homecare workers and is set in the context of severe cuts to public spending which have followed the global financial crisis of 2008. Unique within the international body of literature about paid caregiving, this is an ethnographic account which places law at work centre stage. It is an imaginative contribution to labour law scholarship and provides much-needed evidence about how law and adjudication relate to working lives and society.

Homecare workers help clients (or 'service-users') with the most intimate and personal aspects of living: eating, drinking, dressing, taking medicine, using the toilet or managing incontinence. Their caregiving also supports people at the end of life by maintaining discreet routines and promoting personal dignity. In line with demographic changes seen in many other parts of the world, the UK population is ageing. The rising demand for elder care has prompted the state to shift financial resources away from institutional care and towards the provision of care in people's own homes.[1] The homecare industry is now a major source of employment. Across the UK there are approximately a million jobs in which workers provide care at home to older and disabled people; the size of the workforce is expected to double within a decade (Centre for Workforce Intelligence, 2013; Skills for Care, 2013).

Homecare employment raises distinct issues in labour law, in part because the work is almost exclusively performed by women, it is low paid and takes place in private homes. As the research in this book testifies, the state has organised and reorganised homecare services in ways that maintain the employment of homecare workers at the margin of its own regulatory capacity. Yet homecare workers are far from being the only low-waged workers in the UK for whom employment protections have little positive effect (Pollert and Charlwood, 2009; TUC Commission on Vulnerable Employment, 2008). The utility of labour law is under active scrutiny in many advanced capitalist countries (Fudge et al., 2012). On the one hand it is discredited for creating supposed business inefficiencies which impede 'free' markets, while on the other it is discredited for being unable to protect marginalised workers from exploitation and inequality.

Women have traditionally been excluded from, or marginalised within, the labour market, in large part due to the gendered assignment of unpaid care work within families. Yet in recent decades, governments in the UK and across the European Union (EU) have actively promoted women's engagement in the labour market as a route to economic growth. In particular, the focus was a shift from out-of-work to in-work welfare schemes, backed up by state provision of support/care services such as childcare facilities, after-school clubs, residential care homes, homecare support, day centres and

---

1 Care needs typically increase with age and about half of the population aged over 75 has a life-limiting long-term illness (Office for National Statistics, 2013b). As the population ages, the length of time for which elderly individuals are living with a disability at the end of their lives is increasing – for men, it is an average of 7.5 years; for women, 9.7 years (Office for National Statistics, 2014b).

meals on wheels provision for the elderly. Now that record numbers of women are 'economically active', states have transferred responsibility for the delivery of support/care services to a rapidly expanding private-sector market and systematically withdrawn from direct state provision (Hayes and Moore, 2017). Hence, labour law sits at the intersection of a regulatory nexus which includes the need of state actors and individual citizens to purchase care services at low cost, the need of corporations to generate profit from caregiving, the need of women providing paid care to have good quality employment, and the need of service-users to have trust and confidence in the quality of care provided. While marketised care services are an international phenomenon, each national system of labour regulation is legally distinct. This is because labour laws are shaped by distinct national welfare systems, cultures and industrial histories, as well as by their legislatures and legal traditions. In this book, I address the unique position of homecare workers in the UK labour market. However, since homecare workers around the world occupy a unique position in national labour markets, my research has a deep international resonance (Anderson, 2003; Bernstein, 2006; McCann and Murray, 2014; Meagher and King, 2009; Smith, 2013; Stacey, 2011).

I have adopted socio-legal methods which are especially relevant for understanding how the work of homecare is perceived, interpreted and influenced in three ways: as an everyday experience, through the legal regulation of work and in the political and economic organisation of care. Each strand generates stand-alone knowledge through which homecare might be credibly analysed. However, by binding these strands together I explain how the impoverishment and the persistent disrespect of homecare workers pass as being socially permissible; how the undervaluation of homecare work has become embedded in the organisation of the industry; and why politicians have so easily evaded responsibility for the inadequacy of marketised homecare services. While the words of film-maker Ken Loach provided inspiration for my research methods, his film *The Spirit of '45* also gave me pause for thought since the voices and stories of women were largely absent from his account of the emergent welfare state. This reflection made me acutely aware that homecare workers' experiences in today's labour market are situated within an historically gendered welfare state, as well as of the contradictions which arise from the juxtaposition of its egalitarian principles with the chronic undervaluing of its female workforce. It has been claimed that contemporary socio-legal research frequently places empirical knowledge in a secondary position to that of theoretical knowledge (Flood, 2005). However, theory is applied in this book as a research tool with which to shed light on social interaction. Homecare workers are not theorised as the objects of legal regulation; rather, they are regarded as the participative and experiencing subjects of law at work.

In the chapters that follow, I sequentially trace how working-class women who make their living by providing care in other peoples' homes are widely judged to be inferior participants in the labour market. Such judgments (whether legal, managerial, political, cultural or otherwise) find expression in poverty pay, disrespect and low social status. I identify the persistent and pervasive judging of homecare workers as a process of 'institutionalised humiliation'. It will be immediately apparent that this term concerns neither an emotion nor the feelings of an aggrieved individual. Rather, institutionalised humiliation captures the failure of respect afforded by the state to homecare workers as a collective group; homecare workers' own recognition of being unjustly treated as a group; and the lived reality of economic and social detriment.

The judging of homecare workers as inferior labour market participants takes many institutional forms. We might immediately think of judicial decisions, which define or redefine the parameters of what is known to be law, impose the will of law on parties in conflict, or establish the standing of individuals as legal subjects. However, politicians serving in Westminster, the Scottish Parliament and the Welsh Assembly also exercise judgments about homecare workers. These are communicated in speeches, parliamentary reports and through the legislation they scrutinise and endorse. In addition, homecare workers are subject to institutionalised judgment by governments, particularly since governments take decisions about the allocation of state resources to express the social and political priorities of the day and establish who matters, whose interests are to be protected and how this will be done. Other judgments about homecare workers are carved and communicated in the formulation of social policy, in its content and promotion. Much of this filters down to the level of local government where, at community level, social policy is put into practice. Homecare workers are also under scrutiny through the communicative power of mass media. Press and broadcasting organisations judge homecare workers, either by overlooking them or through news or current affairs programmes that question their competence and motivation.

The multidimensional expression of institutionalised humiliation is a common thread which weaves together the elements of law and legal reasoning, poor quality employment and the stripping away of social care provision, with which this book is concerned. My methodological approach is founded on a basic proposition: that individual experiences of working life in the homecare industry are shaped by social assumptions about the personal qualities, motivations and character of homecare workers as a collective group. It is by showing how these assumptions are expressed in legal doctrine, and how employers, politicians and judges act upon them, that I explain how institutionalised humiliation is created and reproduced.

A process of institutionalised humiliation underpins many of the failings of Britain's homecare services for older and disabled people. In a contemporary context, age-old sexist ideas about the inferiority of women are reinforced and reaffirmed as sexist ideas about the inferiority of homecare workers. Gendered messages about the low status of care work are not monophonic. This interdisciplinary study draws evidence from the accounts of homecare workers, from case law and statutory instruments, from media reports, parliamentary debates and social policy documents. However, my primary focus is on connecting experience of working life to the legal doctrine and statutory provisions that give legitimacy to wide-ranging judgments of inferiority. Consequently, I explore the role of law at work in the subordination and disadvantaging of working-class women.

Poor-quality employment in homecare

Unprecedented cuts to public spending in the UK have followed the financial crisis of 2008 and fiscal austerity programmes have been implemented by successive governments. Severe cutbacks in adult social care provision since 2010 have resulted in about one-third of elderly people who would previously have been entitled to state-funded care now being ineligible (Age UK, 2015).[2] Some people pay for additional hours to top up minimal state provision, others entirely self-fund their care. However, a growing number of people face the consequences of neglect because they are too poor to pay and family support is either unavailable or insufficient to meet their needs.

The provision of paid care at home is absolutely essential to meet the care needs of older and disabled people in contemporary society yet employment rights abuse in the homecare industry is widespread and terms and conditions are poor. The occupation is culturally aligned with expectations of privacy because work is located inside the homes of service-users and the intimate nature of personal care also marks it out as a 'private' undertaking. Nevertheless, there is a wealth of publicly available evidence that hundreds of thousands of homecare workers are paid so little that their wages do not meet the minimum amount required under national minimum wage law. The workforce is predominantly engaged by private-sector employers and is subject to contracts that offer no guarantee of regular hours and make wages insecure; earnings are irregular, as well as insufficient to meet basic economic needs.

---

2 Central government spending on adult social care fell by 26 per cent between 2010 and 2015; further cuts in 2015/2016 were approximated at £1.1 billion; and services for the elderly were the most severely hit of all social services (ADASS, 2015).

The homecare industry is financed predominantly via the public purse (estimated to be worth £5.2 billion annually, of which 80 per cent is state-funded (Francis, 2013a, p. 7; Holmes, 2015, p. 10). Local authorities have a legal duty to meet the assessed care needs of older and disabled people. Since the 1990s, local authorities have reduced the proportion of homecare they provide directly and instead contract with commercial care companies and trading charities. These organisations engage in competitive tendering exercises and act as 'care providers' within local authority areas. In Scotland and Northern Ireland, approximately two-thirds of jobs lie outside of the public-sector; in Wales, four-fifths of homecare employment is no longer with local authorities (Holmes, 2015). The privatisation of homecare is a process for which there is no foreseeable possibility of reverse; it is most pronounced in England and available figures suggest that in England, when the care at home workforce is considered in its entirety, a mere 3 per cent of jobs remain with public-sector local authorities.[3]

Of all Britain's low-waged sectors, including the sizable retail and hospitality sectors, it is the adult social care sector that now employs the largest number of women in low-paid jobs (Hayes, 2015a). As a whole, the sector includes care provision in nursing/residential homes, day-care services and meals on wheels, yet homecare is its largest and fastest growing occupational group. When the Equality and Human Rights Commission (EHRC) undertook an investigation into the extent of disregard for human rights in the provision of homecare it noted that service delivery contracts between commissioning local authorities and care providers very rarely include any reference to terms and conditions of employment, even though local authorities are aware that low pay impacts on the quality of care services (EHRC, 2011, pp. 73–4). In over 90 per cent of local authority areas, the hourly rate at which homecare services are commissioned falls below the rate the industry claims is necessary to fund its compliance with minimum labour standards (UKHCA, 2014). Given the poor quality of employment on offer, it is perhaps unsurprising that the homecare industry suffers from a higher annual turnover of labour than any other sector in the UK economy. Over one-third of workers leave their jobs each year and about half of all new recruits move on to a new job within less than 12 months.[4]

Two-thirds of older people think that the standard of social care in the UK is inadequate and an even higher proportion believe that politicians consider the needs of older people to be a low priority (Age Concern

---

3 Between 1993 and 2011, the proportion of state-funded homecare delivered by the non-public, 'independent' sector (some charitable, but mainly private companies) rose in England from 5 per cent to 90 per cent (HSCI, 2012, p. 46). From 2011 to 2015, the number of direct caregiving jobs with local authorities fell by a further 32 per cent (HSCI, 2016).

4 In 2015, annual labour turnover in the private sector was 32.4 per cent (Holmes, 2015, p. 34).

and Help the Aged, 2009; TNS, 2015). However, despite these difficulties, the homecare industry is booming. Care companies provide employment to many hundreds of thousands of women (and some men); many thousands more are employed directly by service-users as 'personal assistants'; and there is an increasingly significant flank of self-employed workers operating through agencies or taking on assignments with their own service-user 'clients'.

The demographics of paid care work

The study of caregiving as a social role traditionally assigned to women has been a central concern within feminist scholarship. Academic attention has predominantly focused on caregiving as the unpaid work of kin within families, and the denigration and undervaluing of care work has been theorised as symptomatic of gendered inequalities between men and women (Duffy, 2005; Graham, 1991). Since the organisation of care is a primary site for the expression of gendered social relations, feminist scholars have tended to conceptualise the work of care as an unpaid activity which is assigned generically to 'women'. As a consequence, the impact of social class on the contextualised assignment of these responsibilities has been underexplored (Glucksmann, 2005; McKie et al., 2002). Hands-on caregiving is not a significant source of employment for *all* women, but rather it is the preserve of the working class. For many working-class women, caregiving responsibilities exist in paid and unpaid forms, giving rise to experiences of gender that lie outside a middle-class frame of reference. In a working-class context, gendered relations of caregiving are relations of employment.

However, in recent years there has been growing academic interest in the paid work of care. This is reflected in important considerations of trade union organising among care workers (Boris and Klein, 2014; Briggs et al., 2007; Lopez, 2004); of the management practices that maintain low pay in the care sector (Bolton and Wibberley, 2013; Palmer and Eveline, 2012; Rubery et al., 2015); of care workers' construction of personal identities (Aronson and Neysmith, 1996; Stacey, 2011); and of the deregulation of caring labour (Bernstein, 2006; Hussein and Manthorpe, 2014; Rubery and Urwin, 2011). Academic literature about paid care work has also been enriched by consideration of its racialised history (Duffy, 2011), the racial diversity of the care workforce (Anderson, 2000; Duffy, 2005; Duffy, 2007) and explorations of transnational 'care chains' through which labour flows from the global south to the north (Fudge, 2011; Hochschild, 2000).[5]

---

[5] My work on the racial experience of homecare work evidenced in data gathered from this research project is the subject of a separate project and forthcoming journal articles.

Prior research about the UK adult social care sector has evidenced that employers rely upon the availability of migrant labour to manage chronic difficulties in recruitment and retention (Ruhs and Anderson, 2010). For example, over 60 per cent of social care workers in London are foreign-born (Barron, 2010, pp. 180–1; McKay, 2013) and 46 per cent of social care workers employed by local authorities in the capital are from black and minority ethnic groups (HSCI, 2016, p. 54). However, outside of London the employment of migrant workers is far less prevalent. In Wales, and in English regions such as the North East, over 90 per cent of paid social care workers are born in Britain (Shutes and Chiatti, 2012, p. 392). The racial and cultural profile of the adult social care workforce also varies by social care setting. Since many migrant workers are better qualified than their UK-born counterparts, they are particularly attractive to employers in institutional care settings where formal nursing skills are in high demand (Skills for Care, 2010). Migrant, as well as black and ethnic minority, workers are more likely to be employed in institutional settings than in homecare (Eborall et al., 2010; Shutes, 2011). In regions such as the South West, available data records 96 per cent of homecare workers as white (HSCI, 2016, p. 10; Skills for Care, 2016). It has been suggested that employers' recruitment practices in the homecare industry reflect the racial preference of white British service-users for white British homecare workers – only 4 per cent of the population aged over 65 are from a black or minority ethnic group (Twigg, 2000, pp. 124–5).[6]

Approximately half of all workers providing care at home to older people are aged over 45 years (Holmes, 2015, p. 36) and local authority-employed homecare workers are typically older than their private-sector counterparts (HSCI, 2016, p. 49). Their work is highly gendered. Less than 5 per cent of the 'hands-on' care workforce are male (Eborall et al., 2010, p. 10) and homecare is the most likely of all adult social care occupations to be undertaken by women (Hussein, 2011).

Gender, class and the study of labour law

As caregivers in domestic settings, homecare workers carry a deep association with feminine identity. Their subordination within the labour market is 'both a statement about the values of a society and the demographic profile of those who perform paid and unpaid care' (Duffy et al., 2013, p. 148). Overwhelmingly, homecare workers are drawn from the ranks of the lower social classes (Hall and Wreford, 2007, p. 23). The UK homecare landscape is dominated by white working-class women who tend not to have academic

---

[6] For information about racism within the sector, see Cangiano et al., 2009, pp. 97–8.

qualifications. Prior work experience is often unnecessary to gain employment and homecare is frequently categorised as an 'unskilled' occupation. Throughout the chapters that follow, I shed light on the gendered experience of paid caregiving as a classed experience. There is a rich seam of feminist legal scholarship concerned with the regulation of gender at work (Busby, 2011; Conaghan, 1999; Fudge, 2013; Fudge and McDermott, 1991; Lacey, 1987). Feminist studies in particular are alert to the potential that labour law can produce unequal and uneven outcomes in relation to men and women because patterns of work are gendered. At an individual level, however, different women experience the impact of the legal regulation of work differently, and issues of race and social class make a significant contribution in this regard (Bruegel and Perrons, 1998; Pollert and Charlwood, 2009).

When law at work entrenches hierarchies of gender, it does so on the basis of class. It is a distinctive feature of the UK labour market that the vast majority of workers in the lowest paid jobs are women (Gautie and Schmitt, 2010; Hills, 2010; p. 128). Labour market economists observe that the UK has a low pay problem which is largely a consequence of political choices made by central and local government because public services are a key source of women's employment (Gautie and Schmitt, 2010; Howard and Kenway, 2004). The social role of a 'worker' has a deep association with 'provider' or 'breadwinner' aspects of masculine identity, and labour law characteristically assumes a paradigmatic male subject (Fraser, 2013, p. 37). The interests of individual parties to an employment relationship have traditionally been represented collectively in bargaining between trade union and employer associations (Ewing, 2005). However, following similar patterns in most other developed economies, collective bargaining coverage in Britain has fallen from a high point of 82 per cent of the workforce in 1976 to 23 per cent of the workforce in 2015 (Hayes and Novitz, 2014). Over that same period, Parliament has created a plethora of statutory individual rights at work. Aside from the need for academic lawyers to explore the legal scope of these rights, there is an urgent requirement to better understand how individual legal rights function in relation to experiences of working life (Barmes, 2015a; Deakin, 2010; Ludlow and Blackham, 2015). A feature (and I would argue a serious limitation) of labour law scholarship is its scant consideration of what is meant by 'labour' and its valorisation of 'law' as a stand-alone topic. The way in which labour is theorised, and the means by which communities of labour are identified, has a tremendous effect on identifying those for whom labour law scholarship is able to speak.

It is to workers with few alternatives and in low-wage or precarious employment that statutory protection is potentially most meaningful. The promise of labour law lies in its potential to deliver emancipatory fair treatment for all, minimum standards such as basic wages or non-discrimination, and protection from unfair dismissal and economic precarity (Blackett, 2011). However, even where worker protection is the apparent purpose of legal provisions, legal effect is not linear, stable nor necessarily protective (Barmes, 2015b). There is a dearth of empirical research in the fields of equality and labour law (Barmes, 2015b, p. 20) and much to be done to uncover and map the contradictory outcomes of law. For homecare workers this means seeking to understand why employment rights are often rendered meaningless in practice. In this book I examine and explore the numerous ways in which the employment protection claims of homecare workers have been rejected; and the ways in which their legal status is downgraded, their economic value and contribution undermined, their economic needs disregarded, their occupational voice diminished, and their autonomy as a social group eroded.

Law at work sets the terms of engagement upon which employers and people in paid work may lawfully relate to one another. It attributes employers and working people with legal identities, and establishes their legal status, responsibilities and entitlements. However, the idea of 'employers' and 'working people' as two distinct 'classes' is too simplistic to be of much use if we want to think critically about employment relationships in the real world. It is more productive to think of employment as situated in a tapestry of differing social relationships, which are legally constituted through the performance of work. Relations of class are manifest in employment relations and law acts as a weaving thread, attaching people to the grand social tapestry that is the labour market. Although it is rarely made explicit by labour lawyers, the study of law at work is a foray into social class relations by which people are able to 'access and control resources for provisioning and survival' (Acker, 2006, p. 444). Class relations are sustained and reproduced through the structuring and distribution of social and economic power. They are reflected in organisational hierarchies which appear to naturalise social and economic inequality. However, like gender, class relations are not merely *reflected* in law but are produced through legal reasoning and by the application of rules that offer justification for social and economic hierarchies.

It is by undertaking a specific and sustained programme of empirical investigation, as well as by examining the detail of law and legal concepts, that I identify how homecare workers come to occupy simultaneously marginal and inferior positions in the labour market tapestry. Representations of homecare workers in law are entangled with homecare workers' discernible experiences of caregiving. Based on the commonality of their work, the way in which homecare workers encounter law at work is distinctive. As is evidenced in this book, law and legal thinking is central to the regard afforded to homecare workers in the labour market; it also influences how they think, and are reasonably able to think, about themselves.

Legal thinking and experiential existence are mutually reinforcing; law and legal concepts shape the circumstances and situations in which paid care is produced. Homecare workers are conceptually located where the very fabric of legal ideas about employment begins to fray. However, 'being' a homecare worker is central to notions of personal identity and to understandings of the value and purpose of labour, community routines and the organisation of time. It is in the imbrications of law and experience – the overlapping, collisions and enfolding – that marginality attains its material construction.

Questions of voice

The homecare workers engaged in my research wanted their voices to be heard – 'whatever it takes to try and make things better in the future', said one; 'I will tell you everything if someone will listen', said another. I have spent eight years trying to better understand how and why homecare workers are pretty much the lowest valued group of workers in the UK. My curiosity has taken me far beyond an interest in legal rules and the detail of individual employment rights. Understanding the varied 'meaning' of homecare work, as it is expressed and experienced by women employed in the industry, was a touchstone to which I continually returned as I wrote up my findings.

My account of the institutionalised humiliation of the homecare workforce gives particular attention to the interweaving of narrative strands in law and regulatory processes, in social policy documents, by politicians and through the media. However, I have found that institutionalised humiliation is also expressed by narrative silence. Before I began in-depth interviews and conversations, I was aware that academic research frequently overlooks working-class women. It is unusual for sociological studies to focus on working-class women as research subjects and this is especially so in the study of law. One reason for this is the predominant view of law as a textual, inanimate object of academic interest: studies of law are disinclined to also be studies of people. Another reason is that men and women are equally subject to the same set of rules; hence the law purports to be gender-blind, even if these rules often privilege male interests. A third reason is that law proceeds by extracting information from its social context in order to establish material fact. Accordingly, legal processes create a rather flattened view of society and legal reasoning finds it problematic to acknowledge that differentials of power, culture, wealth or other resources influence human behaviour.

Despite, or perhaps because of, these conventions in the study of law, I was conscious that the opinions of working-class women are rarely published, reproduced or afforded formal regard. It is also the case that the *work* experiences of working-class women are under-explored in sociology, industrial relations and studies of labour law (Forrest, 1996, p. 409; Hebson, 2009). This is problematic because what is said by people who are the objects of regulation can profoundly challenge assumptions made about its utility and impact (Barmes, 2015b, p. 25). Further, despite a reasonable presumption that homecare workers will have specialist knowledge about social care, there are few books in which their words or opinions are considered noteworthy. Scholarship about education and class would suggest that their knowledge counts for little because it is acquired through the trials and errors of life, through hands-on experience and through verbal rather than written guidance, passed down by women over generations (Livingstone and Sawchuk, 2005; Wheelahan, 2007). When society seeks out authoritative voices, it turns to people such as politicians, judges, newspaper columnists, business owners, religious leaders, academics and senior civil servants. These are the holders of 'received wisdom', a term closely connected to that of 'received pronunciation' and denoting that which is generally accepted within Britain as credible and intelligible. Arguably, it is advantageous to society to privilege the voices of people who have access to sources of objective knowledge, those who have been formally educated, command social resources that give weight to their opinions and are enabled to communicate in a manner that is highly valued. However, authoritative voices may lack practical insight, are typically male and are unlikely to be working-class.

Homecare workers are a social group who lack recognition as knowledge-holders and command neither the social resources nor status which typically marks out society's knowledge-producers. The knowledge of homecare workers is largely overlooked in research orientated towards the development of social policy. By way of contrast, the opinions of employers (euphemistically categorised as the opinions of care 'providers') are frequently courted by government and industry regulators. This privileging of already-powerful voices obscures the common-sense observation that managers and company owners do not themselves provide care.

As I reviewed prior research in which UK homecare workers were explicitly included, I noted a tendency for interviews to be of a short duration and for the research itself to be conducted in response to industry-defined priorities and commissioned by branches of government. Samples contained large numbers of social care professionals or managers within the research population, engaged with very small numbers of hands-on paid workers, or had subsumed homecare workers within a generic field of care workers. In some instances, researchers had relied upon managers to identify homecare workers and make them available as research participants in working time. This gave me reason to question the extent to which homecare workers had felt free to express their views and I began to notice other instances of homecare workers, and their interests, being silenced. The examples I review in the following paragraphs also serve as contextual insights into the functioning of the social care industry.

Behind the receptionist's counter in the offices of a homecare company I visited was a notice clearly intended for workers who came in to top up their supplies or submit expense claims. It read: 'Please don't ask for holiday as refusal often offends!' The receptionist told me that all available summer holiday leave had already been allocated. It was February, and I wondered how women with dependent children could manage within the confines of such a stringent system. I also found it remarkable that workers on zero-hours contracts, for whom there is no guarantee of work from one week to the next, were instructed by a notice on the wall not to ask for holidays from work, despite the existence of legal entitlements to paid leave.

I read on the Internet about an organisation entitled the Care Professionals' Benevolent Fund that aims to relieve 'financial hardship or sickness' among current, former and retired 'care professionals'. Founders include the biggest corporate care providers in the UK and the fund's website outlines its support for impoverished care workers, such as the provision of a crisis grant following a car accident, transport for a care worker's disabled babies, and a grant for a cooker and washing machine following job loss for reasons of poor health (Howard, 2012). I found it curious that corporations representing an industry notorious for low wages, insecure contracts and a lack of occupational sick pay would characterise care workers as victims of circumstance.

A homecare worker told me that she was taking a box of her unwanted toiletries to a car boot sale in the grounds of a local residential care home. Proceeds from the sale would benefit the care home, which had charitable status and was in need of additional funds. I knew that staff at this care home worked 12-hour shifts and were paid only the legal minimum. Nevertheless, the care home was one of hundreds of similar facilities owned by a multinational corporation which reported an underlying UK profit of £175 million that same year. It seemed to me that care workers' own identities as labouring subjects, and an appreciation of their status as workers, could be lost where the commercial nature of the care industry is confused with the idea of caregiving as a charitable endeavour.

A ground-breaking TV documentary about homecare services in Birmingham was broadcast by the BBC. Episode One of *Protecting our Parents* emphasised how risks to older people were managed in practice. The early part of the programme introduced viewers to a family in which a daughter had stopped making daily visits to her ailing dad who was living at home. She explained 'it takes its toll on you' and was clearly distressed because she could not provide him with sufficient support. She had a school-aged daughter to look after and relied on bus services for transport because she lived in an adjacent town. Meanwhile, when asked, her dad expressed his desire to stay 'in one's own surroundings' and he suspected that the local authority social workers who came to assess his needs were intent on 'taking away [his] independence'. They advised that he needed to go into a nursing home but his daughter was fearful of the consequences: 'I saw my mum in a nursing home and I don't want to see my dad in one too.' She spoke as though an unwilling witness to her parents' decline and sought to maintain her dad's privacy. Yet choice was overtaken by necessity when her dad fell on the stairs and was admitted to hospital. The risk of falling over at home was traded for the risk that he would contract a hospital-acquired infection; viewers were encouraged to consider just how vulnerable older people are to their environments.

The second part of the programme invited viewers to consider the case of Jim, who had recently left hospital. Footage taken in Jim's house showed a man's hands writing on a care plan and then, with his back to the camera, the man spoke reassuringly to Jim, saying, 'someone else will come at tea time'. From this, viewers might have deduced he was one of several homecare workers involved in Jim's care. A feature of the next sequence of film was part of the side of the face of another homecare worker who said, 'I won't see you tomorrow, you are not on my programme to come tomorrow so I will see you when I can'. These fleeting glimpses were the only portrayal of homecare workers in the entire programme. The occupational concept of homecare was merely implied; homecare workers did not speak to the camera and were shown only at the point of leaving.

Episode Two explored the allocation of state-funded care as a limited resource. It featured the deliberations of a hospital consultant, a clinical psychologist and a general practitioner (all male) in a case review meeting. Female social workers offered supplementary advice, but did not make decisions. Footage of a visit to a bed-bound elderly woman living at home showed a social worker in a bright red coat stooped over the bed. It seemed to me that by keeping her hands in her pockets throughout their brief exchange, the body language of the red-coated social worker emphasised that she was not a 'hands-on carer' but maintained an air of detached professionalism in order to observe and advise.

Protecting our Parents offered a sensitively drawn, intimate portrait of the terrible dilemmas that families face as health deteriorates with old age, as individuals lose their survival skills and as life at home can only be maintained with intervention. It also offered a powerful indication of the hierarchies of class and gender at play within systems of social care. Professional men were constructed as decision-makers and the work of hands-on paid caregivers was erased from view. An untold story lay in the interaction of homecare workers with their service-users. The unheard voices were those of homecare workers, rendered invisible by editing decisions that portrayed them as mere functionaries lumped at the bottom of a heap of administrative processes. In silencing homecare workers, this documentary was following a well-established pattern.

The knowledge of homecare workers is not framed as a primary commentary on the industry in which they work, nor even on the subject of their own agency or motivations as paid caregivers. One powerful example is the documented fact that, of the hundreds of thousands of social care workers who leave their employment each year, dissatisfaction with pay is recorded as a reason for leaving in only 3 per cent of cases (Skills for Care, 2015a, p. 52). Since unlawfully low pay is endemic within the industry, this statistic is surprising. Skills for Care is the workforce and leadership development body for adult social care in England. It manages the National Minimum Data Set on Social Care on behalf of the Department of Health and data is collated from employer returns. By this method, employers (rather than homecare workers themselves) control the reporting of the reasons why homecare workers are leaving their jobs in droves. Although Skills for Care notes that the validity of the statistic should be treated with caution, it is nevertheless reasonable for us to question why employers are asked to collate information on this topic at all. It points to the political desirability of an official narrative in which homecare workers' dissatisfaction with pay is presented as if it were a marginal issue for the industry.[7] Data collection processes which do not actively seek out the opinions of homecare workers, and do not actively support the free expression of those opinions, produce data with the potential to silence further the voices and interests of homecare workers.

The structural silencing of homecare workers is also evident in a social policy context. Social care policy rarely even acknowledges the existence of a homecare workforce and fails to address their employment interests. However, on occasions, soundbite-style quotes attributed to an individual homecare worker are published alongside warm-faced photographs to craft the appearance of general 'street-level' endorsement for social policy initiatives. Momentarily, the fog of silence is lifted; yet, at the same time, the very idea that homecare workers *should be* recognised in relation to social policy is manipulated. In these instances, homecare workers acquire a symbolic status in which their words appear as a cipher of authenticity. They are not recognised as knowledge-holders but rather are constructed as a hollow source of endorsement for social policy, in which chronic underfunding, structural problems and poor-quality employment are airbrushed out of the picture.

---

7 See also data from the National Care Forum which similarly records, from employer returns, that 1.52 per cent of care workers leave their employment for reasons of low pay (National Care Forum, 2015, p. 12).

As a researcher, it is necessarily my privilege to determine what counts as 'knowledge' in my own work, and I carry responsibility where my choices may perpetuate the silencing of already-marginalised voices. My task as a social scientist is to tell 'the truth of this world, as can be uncovered by objectivist methods of observation, but also showing that this world is the site of ongoing struggle to tell the truth of this world' (Wacquant, 1989, p. 35). Poorly designed data collection or consultation processes can contribute to the injustices faced by the homecare workforce. This assessment has influenced my decisions about research methods, which include the way in which I have chosen to present arguments. I have approached this book as the product of my research *with* homecare workers – as an opportunity to illuminate and share their accounts of frustrations, injustice, determination and of joy.

Research design and participants

Considerations of class, gender and law presented in this book draw on contributions made by a research cohort of 30 working-class women, all living in the same city in southern England, far away from London. To recruit research participants, I involved myself in community networks and events in the hope of engaging with homecare workers independently of their employment. The ethnographic foundations of the arguments presented in this book lie in my commitment to understand how paid caregiving is experienced by homecare workers. Between 2012 and 2014, I gathered data from loosely structured interviews with homecare workers whose employment situation fitted my research plan. However, these interviews built on more than a decade of prior work. Before becoming an academic, I had worked in a trade union context, representing and organising homecare workers. Activities I led or participated in ranged from running community-based training programmes, to wage negotiations, and to visiting homecare workers to talk about issues such as personal debt. Over a period of many years, I was helping homecare workers access literacy, numeracy and computer skills courses; organising mass meetings with them; representing individuals in grievance and disciplinary meetings; accompanying them at meetings with occupational health consultants; and negotiating with their managers about work scheduling, shift patterns or pay. Being involved with homecare workers also meant spending time together having a laugh in pubs and cafés, organising marches and demonstrations together, and standing in the pouring rain on pavements while leading chants in support of better funding for care services.

Ethnography is often recognised as a source of knowledge about the world based on 'rich description', which requires insight, considerable effort and exceptional degrees of access (Liebling, 2015). It begins with concerns about how to gain 'entry' to particular social communities, questions how to develop trust and empathy, ponders how best to record social interaction and explores how to make sense of the data which is generated. The first three of these concerns is largely absent from research which is not ethnographic (Flood, 2005, p. 40). Before I embarked on interviews I was well-versed in the vocabulary with which homecare workers typically talked about their jobs; I was accustomed to discussing employment concerns with them; I was familiar with many of their motivations; and I knew my way around several of the housing estates where homecare workers lived and worked. All this assisted my efforts to secure access. Even though I was approaching women who were complete strangers to me as individuals, I was confident in my ability to communicate the authenticity of my interest in them as homecare workers. I knew my questions would sound credible since my prior experience supported the integrity of my research plans. It had taken several years to train as an academic, I did not talk to any of the research participants about my earlier work as a trade union official and only two of the women I engaged in this research were known to me previously.

The roots of ethnographic method lie in a desire to integrate first-hand empirical investigation with a theoretically informed interpretation of a community's social organisation and culture (Hammersley and Atkinson, 2007). My initial ethnographic task was to engage with homecare workers in order to share in their knowledge. I was interested in listening to women of any age currently providing paid care in the homes of older or disabled adults in the city where the study was based. They were working in a wide range of employment situations: for a local authority, for private companies, employed directly as personal assistants to clients, working as self-employed or engaged informally on a cash-in-hand basis. As I discovered, the working patterns of some women varied from week to week. Others were working in different forms of employment, or for different employers on different days, and this variety meant I could not neatly define their employment position. Often the boundaries between one 'job' and another were blurred. However, what mattered most was to achieve a balance across the research group to reflect what was happening within the homecare labour market; hence the messiness of real life was to be welcomed.

Creating an atmosphere in which informed consent was a rolling and participative process was of central importance to the research. I wanted all participants to feel in control of the information they shared and sufficiently confident of anonymity that they would talk openly. It surprised me at first that almost all of the women were willing to meet me in their own homes. With time, I came to understand that I was mirroring how they organised their own work. It enabled us to engage in an intimate space where they were in control: I was the guest, and we could talk for as long as their available time or patience allowed. Of the 30 women interviewed, two preferred that we talk elsewhere and, in those instances, I booked a room in a community centre. The research design and documentation had university research ethics approval and participants were keen for the work to be published, in the hope that homecare services might improve if people outside the homecare industry understood it better. Before each interview began, I obtained written consent to use data, advised that participants could withdraw from the research without giving a reason and offered to send a copy of the transcript for their comment or correction. Interviews lasted for between two and four hours and data was adjusted in transcription so as not to contain information through which participants, users of services or other persons could be identified.

The women I spoke to in the early stages of my research subsequently spoke to their friends and made recommendations about how I might recruit new participants into the study. One suggestion was that I should place a free-of-charge classified advert on a particular website where many personal assistants and self-employed care workers looked for new clients. Another was to set up a Facebook page about my research which homecare workers could share. Both of these ideas turned out to be fruitful ways of engaging with the more informal and self-organised parts of the homecare labour market.

The age of my research participants ranged from 25 to 64 years, with the average being 47 years. The following table provides a summary of information. The left-hand column records the name I have assigned to each participant as a pseudonym. The column to the right of this shows the name I have assigned to protect the real identify of their employer. The third column shows the type of employment in which they were engaged; the fourth, the form of contract under which they worked; and the final column gives an indication of their age. The first two research participants listed, Donna and Heather, took on assignments through a labour agency and they were both of mixed racial parentage. A further two women, Rosa and Abbi, made their living at that time by combining formal employment and agency or informal (cash-in-hand) work. One was an immigrant to Britain as a child; the other was white British. There were eight local authority homecare workers with an average age of 50 years, who were each employed by the same local authority. They were going through the experience of losing their jobs as their service was closing down; all were white British.

Name	Employer	Job	Age	Contract
Employed by a labour agency				
Donna	Tempco	Care worker	30–34	Zero-hours
Heather	Tempco	Care worker	55–59	Zero-hours
Employed by private-sector care providers				
Debbie	Towncare	Homecare worker	40–44	Zero-hours
Claire	Assico	Homecare worker	25–29	Zero-hours
Cathy	Healthhelp	Homecare worker	45–49	Zero-hours
Lucy	Abcare	Homecare worker	40–44	Zero-hours
Kath	Oaktree	Homecare worker	45–49	Zero-hours
Gina	Care4U	Homecare worker	50–54	Zero-hours
Trish	Redbird	Homecare worker	55–59	Zero-hours
Lynn	Alphacare	Senior Homecare	40–44	Guaranteed
Beverley	Bridgecare	Supervisor	25–29	Fixed hours
Ann	Bridgecare	Supervisor	40–44	Fixed hours
Rebecca	Bridgecare	Owner/manager	55–59	Fixed hours
Employed in multiple categories				
Rosa	Various	Homecare /PA	45–49	Fixed / ad hoc
Abbi	Various	Homecare /PA	40–44	Fixed / ad hoc
Employed by a local authority				
Marilyn	Local authority	Homecare worker	55–59	Fixed hours
Carol	Local authority	Homecare worker	45–49	Fixed hours
Michelle	Local authority	Homecare worker	50–54	Fixed hours
Nadine	Local authority	Homecare worker	55–59	Fixed hours
Samantha	Local authority	Homecare worker	35–39	Fixed hours
Katy	Local authority	Homecare worker	60–65	Fixed hours
Janet	Local authority	Supervisor	45–49	Fixed hours
Sophie	Local authority	Homecare worker	40–44	Fixed hours
Working directly for service-users				
Sindy	Various	Personal assistant	55–59	Self-employed
Jane	Various	Owner-manager	50–54	Self-employed
Carrie	Various	Personal assistant	40–44	Mixed status
Sasha	Various	Personal assistant	35–39	Mixed status
Kim	Various	Personal assistant	35–39	Self-employed
Philippa	Various	Personal assistant	60–65	Self-employed
Hazel	Various	Personal assistant	45–49	Self-employed

The 11 private-sector homecare workers taking part in my research were of white British heritage, had an average age of 43 years and were employed by nine different care companies. This included three women who comprised the management team at a small homecare provider I have called Bridgecare. Their inclusion happened rather by accident. I was made aware of an owner-manager who had been a hands-on caregiver. I contacted her and she readily offered to do an interview. I also interviewed two members of her supervisory staff. Together, these three unexpected participants brought a new dimension to this study: as women who were responsible for the recruitment, discipline and supervision of others. I balanced this private-sector insight with the inclusion of a homecare supervisor working for the local authority, as well as an owner-manager of a small business that organised work for self-employed personal assistants. Among my research group, there were eight women, with an average age of 49 years, who were working directly for service-users on either an employed or a self-employed basis. Two of these women were immigrants – one from Eastern Europe; the other from a former British colony. Both were white.

Data collection and analysis

It is a well-established practice in the 'phenomenological' tradition of social science for researchers to steer interview conversations towards the generation of personal narratives (Moustakas, 1994; Pollio et al., 1997; Sanders, 1982). Each of us lives 'storied' lives and uses narratives as a communicative device with which to express our place within the world and our experiences of it (Connelly and Clandinin, 1990, p. 2). Narrative research methods recognise that what we know about ourselves, and the knowledge we create as living persons, is nestled in these stories (see, for example, Ewick and Silbey, 1998, pp. 28–9). For ethnographic researchers, narrative communication is particularly valuable because it captures the contested, ambiguous and inchoate dimensions of social interaction. I knew, through my preparatory investigations, that homecare workers were disadvantaged as a group by demeaning representations and assumptions. I was also aware that if my response was to adopt a simplistic sympathy for their position, my research risked being highly condescending and one-dimensional. By encouraging research participants to talk in storied form, I could promote and uphold respect for the complexity of their relationships with work colleagues, managers, service-users and service-users' families. Instead of asking about whether or not something had happened, or what they thought about a particular statement, or why they held a particular view, I structured my questions to encourage storytelling. For example, I would ask:

What happened on your first day as a homecare worker?

Can you tell me about a time when you felt really appreciated at work?

What did you say when a service-user asked you do something unexpected?

Paying attention to personal narratives enabled me to listen carefully to the ways in which homecare workers communicated a sense of identity and relayed rich details about their lived experience. Their narrative accounts had a political quality and they shared stories which shed light on how they had dealt with actual situations, how they regarded one another and how they saw themselves. As I gathered these stories, it was rapidly apparent that if my analysis simply repackaged this 'data' into a purportedly objective summary of general themes and inclinations I would compromise the intellectual and ethical credibility of my research. Rather, I would need to communicate my findings using homecare workers' words, respecting their choice of vocabulary and producing an account that served to amplify, rather than depoliticise, the contribution they made.

Taking an ethnographic approach to analysis requires researchers to interpret social meanings. Ethnographic analysis also seeks to understand the intended functions and consequences of human actions, and the impact of institutional practices, and then attempts to set them into wider context (Hammersley and Atkinson, 2007, p. 3). When I began to analyse the research data, I categorised narratives under different topic headings in order to try and make sense of what was being said by research participants as a group. There were significant similarities in the content of the narrative accounts, and individual stories pointed to social assumptions being made about homecare workers as a group. I had anticipated that women from comparable social backgrounds, working in the same industry, in the same city, would draw on similar experiences to talk about their work. However, although examples of contradiction between the accounts were few, contradictions *within* individual accounts were commonplace. What intrigued me was that these contradictions were so alike and that they cropped up repeatedly during interviews with different women. For example, there were stories about homecare work being personally rewarding, yet the same storytellers would move on to narrate an account in which homecare work gave rise to feelings of personal worthlessness. Some would describe the discomfort of being poor, but take apparent pride in being willing to work without pay. Others talked about the frustrations inherent in making difficult choices without adequate management guidance, yet also insisted that they were unconcerned at the prospect of being covertly filmed via CCTV in service-users' homes by unknown observers with fears about elder abuse.[8]

---

8 I have written about this elsewhere (see Hayes, 2015b).

Inevitably, homecare workers' understandings of their work are shaped by its social context and there are tensions and ambiguities in how we all think about our daily lives. Homecare workers are as influenced as anyone else by prevailing discourses about the different values placed on men's and women's work, about the undervaluing of care, practices of class-shaming, racism and the social values associated with good citizenship. However, because I had encouraged research participants to talk in a narrative style, I gauged that they often talked about themselves through the eyes of others. Narrative accounts, and their symbolic qualities, are significant for establishing perspectives that are counter to, yet infused by, background conditions of social inequality (Clough and Barton, 1998). Homecare workers occasionally slipped into a type of discourse that the early-twentieth-century civil rights philosopher W. E. B. Du Bois called the 'double consciousness' of people who measured their own lives using the 'tape of a world that looks on in amused contempt and pity' (1903, p. 3).

For example, it was a common feature of my research encounters that women would tell me that their job did not involve cleaning, while at a later point in the conversation they talked about times when their job required them to do cleaning. Almost all the homecare workers complained to me about people who wrongly assumed homecare jobs involved domestic cleaning, but then also told me stories in which they either resented having to do cleaning or said they didn't mind the cleaning tasks they performed. By analysing the storied meaning of their narratives, I came to understand that this inconsistency expressed their negotiating of the social stigma of domestic cleaning. It symbolised the extent to which they did not want to be represented, portrayed or classified as 'cleaners', regardless of whether they actually engaged in cleaning tasks. This insight gave me an appreciation that category labels such as 'carer' or 'cleaner' lose their precision in relation to daily life experience and might, for example, be used to communicate stigma rather than function. It was a valuable lesson to add to my existing appreciation that the labels giving doctrinal meaning to paid work in law bear little resemblance to the social relations that connect individuals to their work. Narrative accounts shed light on the ways in which category labels, legal or otherwise, are challenged in the construction of social meaning.

Learning from others' experience is undoubtedly a messy terrain and it is a perpetual challenge in empirical data analysis to resist oversimplification. Clearly researchers cannot read minds and cannot know or verify the internal mental state of another person, but that is not the purpose of ethnography. Ethnographers attempt to understand a community or issue better than prior to undertaking fieldwork (Flood, 2005). Opportunities to present subjects as complex and multidimensional are particularly valuable to researchers interested in disrupting or challenging existing norms, legal or otherwise, about gender (Hunter, 2013, p. 18).

From my concern about categorisation, contradiction and narrative complexity I began to wonder how best to bring to life the sexism and class biases that emerged in homecare workers' narratives. I wanted to engage in an analysis that could address the commonality of content, yet retain, rather than overlook, narrative contradictions. By stepping back from seeing each story as an individual account, I could attempt to understand what was being communicated about homecare workers collectively. As a whole, the stories spoke to the various social roles performed by homecare workers; the obligations they owed to clients and employers; the routines they were required to adopt; the rights that they expected to exercise; and their anticipations of economic reward.

As I decoupled each story from its original place within an individual interview and connected it to similar stories told by others, I began to identify a number of distinct thematic 'voices' that were audible at a collective level. I rigorously analysed data in order to establish the dimensions of these voices and build a multifaceted understanding of working in homecare. This resolved the problem of how to deal with contradictions because I could attribute them to the idea that individual homecare workers each used a number of different storyteller voices. Experience is complex and *any* reduction to a singular narrative would constrain analysis and make representation partial (see Davies, 2013, p. 69). If experience could be vocalised from different perspectives, it was entirely plausible (for example) that homecare work could be both personally rewarding and conducive to feelings of worthlessness, depending on which voice a homecare worker adopted to tell a particular story. I identified four narrative voices which appeared to represent the different ways in which the collective reality of working in homecare was presented, told, retold and represented. Aside from a plotline, characters are the most obvious components of what makes a story. When storytellers embark on stories about themselves, they are often the most significant character in the narrative, even if their identity, or characteristics, is not made explicit. By 'characterising' the voices, I could highlight stories about gendered inequality or class bias and use them as viewpoints from which to contextualise my doctrinal assessments of law at work. Narrative was both a method and a product of this research. The structural backbone to this book comprises four 'character narratives' – Cheap Nurse, Two-a-Penny, Mother Superior, Choosy Suzy – which I use to illuminate the role of law at work in the institutionalised humiliation of the homecare workforce.

Character narratives

Experiential truths about the world are highly personal, yet universally human, for we have all encountered hurt and pain, joy and love. To connect such truth of living to the 'stuff' of law requires a methodological imagination. The character narratives I have devised are a bridge with which to connect legal scholarship to the unequal, incomparable, ecologically unique and historically contingent mess of human existence. Each chapter begins with a narrative, relayed as though a separate and distinct 'character' is speaking about her experiences. These chapters were written with the intention of being read sequentially, since the book is designed to be understood as a whole. Although each is different, when read together the characters present homecare workers as complex actors in the world of work.

Experiential truths about the world are frequently lost in legal process. Law seeks to shape and justify its imposition of social order by an appeal to rational thought. It tends not to trade in the truth of subjective experience but rather sets out how our relations to one another *ought* to be. However, law is not a distinct social realm, but a socially embedded system of interpretation and adjudication (Lacey, 1998, pp. 5–12). Examining the form and function of law is one way of explaining how oppressions of gender and class are made 'real'. Sexist or class-biased stereotypes are imported into legal processes, interpreted as legal fact and constructed as 'truth' by judges, legislators, bureaucrats, managers and so forth (Davies, 2013, p. 72). Gendered depictions in law are subsequently carried into social life more widely because law has material consequences (Conaghan, 2000, p. 363). By prioritising the experiences of homecare workers as a basis from which to proceed in my analysis of law, I establish that law at work is not separate from, but is intertwined with, the materiality of paid caregiving.

While the content of each character narrative is true, the character herself is merely an imaginative device. To be clear, the character narratives I have created do not represent individual homecare workers; I am not in any way suggesting that homecare workers are 'like' these characters. What the characters represent is my categorisation of the *stories* that were told about homecare work, and the stories that homecare workers told about themselves. The characters are not real, but they are 'true' – by which I mean that everything 'said' in a character narrative was said to me by a homecare worker; every event had been experienced in real life; and every emotion felt. My efforts to characterise interview data acknowledged that although experience is individually embodied, it is rarely made explicit as a collective body of knowledge. I matched data to ensure that the stories which made their way into character narratives were not 'one-offs' but communicated shared experiences.

The character narratives conjure up a series of word pictures that enabled me to connect legal concepts with the stuff of everyday life. They each portray institutional humiliation in action by establishing how judgments of inferiority achieve legitimacy through law at work. Making pictures and telling stories are springboards for intellectual journeys that deepen our understanding. My assessment includes equal pay and sex discrimination law; the right to employment protection in the event of unfair dismissal or a transfer of undertakings; the UK's national minimum wage scheme; and the organisation of social care according to the Care Act 2014. Each character narrative serves to challenge gendered and classed assumptions about homecare workers that are reinforced or imagined in law. Each assessment of law shows that legal entitlements, protections or standards are underpinned by criteria that do not recognise, or worse, recognise but denigrate, the experiences of women in the homecare industry. Harmful assumptions about gender and class both reflect and inform social norms which are 'skewed in favour of values associated with masculinity' (Davies, 2013, p. 65).

In Chapter 1, the character narrative of *Cheap Nurse* represents the voice of homecare workers as they talked about being misrecognised, undervalued and assumed to lack distinct skills. The stories that I brought together correspond with stereotypes about working-class women as secondary earners who lack commitment to the world of work and have little economic worth. The chapter addresses homecare as a low-waged occupation. I set the Cheap Nurse narrative in the historical context of the development of homecare services and the evolution of equal pay law in the UK. I draw on theoretical insights about the invisibility of women's work, and caring labour in particular. This informs the method I use to explore law in this chapter, namely examining the framework of the Equal Pay Act 1970 and measures in the Equality Act 2010 that purport to tackle sex-based discrimination in wage-setting. I find that the invisibility of women's labour is echoed in the architecture of equal pay law and that the inadequacy of non-discrimination provisions has influenced the organisation of homecare jobs as low-waged, discriminatory and precarious. My argument is that the structure of equal pay law is based on sexist ideas about women's supplementary role in the labour market, and that equal pay law has both incentivised and justified the privatisation of homecare services.

In Chapter 2, the *Two-a-Penny* character narrative communicates what it feels like to work on a zero-hours contract and the damage done to homecare workers' self-confidence by their lack of economic security in the labour market. It represents stories about being forced to work overtime, being tricked by employers into taking jobs on false pretences, of being short-changed, but above all, stories about being fearful of instant dismissal. Two-a-Penny is a narrative device that focuses on understanding homecare work as insecure employment. From this perspective, the chapter offers a gender sensitive account of employment protection law. My methodological approach is to analyse judicial doctrine relating to unfair dismissal law as well as to analyse doctrine that has arisen from the adjudication of the Transfer of Undertakings (Protection of Employment)

Regulations 2006. I build on scholarship about sexist justifications for women's social inferiority to argue that employment protection law normatively assumes, and then facilitates, the stability of male employment in ways that reflect notions of female inferiority. By examining employment protection law in the light of the Two-a-Penny character narrative, I show how homecare workers are negatively impacted by judicial doctrine, which distributes the advantage of employment security towards forms of employment in which men are typically engaged.

The next character narrative is that of *Mother Superior* and, in Chapter 3, I explore homecare work as unpaid labour. Stories fitting the Mother Superior character narrative are those in which homecare workers present themselves as being morally 'good women'. The narrative characterises how homecare workers express their caring competencies in terms that emphasise motivations of love rather than economic reward. I draw on aspects of a vast literature about caring labour to connect the gendered framing of care for family as unpaid work with the prevalence of unpaid work in the homecare industry. The ensuing discussion reveals the extent to which understandings of caregiving are influenced by middle-class ideals of maternal nurture and emotional engagement. It is from this perspective that I integrate homecare workers' accounts of intimacy and altruism with an assessment of the statutory right to a minimum wage. I show how the legal rules set out in the National Minimum Wage Act 1998, and the supporting National Minimum Wage Regulations 1999, reflect and reinforce normative expectations that care at home ought not to be provided for the reason of economic reward. I argue that these rules are gendered and fail to fully recognise caregiving as work. Judicial interpretations of national minimum wage law justify constructions of paid caregiving as an unpaid activity and serve to validate the organisation of homecare work in ways that squeeze unpaid labour from working-class women.

In Chapter 4, the character of *Choosy Suzy* narrates the determination of paid care workers to promote the choice and independence of their service-users. It focuses on neoliberal understandings of social care provision as enterprise. I critique core provisions of the Care Act 2014 which point to the erosion of paid caregiving as a form of labour which is recognisable in labour law. My method in this chapter is to identify and analyse research data as 'discourse'. I find that a discourse of choice underpins the Choosy Suzy narrative and finds statutory expression in the Care Act 2014. It validates a step change in the marketisation of care by requiring local authorities to promote service-user choice and control over care as a matter of statutory principle, as well as by requiring that they stimulate and support local care markets. Despite a rights-orientated language of 'empowerment' and 'choice', the marketisation of social care carries political meanings that are antithetical to the interests of women paid to provide hands-on care. Hence, I argue that a discourse of choice points towards a reconfiguration in the gendered exclusion of paid caregivers from the scope of labour law. Through the lens of Choosy Suzy, I show how a discourse of choice reduces the occupational craft of caregiving to one of care-for-hire and advances the deregulation of labour by combining the unregulated qualities of familial care with the economic qualities of enterprise.

Democratising voice and politicising the provision of paid care

There are several ways in which this book offers something new. Firstly, it provides an assessment of the 'crisis of care' in the UK as a crisis in the legal regulation of caring labour (although I dislike using the term 'crisis' to describe a situation which has in fact been deliberated, crafted and managed by our elected politicians). I argue that the homecare sector offers an ideal vantage point from which to observe the gendered inadequacy of labour law in action. Homecare workers have fewer legal rights and fewer legal freedoms than do other workers and this harsh reality reflects the ongoing institutionalised influence of stereotypes of gender and class which are also racialised.[9]

Secondly, the book offers a rare window on the experiences and opinions of working-class women, a social group who are frequently overlooked in sociological research (especially in examinations with a legal dimension). It illustrates that law at work marginalises homecare workers' economic interests, facilitates stereotyping and upholds a social hierarchy in which their silencing in social policy debates appears justified. My research makes a specific contribution to understanding how gender is produced and sustained in the day-to-day experiences of working-class women through the functioning and impact of law.

Thirdly, in its approach to the substance of law, this study is distinctive. It not only examines the application of employment rights in the context of homecare work, it also critically explores what the law *does*, both directly and indirectly, to the social standing of homecare workers. I consider the performative power of law and its justificatory support for the institutionalised humiliation of homecare workers. My assessment of law at work offers a critique of the gendered structure of employment rights in the UK, and argues that inequalities of gender and class are 'written into' rules and reasoning deployed in law as well as in the everyday experiences of homecare workers. This leads neatly to my fourth point. The research methods I have used to capture the knowledge of homecare workers have embedded this study in their everyday lives. My combination of ethnographic methods

---

9 I analyse the racialised aspects of my research elsewhere, see footnote 5 above.

with doctrinal legal analysis and social theory breaks new ground. Through attention to narrative, I have been able to identify social attitudes, legal structures and political motivations which ignite and support the degradation and subordination of working-class women who make their living by providing care in other peoples' homes.

Over several years, a steady stream of data about the inadequacy of the social care system in Britain has developed into a torrent of information. Paid care workers affirm the deterioration of service provision and it is not for a want of evidence that little has changed in the widespread assignation of social care as a system in crisis. The character narratives upon which this book is based each testify, in different ways, to the institutionalised humiliation of homecare workers. At an individual level, the erosion of social care provision harms citizens on the basis of disability, ill-health or frailty; it harms the women represented in this book; and, as state support ebbs away, the interests of unpaid familial carers are also harmed because they have fewer choices available to them. However, at a collective level, the undermining of social care breeds inequalities of race, sex and class which harm us all.

I have lost count of the number of times that someone has shared with me their frustrations in arranging care at home for a relative, and their subsequent realisation that homecare in the UK is under-resourced and badly organised. Far from being disengaged, I find that people continue to believe in our social capacity to care for one another and are not uninterested in the quality of care provided to vulnerable adults who are not part of their own families. Rather, they seem confused about how we have ended up with a system of adult social care that doesn't seem fit for purpose; they don't understand why employers are able to get away with paying such terribly low wages; and they don't know who or what is responsible for the feeble state of adult social care.

The current texture of political debate, and a constant stream of 'bad news' about the provision of homecare, seems as if it is designed to lower public expectations about the quality and availability of state-funded social care. Since the financial crisis of 2008, there has been a substantial reduction in the provision of state-funded social care across the UK population. Government spending cuts have left over a million older people who need help with day-to-day living with no help at all and the charity Age UK reports that they 'struggle alone' (Triggle, 2015). There is a reported surge in preventable illnesses and infections among the UK's elderly population, and a growing body of statistics points to longevity now being in reverse for men and women aged over 75 (Dorling, 2014; Mortimer and Green, 2015). Yet the problems of those who are *without* state-funded homecare services ought not to be viewed in isolation from the problems faced by those who fall *within* the ambit of the homecare industry. Deprivations of care can, and do, arise in either circumstance. Industry regulator the Care Quality Commission reported that homecare services were 'inadequate' or 'in need of improvement' according to statutory minima in one-third of its inspections (Care Quality Commission, 2015, p. 19).

It would seem that to effect change, public outrage is urgently required. However, if such outrage is to bridge the gap between the existing state of paid caregiving and the social care provision we need, political demands for change must take account of social care as a *socialised* and multidimensional concern. It is only with such an approach that the gendered crisis in the regulation of work which is being played out in the homecare industry can be brought to the fore. Political discussions about paid caregiving are too frequently hampered by questions about who pays for care, how much it costs and how it ought to be paid for. These are questions which fail to acknowledge that social care 'happens' in the socialised interaction of people in need of care and the women who are employed, in one way or another, to do the work of caring. Consequently, we rarely get to the point where discussions about social care are animated by legal questions about women's equality and their economic and social entitlements in the labour market. It is with the intimate connection between a politics of social care and the gendering of labour law that my concluding chapter is concerned.

As a film-maker, Ken Loach's ability to 'make pictures' in his work is clear. This book is the culmination of my own efforts to make pictures. I do not claim to provide a definitive account of paid care work, but I have aspired to set out *better* pictures than those which have gone before. It is my hope that by adopting a progressive methodological lens with which to look at labour law and care work, this book will advance the case for legal protection to be fully realised in the labour market and for the building of entitlements consequently able to overturn hierarchies of gender and class bias. We must aspire to legal reforms which can transform the labour market. A key test will be if homecare workers are able to cast off the legacy of institutionalised humiliation, access the full suite of employment rights and begin to engage in effective collective bargaining across the social care sector, so as to secure improvements in their working lives. The terms on which homecare workers are employed are not a private matter and they warrant urgent public deliberation. What homecare workers do, who they are, and how they are employed is of vital importance to the social foundations of paid caregiving and to the legal foundations of a labour market with the emancipatory potential to free all its participants from degradations of class and sex.

1
Cheap Nurse

At the end of the day, I think we are cheap nurses. If you ask me about fair pay for homecare, the pay is not fair. The homecare workers are out there on their own, doing their own workload and doing all the work by themselves. The morning calls is from seven. Getting people up; showering or personal care; incontinence care; emptying leg bags; getting them clean; putting on fresh clothes if they want it; breakfast, cup of tea; medication ... all in under half an hour; and on to the next. It's exhausting; sometimes there are nine service-users to do on a morning. If there are lunch calls, they might start at midday but in-between there might be a person's shopping to do, there might be some laundry. At five o'clock it is tea calls. People also need pads changed or bags changed. We see some service-users four times a day ... rush, rush, rush. From seven o'clock is night-time calls; obviously many of our people are bedridden but not everyone is necessarily going to bed so early, they might just have their pyjamas or nighties put on.

We write everything we do down on daily log sheets. We sign for medication, to say they have taken it in front of you, these are legal documents. Sometimes it's even controlled drugs like patches, morphine. We have bowel charts, so we can keep an eye out that they have their bowels open often enough and are passing urine. We have food charts for people who don't eat that well, or if there is concern they're losing weight, we can monitor what they are eating. To me, they are not disabled; they are just people who have had strokes, some have got dementia, or are end of life. A lot of the palliative care is mainly cancer. People either want to stay at home or they have to stay home because there is not enough money in the system. The care homes are closing down and there is nowhere for them to go.

One lady I go to is in a wheelchair, diabetic, she can't walk. Every manoeuvre she needs, you've got to do it for her. You get her up in the morning; it's all ceiling hoists; all sling work. Hoist her to her chair;

wheel her to the bathroom, which again is a hoist job to get her on the toilet. Then she will want her breakfast sat on the toilet. She can't hold things very well enough in her hands, so cups of tea you've got to feed her fingers through the handle. She wants her medication sat on the toilet, and that'll be her tablets and her insulin, I inject her. And then it's hoist into the shower. Get her dressed in the bathroom and then put her back in the wheelchair and put her splints on her hands to keep her hands straight. It would take you two hours to get her up and dressed in the morning. It is extremely hard work.

What we do is probably not a lot different from nursing. I've done loads of training: manual handling training; vulnerable adults training; food and hygiene; medication training; peg feeding training. Some of the cases is bad though, with dementia it could be aggressive; we may get scratched, spat on, what have you. One of the first times I remember, this poor woman was covered in shit, in the hair, the face, you name it, it was everywhere. We had to shower her and she was fighting with us and shouting at us saying, 'don't bloody touch me, get off me you dirty cows'. They can call you all the names under the sun, because you are invading them and their body, but we have to intervene, you can't leave that person like it. But the personal care side of it is actually really rewarding. We go to a lady now, don't ask me what she has got because it's a great big long word I can't pronounce. She was in a bed in her living room and her curtains was closed, she never had no TV on, no radio on. She didn't really eat any food; she was peg fed. Didn't really speak, didn't laugh. She was quite incontinent and she had really grey hair. We started working with her and her improvement isn't just down to me, it's about all the girls that go into her. She is now upstairs in her own bed. She's had her hair coloured to cover all the grey. She laughs, she talks. She has all the curtains and the windows opened, and she eats food. Twice a day she uses her own toilet, which is a massive achievement for her because she thought she would never sit on her own toilet again. She started wearing a bra again; she hadn't worn a bra for years. She is doing lots of physio and we've got her walking just a couple of steps. That's why our jobs are so good.

I used to be frightened that I would find someone dead. I thought, 'What if someone dies on me, what would I do', and then it happened to me. I was amazed at how calm I was. Have you heard it said that when someone is dying, that a veil comes over their face? Well, that's what happened, and she just flopped. And after that, I wasn't frightened of seeing anybody dead. Yes, it is nursing, we are nursing but I *think we are still seen as domestic workers. I don't think we have ever been recognised. Years ago the district nurse would do a lot of what we do but now it's cheaper to get us to do it. Whereas some would say district nurses were a bit revered, we've never been seen as specialised. It's just seen as though we go in and do a bit of body washing, and that's it really. I think probably we do more hands-on than what nurses do now. We're just not recognised enough because without us, nothing would run; nothing. But people have more respect for a nurse than they would for me. If you put us both together, you know, in uniform, I am not respected. A nurse, well she is more qualified, and that nurse had to work hard. The majority of them now go to university don't they? I think, yeah, she should get better pay than me, but a lot of people still look at us as cleaners or the general dogsbody.*

I'm not saying nurses are rubbish, they're not, but the people up the top haven't got a clue. They have probably never been out and seen what a homecare's work involves. I don't know what their names are, but the people in social services, the politicians, every single one of them, they haven't got a clue. It's all about saving as much money as they can and squeezing as many people in as possible. They say they can't afford to pay us more, according to them we are expensive! I believe our pay should be much higher but I just want to be a carer to the best of my ability. I love care. I love being with the people. Some of their stories are bloody lovely, some are really sad but you take the good with the bad. In this job you are making a difference to someone's life.

I don't like being under pressure to work on my own but lone working saves money, and management have dwindled us down so we are solely on our own. There was a lady whose dementia was really bad and she couldn't remember how to bear her own weight and we had to say to the office that she needs two of us because it was so bad for our backs. Another lady didn't want to be washed and could be very difficult, but when there was two of you somebody else could come at it from a different angle to try to persuade her to be calmer. Now all that is gone, all the office want is the cheapest option, the very cheapest option. It's sad when you are working under pressure to get out as quick as possible and get on with the next one because you are not allowed to do professional caring for people.

You know, people think women aren't worth much, and it's a woman's role really because its cleaning and all the rest of it. It goes back years, but it still goes on. The trouble is that a lot of older women would not have a male homecare come in to them. Even if it was acceptable to them, people think men ought to be paid more than the rate for this job. The majority could tell you that we either prepare meals or do cleaning, they don't realise that we do so much hands-on personal care. My ex-husband fixes cars, and I fix people. Like lots of men he says 'I couldn't do the job you are doing', but I couldn't be a car mechanic. So why should he get more money for being a car mechanic and me get less for actually keeping a person independent in their own house?

Women in this day and age shouldn't need to rely on a man. You know, they're just as determined as what men are and we should be paid exactly the same as a man. I am the wage earner in this house and, well you wouldn't expect a man to live on what I have to live on every month. As a single parent, I have struggled bringing up children. I know money is not everything but it would have been nice to have a little bit for all the hard work I've given – in bloody Asda they get more than what I do. I am living on an overdraft and there is always some reason why I can never seem to get ahead with my money, never. But I wouldn't describe myself as poor because I don't need the latest technology. I don't need a brand-new kitchen; I am not starving; I can have the heating on; so no, I am not poor. But it's very hard being someone on the homecare wage. I know a woman is worth just as much as the man is but people don't realise what we do. You have got to be so many different people in this line of work, so if you broke down each one of those roles – alright then, as job descriptions – then yes we should get more money. Other people would probably look at it and say, 'Well you get paid what you're contracted for', but the point is, you have to have some sort of incentive to feel you are worth it. Unless you are actually in the thick of it and you are actually walking in the shoes of a homecare, you do not know. I can look at the lovely things of my job, but sometimes, when I come home ... the thought of poo ... it's up my nose; I can smell it, I can taste it and it makes me feel sick. Does anybody pay me for that?

Cheap Nurse and equal pay law

Early on in my research it was evident that homecare workers were being represented, and indeed presenting themselves, as cheap nurses. Clearly, I would need to find a way to communicate what was being lost in the clamour for cheapness in social care. Bringing together stories through which homecare workers expressed their professionalism and competence was a first step. Women who were hugely experienced, wise to the world and knew what they were doing when it came to caring for older people were either losing their local authority jobs or had lost them some time ago and were now working for private care companies. I built the 'Cheap Nurse' narrative by blending aspects of conversations in which homecare workers talked to me about caring and about curing – of giving medicines, providing rehabilitation and soothing troubled minds. These were their accounts of skill, dedication, commitment and expertise.

Considerable changes in the delivery and organisation of social care since the 1990s have shifted care of the elderly from hospitals and residential institutions into personal homes. In addition, social care has been marketised, homecare provision has been privatised and the employment of paid care workers has moved wholesale from the public-sector into corporate hands. The narrative figure of Cheap Nurse is set in the context of such shifts. She is well acquainted with the economic injustices of sexism, by which I mean the subordination of women which puts men at an advantage and prioritises the meeting of their needs above those of women. Paid care work carries little by way of social status and it will be evident in my discussion of the Cheap Nurse character narrative that decent terms of work have been readily dismissed as unnecessary in the organisation of the homecare industry. Across the UK economy, jobs in which women are most likely to work are also those most likely to be low paid (Low Pay Commission, 2011). The skills of women without formal qualifications carry little economic value while the skills of men with similar educational outcomes have much greater economic worth (e.g. construction workers, gardeners, scaffolders and lorry drivers, see Rubery and Grimshaw, 2007). The undervaluation of women's labour means that care work in particular does not yield a wage commensurate with otherwise comparable, non-care-based jobs.

Homecare workers who talked to me about being made redundant from their local authority jobs were aware of sexist attitudes about 'women's work' and sexist assumptions that undermined their rates of pay. Despite the economic devaluing of their skills, they passionately defended the worth of their caring capabilities, effectiveness and knowledge. In this chapter, I question how a low-cost homecare workforce has been created and maintained. I use the character of Cheap Nurse as a central device with which to explore local authority homecare work as a public service stripped of wage value in the push to create a competitive market in care provision. I demonstrate how relations of sex discrimination are linked to relations of employment, as well as to relations with service-users. It is evident that experiences of paid caregiving are infused with experiences of sex discrimination and I give particular regard to explaining how sex discrimination in pay is legally recognised, legally regulated and when it is legally permissible.

By drawing on the idea of homecare work as 'invisible' labour, the chapter weaves together a discussion about the origins of the homecare service with an account of the legal architecture of equal pay law. My purpose is to position the character narrative of Cheap Nurse within a wider historical and legal context. Pay equality between men and women is the foundation of a fair and open labour market; it is a first step towards wider equality in society and it is a prerequisite of social justice. To fully appreciate the negative economic influence of the sex discrimination to which homecare workers are exposed, we must recognise sex discrimination at work as a legally regulated relation. From my assessment of the Equal Pay Act 1970 and the Equality Act 2010 which replaced it, I make two key observations. Firstly, equal pay law offers only partial freedom from sex discrimination and its benefits are not available to all women because it does not extend its scope to all places in the labour market. Secondly, the legal architecture of equal pay law incentivises the privatisation of homecare services. I argue that equal pay law provisions are framed by sexist assumptions which marginalise the economic needs of women in paid care work. Low pay in homecare is not an accidental by-product of history but rather the framing of equal pay law has actively shaped this low-waged industry.

The 'worthlessness' of homecare work is also evident in the lack of regard which the state gives to relationships between homecare workers and the people for whom they care. Marketisation has created circumstances in which the substance of caregiving relationships is not recognised as being valuable and not assigned an economic value. This reflects sexist assumptions that there is little community significance to the economic contribution of homecare workers. It strikes me that the injustice of sexism finds expression in the personal and community traumas that flow from the transfer of homecare work from the public to the private sector. However, these are rarely acknowledged in either sociological or legally orientated research, nor by politicians or the local authority managers responsible for implementation.

Homecare as invisible labour

The terraced house where Michelle lived was remarkably busy. After three o'clock on the afternoon she shared with me, her home began to swell with family: children, grandchildren, two dogs and her partner coming in from a scarce day of casual work on a construction site. To give us privacy to talk in the kitchen, they crammed into her lounge and pretty much minded their own business, coming in occasionally for an orange squash or a biscuit. Both Michelle's children were grown up and had left the family home, but Michelle's house continued to be the place where they, their children and friends came together every day after nursery, school or work. Michelle's partner had been unemployed for the best part of 18 months and there didn't seem to be much hope of regular work for him on the horizon. Her place at the 'head of the family' was conspicuous and tangible. For most of her life, Michelle had raised her children as a single parent and she was incredibly proud to work as a local authority homecare assistant. However, Michelle and her colleagues were about to be made redundant because the local authority had decided to contract out all their work to private companies. When I asked her to describe her job to me, she was adamant: 'I am a cheap nurse. End of.'

Like others with whom I spoke, Michelle was both angry and confused about losing her job. She saw herself as a public servant and her labour as a public service. Yet it seems to me, that when paid care is organised in domestic homes it is particularly vulnerable to being undermined as a public duty or a social good. Despite the shaping of family life by taxation and legal norms, and the shaping of living spaces by social welfare and housing policy, there is a commonplace regard for domestic homes as private, personal places where people live so-called 'private lives'. Similarly, despite the investment of the state in education, transport, infrastructure and the general conditions which enable private businesses to thrive, economic markets are considered 'private', in contradistinction from the state. Regard for paid care as a public good seems incommensurate with understandings of both the home and the marketplace as 'private' spheres. Furthermore, caregiving at 'home' is culturally associated with unpaid family responsibilities, typically shouldered by women. Social expectations of care as the natural, freely available and inevitable outcome of families, marriage and having children, sit uncomfortably with the economic reality of 'homecare' as a multibillion-pound industry. The privatisation of homecare work has mixed the economically 'private' realm of the market, together with the socially 'private' realm of the home. The consequence is a concoction in which ideas of public service, state responsibility, democratic control and legal accountability seem out of place.

Michelle was in a state of disbelief. In her experience, the local authority had not paid her fairly for her skills and effort, yet she was now trying to comprehend a future in which her job would be done for an even lower price in the private sector. Michelle was certain that the service would deteriorate and the only way she could reconcile her anger, with her confusion, was to conclude that homecare work was grossly misunderstood by the public:

> I think if we would have been more recognised by the public, for what we actually do, within the home, and the training that we have got and have to do as well. I think that if that had of been put out for public knowledge, I don't think that our jobs would have been taken away.

Michelle's reflection on the local authority's decision to cease providing a public-sector homecare service framed the public as critical, if poorly informed, actors. In her view, public opinion might have been able to prevent the dismantling of the local authority homecare service, but there was a catastrophic lack of public awareness about what it was that the public was about to lose as a consequence of homecare privatisation. It is indeed remarkable how marginalised the topic of care is within mainstream political discussion (Lawson, 2007; Tronto, 2013). Caregiving has been attributed an 'aura of invisibility' on the grounds that, while it is fundamental to everyday existence, care is so familiar as to be easily overlooked and taken for granted in public debate (Bowden, 1997). Yet in contemplating the idea that care lies undetected within everyday patterns and routines, we should not lose sight of the social ties that bind women to caregiving practices and should ask ourselves if caregiving lacks the recognition it deserves because it is carried out by everyone, or because caregiving is the work of women?

Forms of labour which are culturally assigned to women within domestic settings do not carry the same level of social respect which accompanies paid labour in the wider economy. Our most basic understandings of what the word 'work' actually means are highly gendered. For example, legal rights and many opportunities for social connectedness are available to 'working people', yet people who undertake 'housework' are excluded, and work without pay rarely seems to count as 'work' at all (Busby, 2011). Theories of 'invisible work' (Kaplan-Daniels, 1987; Marx-Ferree, 1976) variously explain the undervaluing of women's paid labour by suggesting that the gendered invisibility of work in the home is carried into the labour market. It is an idea which has been applied in cases where women's contribution to the labour process is physically hidden from public view (Thomson et al., 2007); where women's skills pass without notice because they are considered to arise 'naturally' in female workgroups (Apel, 1997; Kosny and MacEachen, 2010); and where the work of women is hidden deep inside contracting chains (Murray, 2013). In such circumstances, the invisibility of women's labour makes it easier for human rights abuses to be disguised and for workers to be exploited, replaced or denied the capacity to assert their true worth (Boris and Klein, 2007; Kotiswaran, 2011).

Invisible work theory has also been applied specifically to the care industry. Paid caregiving has emerged as a market-based activity in countries around the world but feminist economists claim that the relational elements of care remain 'invisible' (Folbre, 1994; Held, 2002; Stone, 2000). The suggestion is that care work can never be fully commodified because it does not wholly fit the language, customs and expectations of commercial markets. While the relational qualities of what makes 'good care' remain unquantified, markets will inevitably fail to account for care on a complete basis and operate on the basis of undervaluation (Folbre, 2001). The 'cloak of invisibility' which surrounds caregiving, both paid and unpaid, makes it possible for homecare work to be disregarded and devalued (Barnes, 2012, p. 3).

When I discussed the issue of low wages with the women who participated in my research, it was generally apparent that they placed their own low pay in the context of the everyday attitudes they encountered – those of service-users unwilling to be cared for by men; of a general presumption that men deserved more money, that women were second-rate; and the degraded perception of homecare as cleaning work. The idea of care work as 'invisible labour' explains in part why homecare workers are so vulnerable to being paid less than they are worth. As I discuss in the next section, the state has persistently failed to recognise a need for quality employment opportunities for homecare workers. I suggest that the gendered processes by which care work is persistently stripped of economic value have resulted in the discontinuation of homecare as a role for public servants.

Sexism, sex discrimination and privatisation

Unusual among the women I interviewed for this book, Marilyn had come into homecare as a second career after working in a commercial environment. When I met her she showed me her brightly coloured, recently decorated living room; she showed me around her beautiful garden and, most special of all, she introduced me to her dad who was watching the television in an upstairs bedroom. Marilyn told me that he suffered from dementia and a number of other health problems. In addition to her paid work in homecare, she was his unpaid carer, and she clearly adored him.

However, by her own admission, Marilyn was now 'an angry woman'. Losing her local authority homecare job because of privatisation had left her 'mentally bruised' and feeling like she was going through 'a big, bad divorce or something like that'. Marilyn's emotional sensitivity was an essential attribute for performing her job well, but it also meant she was vulnerable to being hurt. She explained, 'to do this job you can't help being human. I'm not a piece of paper, not a bit of metal, and if you slap me I am going to hurt, do you know what I mean?' As Marilyn saw things, her work as a homecare assistant made an enormous contribution to her local community and she was owed more respect from the public at large than she had been shown. In Marilyn's opinion, homecare workers were treated as cheap nurses because women were undervalued by men. She directed her anger at the data recorder on which I was taping our conversation, as though she were involved in a live radio broadcast. Perhaps in the hope that someone with power and influence might eventually listen to what she had to say, she announced,

> I will tell you something about valuing women. Well, I say to all you men out there, 'This is Mrs Churchill speaking, Winston Churchill's wife. I shall say to you. You *do* devalue women. Take women out of the equation and let's see how this country runs for 24 hours because I am telling you now. It won't!'

Marilyn's appeal to Churchillian rhetoric is not as out of place as it might at first appear. Public services in Britain continue to be shaped by the ongoing impact of government decisions taken during World War II. Conscripting men into the armed services through the National Service (Armed Forces) Act 1939 created labour shortages in factories and engineering plants. However, the government feared that if it put women into 'men's' industrial jobs, employers would respond by lowering wages and this would destabilise the future earnings potential of husbands and fathers (Smith, 1981). As an alternative strategy, men who were working in the civil service were required to take up industrial jobs, and women were expected to provide replacement labour in the civil service (Summerfield, 1998; Weiler, 1993, pp. 113–14). Yet this proved insufficient as a remedy for labour shortages. As the war progressed, the government felt compelled to directly conscript women into industry, requiring almost a million women with heavy domestic responsibilities to work on a part-time basis (Smith, 1990, pp. 214–16). Families were depleted of the customary care and day-to-day efforts of wives and daughters at home and some were left in dire straits. The War Office ordered local authorities to keep a register of women who were willing and able to act as domestic helpers (Means and Smith, 1985, pp. 91–4).[1] This is how the 'home-help service' was established. While local authorities sourced the labour, the Ministry of Health met 'reasonable expenses' because most families could not afford to pay.

Both the government and trade unions were concerned at the likelihood that employers would use women as cheap labour. However, determined that trade union influence would not be undermined, Parliament turned down the opportunity to introduce equal pay legislation during the war. Employers and unions were instead encouraged to bargain collectively over women's pay rates and to use systems of job evaluation as a mechanism for pay-setting (Minutes, *War Cabinet,* 28 March 1944). When the war ended and men returned home from the frontline, the government closed down state-funded childcare and implemented a propaganda campaign calling on women to vacate industrial jobs as a matter of patriotic duty (Smith, 1990, p. 222). However, the home-help service continued, not least because many people now faced a life of disability as a consequence of wartime injuries.

Women's work as invisible labour in law

Legislation passed by the post-1945 Labour government put in place the legal infrastructure of the welfare state. The National Health Service Act 1946 imposed a duty on the Minister of Health to establish a health service

---

1 See for example Circular 179/44 issued by the War Cabinet under the Defence Regulations 1944.

to prevent, diagnose and treat mental and physical illness. The National Assistance Act 1948 included a requirement that local authorities provide support at home to older and disabled people. In lieu of industrial employment, the government offered women the opportunity to take up low paid, part-time positions in local government, health and education. One such 'opportunity' was to work as a home-help. The job was only partly paid, it was casual work and yet it was regarded as a way for women to earn a little money in return for their good 'neighbourliness' (Clarke, 1984; DHSS, 1976, p. 37; Land and Himmelweit, 2010, p. 7). In the context of rapid social transformations, the state was able to turn widespread social acceptance of women's subordinate status into political expectations of a low-cost public-sector workforce.

Sexist attitudes towards women as workers were by no means the exclusive preserve of the British government, but sexism was especially prevalent in Britain's home-help provision. In other European states, as far back as the 1950s, home-help workers were expected to engage in training programmes that combined academic study with practical experience (Dexter and Harbert, 1983, pp. 178–9). In Britain however, the state positively chose *not* to train women working as home-helps, a decision that was justified on the grounds that married women were already experienced in 'household management', they would be stripped of 'initiative' if they were trained and would become 'status conscious' and unwilling to perform 'less pleasant tasks' (Institute of Home-help Organisers, 1958, p. 20). The job of a home-help was crafted as part-time work for middle-aged women without formal skills and the state sought to prevent women from advancing their social standing when they entered the labour market as paid care workers. Being a home-help was regarded as an 'expression of society's conscience' and home-helps were expected to regard each 'client's burden [as] their own', an expectation that women were sufficiently conditioned to their social role as unwaged caregivers in their own families as to willingly shoulder additional care responsibilities in the service of the state (Dexter and Harbert, 1983, p. 204).

The state's desire to define women differently from men in the labour market was reflected in the design of statutory employment rights. Scholars of labour law widely regard the Contracts of Employment Act 1963 as the advent of 'modern' statutory employment protection (Brown et al., 2000). It created an individual right to receive notice of termination of employment and imposed a duty on employers to provide employees with written terms of employment. When debated in the House of Commons, its provisions were said to promote an ideal in which 'every employee has the right to be treated like a human-being and not be cast aside unnecessarily or without adequate notice' (Mr Diamond MP, House of Commons, Hansard, col. 1100, 1 May 1963) However, this ideal only extended to people working for 21 hours a week or more and, later in the same debate, parliamentary secretary to the Minister of Labour, Willie Whitelaw MP, clarified the government's position as, 'trying to ensure that *men* are treated like human beings, that they are given proper notice and that they are not put out on the street at a minute's or an hour's notice' (col. 1113). I have emphasised his use of the term *men* because Whitelaw proceed to justify the threshold of 21 hours a week as a measure intended to exclude 'women with domestic responsibilities [to whom] the employment relationship is not of substantial importance'. Such legal framing provided institutional support to a sex-based hierarchy in which women were, and continue to be, constructed as inferior citizens. It is an example of how sexism becomes institutionalised through statutory measures and how sexism is communicated in legal doctrine.

The routine exclusion of women from the benefit of employment protection rights has been described by labour law experts Kilpatrick and Freedland (2004) as 'almost mechanical' until the UK responded to pressure from the European Union (EU) in the mid 1990s. Labour market regulation in Britain was deliberately fashioned so as to mark out a subordinate class of labour, mainly comprised of low-waged women. The sexist inclinations of employment protection law are especially laid bare when we consider that legal measures designed to protect women from being paid less than men were also exclusory. In the discussion which follows, I argue that the right to equal pay, a legal entitlement which one might expect to level the playing field for women in low-waged work, has been blighted by sexism. The qualification rules established in equal pay law ensure that its protection is only available to women who work in close proximity to men, and in work which is comparable to work performed by men. The Equal Pay Act 1970, and provisions in the Equality Act 2010 which replaced it, were designed to offer very little to women working solely alongside other women, or to women working in occupations such as caring or cleaning which are devalued and derided as 'women's work'. Sexism, being the subordination of women to the needs and interests which serve to put men in a position of advantage, is central to the gendered rationale underpinning equal pay law. As I will illustrate, legal provisions construct work such as homecare as 'invisible labour'.

Tackling sex discrimination with equal pay law

The Treaty of Rome 1957 set out the legal foundations of the European Community (EC) and a Court of Justice was established to support its implementation (then known as the European Court of Justice, now known as the Court of Justice of the European Union). Article 119 of the Treaty asserted the principle of equal pay between men and women. It provided an assurance that competition between member states could not be 'distorted' by differences in labour costs between those states that permitted sex discrimination in pay-setting, and those that did not (*Defrenne* v. *Belgium* [1974] 1 CMLR 494). Council Directive 75/117/EEC subsequently set out how Article 119 was to be implemented and it made clear that all EC member states must pursue 'the elimination of all discrimination on grounds of sex with regard to all aspects and conditions of remuneration'.

Prior to the introduction of equal pay law in Britain, there was nothing legally amiss when employers discriminated against women by paying them less. The idea of a male 'family wage' held strong historic appeal and women in mixed-sex workplaces were typically paid 50–85 per cent of the relevant rate for men (Friedman and Meredeen, 1980). Judge-made common law supported employers' freedom to make decisions about pay howsoever they chose, as long as a pre-existing contractual term was not infringed (*Allen* v. *Flood* [1898] AC 1 HL). Hence parliament's decision to legislate in order to protect women's pay from the negative influence of sex discrimination was groundbreaking. Following almost a century of campaigning by feminists, a high-profile strike by sewing machinists in 1968 at the Ford Motor Company in Dagenham galvanised popular opinion in support of statutory action on equal pay. The Labour government of the day acted on this political momentum while shepherding equal pay legislation through the House of Commons. Both Labour and Conservative politicians committed to address the detrimental treatment of women as a source of cheap labour (see, for example, House of Commons debate, Hansard, cols. 913–1038, 9 February 1970). However, the legal context for the introduction of the Equal Pay Act 1970 was that equal pay law was required for membership of the EC.

The UK joined the EC in 1973 and by 1976 the European Court of Justice had ruled that Article 119 could be relied upon directly by citizens in all EC member states (C–43/75 *Defrenne* v. *Sabena* [1976] 2 CMLR 98). In the UK, it meant that women could bring claims in the UK courts based on their EC rights and advance these claims on appeal through the ordinary courts, up to the European Court of Justice for a final decision to which the UK courts were bound. However, as originally enacted, the Equal Pay Act 1970 fell short of EC requirements. Following a successful legal challenge by the European Commission, the Equal Pay Act was amended to permit claims of 'equal pay for work of equal value' (Equal Pay Act (Amendment) Regulations 1983 see C61/81 *Commission of the European Communities* v. *United Kingdom* [1982] ECR 601).

The Equal Pay Act 1970 was exclusively concerned with eliminating sex discrimination in pay. It introduced an 'equality clause' into the contract of every worker and, within its rules, enabled them to draw on the equality clause in the event that a person of the opposite sex was employed on more favourable terms. The law gave both women and men the opportunity to expose 'his and hers' contracting practices and claims could be brought before an employment tribunal while employed, or within six months of their employment ending.[2] Since the problem that the law sought to address was the underpayment of women, I will discuss potential claims from the perspective of female claimants. What mattered in law was not the *total* amount of a woman's pay but her individual contractual terms; each could be assessed in relation to corresponding terms in the employment contract of a comparable man (*Hayward* v. *Cammell Laird Shipbuilders* [1988] ICR 464 HL). Identifying a resulting pay difference was not enough to bring a successful claim; a court or tribunal had to find that the *reason* for the difference was because of sex discrimination. The term 'sex discrimination' thus denotes a specific legal relationship through which an adjudication about individual pay can ensue. In law, such discrimination can be identified as either 'direct' or 'indirect' with the key legal difference between them being that direct discrimination is always unlawful, while indirect discrimination is lawful if it can be justified.

Direct discrimination occurs if an employer pays a woman less than a man for the reason that she is a woman. Paying a woman less than a man for a *different* reason, however, is within the law. So employers rebutting equal pay claims often argued that the reason for a pay difference was not one of sex. This became known as a 'genuine material factor defence' and each case was assessed on its individual merit by tribunals and courts. By looking back at the case law we can see that claims could be defeated with the following arguments:

- The higher paid man had greater productivity or responsibility (*Villalba* v. *Merrill Lynch* [2006] IRLR 437 EAT):
  — He had longer service (*Shields* v. *E. Coomes Holdings* [1978] IRLR 263 CA; *Wilson* v. *Health and Safety Executive* [2009] EWCA Civ 1074; *Skills Development Scotland* v. *Buchanan* [2011] Eq LR 955 EAT).
  — He had more experience, was better educated or other pertinent factors applied when his period of employment first began (*Bowling* v. *Secretary of State for Justice* [2012] IRLR 382 EAT; *Shields* v. *E. Coomes Holdings* [1978] IRLR 263 CA; *Glasgow City Council* v. *Marshall* [2000] IRLR 272 HL).
- The higher paid man was recruited at a time of labour shortage:
  — He filled a need for specialist skills (*Ojutiku* v. *Manpower* [1983] ICR 661 CA; *Rainey* v. *Greater Glasgow Health Board* [1987] IRLR 26 HL; *Benvenista* v. *University of Southampton* [1989] ICR 617 CA).

---

2 Cf. *Abdulla* v. *Birmingham City Council* [2012] UKSC 47 which established for the first time that it is possible for claims to be brought in the ordinary courts within a six-year limitation period, as is standard in claims for contractual breach.

The first group of reasons relate to instrumental value; the man in question is doing work for which a woman would have received equal pay except that the man exhibits qualities by which he is regarded to be of greater use to the employer. The last two reasons relate to market forces – instances where particular demand requires an employer to inflate wages in order to secure skills or talent. Once a genuine material factor is accepted as the reason for a pay difference, continued economic inequality between a claimant and her male comparator is legally permissible. If a man, lawfully, is appointed on a rate of higher pay than a woman in equal work, the passage of time has no impact on the lawfulness of the reason for so doing. It seems that an employer may continue the pay difference *ad infinitum* without any requirement for wages to be equalised even in the medium to long term (*Nelson* v. *Carillion Service* [2003] EWCA 544; *Bowling* v. *Secretary of State for Justice* [2012] IRLR 382 EAT). In such circumstances, the law provides no route at all through which pay inequality can be remedied, because the woman's lower pay is rendered legally invisible. However, we should also bear in mind that judicial determinations of what counts as acceptable instrumental value or market forces explanations are subject to ongoing revision, reflecting wider social and attitudinal change. The classic example of this lies in judicial assessments of part-time work.

Social expectations that women work in 'support' of men, supplementing the male wage and providing unwaged labour at home, together with the state's historic construction of the public service workforce, have funnelled women into part-time work which is also low-waged. While the number of women in paid employment has steadily increased since the 1970s, the proportion of women in part-time employment over the past 30 years has remained consistent at about 45 per cent (Office for National Statistics, 2013a, p. 1). However, in the 1970s and early 1980s it was legally permissible for employers to pay a woman working part-time an hourly rate which was lower than that paid to a man, in the same job, working full-time (see, for example, *Handley* v. *H Mono* [1978] IRLR 534 EAT; *Clay Cross (Quarry Services)* v. *Fletcher* [1978] 1 WLR 1429 CA). In the event of an equal pay claim, it was open to employers to argue that full-time workers had greater instrumental value because the administrative costs associated with employing part-timers were proportionately larger. Alternatively, employers could rely on a market forces approach and argue that full-time workers were in higher demand because they made more extensive use of equipment or machinery in which a firm had invested. However, this jurisprudence was overturned by a ruling of the European Court of Justice in *Jenkins* v. *Kingsgate* ([1981] ICR 715). Accordingly, paying lower rates to women who were working part-time than to men working full-time was a form of indirect discrimination which had to be legally justified if it was to be accepted as lawful.[3]

Indirect discrimination occurs if an employer introduces a 'provision criterion or practice' which puts women at a 'particular disadvantage' when compared with men (most recently set out in s 19 Equality Act 2010). Examples of initiatives which a court has treated as a relevant 'provision, criterion or practice' include policies excluding part-time workers from occupational pension schemes, or bonus schemes which reward productivity in jobs done by men but do not equally apply in jobs done by women. Once a disadvantage of indirect discrimination is established, an employer has the opportunity to show that the factor in question is 'a proportionate means of achieving a legitimate aim'. The ability to justify indirect sex discrimination is a legal strategy which makes pay inequality between men and women appear 'invisible' in the light of business needs. Employers can lawfully justify wage systems which reward men more favourably than women, so long as they can establish that the indirect sex-based pay disadvantage to which women are exposed fulfils a business aim and is proportionate to its business benefit (*Haq* v. *Audit Commission* [2012] EWCA Civ 1621).

A limited right to equal pay

In relation to both direct and indirect sex discrimination, strict qualifying provisions in the Equal Pay Act 1970 set limits on the ability of women to bring legal claims.

Consequently, a claimant cannot compare her pay with any man of her choosing; a court or tribunal had to approve the comparison according to statutory rules which excluded many women from making successful claims. According to s 1(2) the comparator man had to be in 'like work' (meaning work which was the same or very similar), or in work that had been 'rated as equivalent' under an objective job evaluation scheme, or (where an employer did not have a satisfactory job evaluation scheme in place) in 'work of equal value' as assessed at the instruction of a court or tribunal. In addition, the comparison had to be with a man in equal work at the 'same employment'. It is a requirement in EU law that potential comparators work in the same 'establishment', a term meaning 'the unit to which the workers (…) are assigned to carry out their duties' (C–449/93 *Rockfon A/S* v. *Specialarbejderforbundet I Danmark* [1995] ECR 1-4291 [34]). Yet the 'same employment' requirement of the Equal Pay Act *also* required a comparator to work for the same employer as the claimant.

---

3 The classic explanation of justification is C–170/84 *Bilka-Kaufhaus* v. *Weber Von Hartz* [1986] 2 CMLR 701. (See discussion in Busby, 2011, pp. 152–3.)

The Equal Pay Act pre-dated the Race Relations Act 1976 (which made discrimination on grounds of race unlawful). The Race Relations Act made it unlawful to segregate people on racial grounds by stating that, in and of itself, segregation constituted less favourable treatment (s 1). However, segregating women from men on grounds of sex was not made unlawful by the Equal Pay Act. As recognised by the House of Lords in *Leverton* v. *Clywd County Council* the statutory framework permits employers to operate 'essentially different employment regimes at different establishments' ([1989] AC 706 p. 746). Employers may organise their workforce at different establishments and permissibly segregate workers in female-dominated occupations into discreet locations. Nevertheless, the arbitrary exercise of pay-setting power by employers was constrained by s 1(6) of the Equal Pay Act. It provided the opportunity for a woman to make a comparison to a man working for the same employer, but at a different establishment, if 'common terms of work apply'. These 'common terms' were those reached through negotiations between trade unions and employers and were set out in collective agreements. In *North* v. *Dumfries and Galloway Council* the Supreme Court found that provisions at s 1(6) enabled childcare workers employed in local authority nursery schools to validly compare their terms with men in work of equal value employed to provide refuse collection, road repairs and groundwork services by the same local authority ([2013] UKSC 45). Even though these work groups were occupationally distinct and geographically separate (being located at different 'establishments'), the law required their pay to be equalised because the 'common terms' of collective agreements spanned across the local authority workforce.

Because of the connections established through union representation, it was possible to remedy in law the sex discrimination manifest in paying more for jobs which required physical strength and the operation of machinery, than for jobs which required dexterity or attention to people. As a consequence of s 1(6), the invisibility of women's labour in traditionally gendered occupations such as childcare, catering and care of the elderly, could be challenged in law where collective bargaining alone had not achieved equal pay. It was in those occupations in particular that women were most likely to be adversely affected by sex discrimination. Where they were employed in mixed-sex workforces with active trade unions there was the potential to benefit under equal pay provisions. However, it has been argued that it was always problematic for equal pay law to make women reliant on historic patterns of union organisation for an effective right to equal pay, particularly because of declining trade union influence and the collapse in collective bargaining coverage across the UK labour market since the 1970s (Fredman, 2008, p. 197). Yet, in homecare, a workforce employed within local authorities had access to public-sector trade union representation and came within the scope of the Equal Pay Act 1970 as a consequence of s 1(6).

The Equal Pay Act was a sister act to the Sex Discrimination Act 1975 (which provided protection from discrimination in hiring decisions, discriminatory dismissal and harassment, and access to opportunities such as training). The Sex Discrimination Act gave women greater scope to establish less favourable treatment than did the Equal Pay Act. Arguably this was because the Equal Pay Act regulated sex discrimination in relation to women's pay, whereas the Sex Discrimination Act was less overtly concerned with economic justice. For example, under the Sex Discrimination Act s 1(1) a person discriminates against a woman if, 'on the ground of her sex he treats her less favourably than he treats or would treat' a man, or if, 'he applies to her a requirement or condition which he applies or would apply' equally to a man but it puts her at a disadvantage or detriment. The key phrases in these provisions – 'would treat' and 'would apply' – enabled women to challenge sex discrimination on the basis that, in principle and hypothetically, a man *would be* treated more favourably. Yet under the Equal Pay Act (and most recently s 79 of the Equality Act 2010) sex discrimination in relation to pay is unlawful only where women can identify an actually existing male comparator on the basis of 'concrete appraisals of work actually performed' by men and women (C–129/79 *Macarthy's* v. *Smith* [1980] IRLR 210; *Walton Centre for Neurology* v. *Bewley* [2008] IRLR 588 EAT).

The design of the Equal Pay Act overlooked the problem that many, if not most, low-waged women are employed at lower rates of pay than are men because employers can treat women less favourably as a collective group, irrespective of the presence of men in their places of work or occupations. Women's earnings are at their lowest in all-female workgroups, when they are working in traditionally 'female' roles, and when employed on a part-time basis (Hirsch, 2005; Manning and Petrongolo, 2005; OECD, 2010). Although the sexist underpayment of women is not predominantly found in the presence of similarly situated men, legal cognition of discrimination is only possible where underpayment is unveiled in relation to an eligible male comparator. The extent to which a statutory right to equal pay is effective, is a measure of the willingness of the state to provide women with a place in the labour market that is not devalued by sexist assumptions or practices. When introducing Equal Pay Act provisions to the House of Commons in 1970, supporters championed its benefit to 'poor women' and its potential to reduce women's exploitation (see for example Lena Jeger MP, House of Commons, Hansard, cols. 968–71, 9 February 1970). Yet, over 40 years later, women continue to be concentrated in the lowest paid jobs and the gendered structuring of the labour market remains in place. The persistence of pay inequality not only suggests that statutory measures have been insufficiently robust, but also points to a lack of motivation on the part of the British state to free all women from the economic impact of sexism upon their wages.

Having explained a little of the post-war origins of the homecare service and provided an overview of equal pay law, I now turn to consider how the legal construct that is 'sex discrimination' relates to the contemporary undervaluing of homecare work. The discussion focuses on how concerns about skills and sexism were raised by the homecare workers with whom I spoke. My purpose is to illustrate that sexist presumptions and a marginalising of women's talents and capabilities are inherent within the organisation of homecare work. I will argue that the statutory design of equal pay law is a prominent factor in the development of a marketised and low-cost homecare industry which fails to recognise or reward caregiving as a skilled endeavour.

The gendered invisibility of 'skill'

Michelle was the first, but certainly not the only, homecare worker with whom I spoke to define her position in society by the phrase 'cheap nurse'. These two words usefully captured the idea of an undervalued yet skilled caregiver and were also used by women I interviewed who worked in the private sector. They were surprised at the technical ability that was needed to do a homecare job well, mainly on account of recruitment adverts that had stressed, 'no experience or qualifications required'. Donna was one such example. She worked for a care agency and thought that her low wages did not reflect the complexity of her work. She explained, 'I am a cheap nurse. Although you're not giving injections and you're not trained [like a nurse] you are fully trained to do certain things that nurses either used to do, or should do.'

Donna was right. From the 1990s onwards, homecare workers across the UK took on much of the work of district nurses. Prior to that, they had been employed as 'home-helps' to provide companionship, to light coal fires, to clean, cook and 'care-take' for older people, but back then there had been little, if any, personal or intimate body-work involved in the job. Donna's responsibilities as a 'homecare', however, were to people with severe disabilities or those who were terminally ill or bed-bound. She would bathe them, change their incontinence pads, empty and replace catheter bags, and position or reposition her service-users so as to manage or prevent pressure sores. A key skill she needed in her job was to persuade people to trust her, even though she was a total stranger in their homes and might never see them more than once or twice.

Donna's employer had a labour supply contract with a private care company, which in turn had a contract to provide homecare services with the same local authority from which Michelle was being made redundant. In Donna's own words, she was a 'gap filler' and provided an intimate service to people she met on a one-off, or at best infrequent, basis. A good way to conceive of the work, she told me, was to throw the nurse role together with a fair sprinkle of the organising of a social worker and the hard graft of a hospital cleaner. The skills required to do her job were constructed as invisible in the recruitment process, did not appear in any job advertisements and were not discussed at interview, and this provided a clear indication that they were also invisible in pay-setting processes.

In my research, I found that like Donna, other homecare workers were prone to selling themselves short when it came to talking in detail about skill. Although they each insisted that homecare work was skilled, their lack of formal education qualifications appeared to present a considerable hurdle. Michelle, for example, was keen to tell me that her choice to work in homecare had been shaped by a lack of access to education. When she was younger, it had been her ambition to be a nurse and Michelle had tried to gain qualifications at night-school, but on each occasion something went wrong (relationship breakdowns, unemployment or financial hardship) and she had repeatedly been compelled to leave her college course. It was neither intellect nor lack of ambition which held her back, but her situation. Her experiences echo those of many working-class women who may fail, or perceive of themselves as failing, in adult education, because they cannot surmount the combined problems of extensive labour market commitments, childcare/domestic responsibilities and insufficient time for study (Reay, 2003). As Michelle put it, 'I've got the ability to train, I just haven't got the lifestyle to be able to give me that opportunity to train because I have always been the mainstay at home.' Disadvantages of gender and class meant that the capabilities she acquired as a mother and an unpaid family caregiver were worth little on the labour market. It was a cruel irony then that fulfilling those roles also prevented her from accessing the education she would need in order to gain alternative, and better paid, employment.

Other women with whom I spoke told me that once it became clear that their hopes of becoming a nurse would never materialise, they settled for a career in homecare as the next best thing. Many had previously worked as hospital domestics, in nursing homes or in hospices. A big attraction of employment in local authority homecare was the prospect of job security, and latterly, its offer of access to training. Yet in Michelle's experience, the training she received as a public-sector worker was not accompanied by the certificates, pay rises and greater autonomy which she had been promised. Unlike nurses, who have a national professional standards body, homecare workers are unaccredited, the effectiveness of their representation through systems of collective bargaining in local authorities has been patchy, they face aggressive cost competition and they lack a clear professional identity. When Michelle described herself to me as a 'cheap nurse' she emphasised that she was indeed trained and competent in basic nursing care, even though her pay did not reflect this and she was not formally accredited with having acquired predefined 'skills'.

All the homecare workers I spoke with were adamant that their work was skilled, but many found it frustrating to try and explain this. Local authority-employed workers could reel off a list of training courses they had attended: dementia, mental health training, bereavement training, first aid, colostomy bags, small dressings and wounds, and incontinence care. Nevertheless, they preferred to talk about 'experience' and being 'up to date' rather than about 'skill'. The concept of skill is historically, rather than biologically or technologically, constructed and reflects unequal structures of class power as well as long-standing inequalities of gender (Jenson, 1989). Although I tried to get homecare workers to talk about their technical competence, it was clear that relational accomplishments were the factors they relied upon to assert their worth. These included the ability to 'be a friend'; to 'get [service-users] to trust you'; 'to know what to look for'; 'be confident in what you do'; and 'respect their wishes and dignity'. The exception however was the administering of medication to service-users and all the women taking part in my research named 'giving meds' as a skill.

Homecare workers are routinely required to empty tablets from a dosset box (which is prepreared by a pharmacist), give the tablets to service-users and record that the tablets have been ingested. The practice carried the status of 'skill' because 'giving meds' resulted in a written record, confirmed by a personal signature, which was regarded as legally significant. It is an area of responsibility for which homecare workers need to be alert and attentive, but the task of 'giving meds' appeared to me to be far less complex and intellectually challenging than the relational work of homecare. Indeed, the status value of 'giving meds' lay with the necessity of a written record, which made it objectively 'visible' to the world outside the domestic home. However, when I asked Michelle to tell me about the skills associated with giving medication she switched from referring to her service-users by their forenames and talked in impersonal terms, for example referring to the 'monitoring of this body'. One reason why homecare workers found it so hard to talk about their skill and technical accomplishment was because such conversations required them to objectify their service-users. Nevertheless, several homecare workers used 'giving meds' as a pay reference point, explaining that healthcare assistants on hospital wards were better paid than them but did not carry the responsibility of working alone. They also noted that employers referred to the practice of 'giving meds' as 'prompting medication', which they regarded as an attempt to degrade their skills and make responsibility for medicine sound less clinical, less responsible and, by implication, less economically valuable.

Manipulating the visibility and invisibility of skills, on the basis of established understandings of gender roles, is a key mechanism through which homecare workers are exposed to pay disadvantage. For example, Michelle had received formal training in how to give eye drops and administer skin creams. Having completed the course at the instruction of her employer, she was entitled to a pay increase in recognition of her greater utility, quasi-clinical responsibilities and the fact that these tasks had previously been undertaken by a university-educated district nurse employed by the National Health Service. She discovered however that the pay rise only came into effect when she visited a service-user who specifically needed eye drops or skin creams. As Michelle put it, 'for administering these potions and lotions I was entitled to an extra 50p a time ... it was so little money, it was a joke'. Nevertheless, she really enjoyed the extra responsibilities and had appreciated the opportunity to train. It was deeply disappointing then that government funding for this initiative ended soon after it was launched. As a consequence, Michelle was specifically instructed to stop giving eye drops, cease administering creams and her manager warned her she was no longer 'insured' for these purposes.

This turn of events – training up Michelle and her colleagues, only to later withdraw permission to act on their new skills and knowledge – made life difficult for them at a practical level. Decommissioning the work was unenforceable because service-users' needs could not be turned off like a tap. So Michelle didn't stop applying the eye drops or administering creams; she simply stopped telling her manager she was doing it, and no longer claimed the 50p. Her account illuminates how sexism is entwined with workplace practices and systems of value. Setting aside the derisory amount of the pay increase, her new skills were only recognised on each individual occasion that they were physically put into practice. This suggests that the attainment of formal skills did not result in an increase in the value of Michelle's labour as a whole; there was no financial advantage for her to gain from additional training, and any suggestion that her financial worth would be enhanced was illusory. The payment system put in place was a classic example of payment for piecework (for type A clients, the standard payment applied; for type B clients, the enhancement). This ethos objectified service-users and thus also denied recognition of Michelle's skill in caring for people as unique individuals with highly personal needs. Michelle's account emphasises how homecare work is practically administered as an activity in which skills have no value and remain unrecognised, even in the context of technical competency. As Michelle described later in our conversation, being trained in skills which were subsequently rejected 'felt like being picked up and praised and then all of a sudden, we were gone, we were too much money.'

It seems that homecare workers are conceptually and practically separated from understandings of medical care and denied the labels of accreditation associated with healthcare knowledge. While the tasks performed by homecare workers clearly entail life-sustaining work which might otherwise take place in medical institutions, the domestic location of their work continues to invoke home-help traditions in which local authorities provided replacement labour for wives and daughters. The failure to credit homecare workers with 'skill' continues to reinforce gendered perceptions of homecare as 'wife-like' work and the sexist assumptions that anchor the value of paid caregiving to the familial labour of care-taking, cooking, washing and cleaning. The occupational culture and discourse of homecare prizes relational informality to the extent that it distinguishes homecare workers from the district nurses who preceded them. This is reflected in an occupational language of 'service-users', 'respect', 'dignity', 'experience' and 'prompting', in contradistinction to a medicalised language of 'patients', 'procedures', 'skills' and 'administering medication'.

Cheap Nurse and the regulation of care

The social care responsibilities of local authorities are set out in law and the pursuit of 'cheapness' has arguably been a theme running through the regulatory design and redesign of public policy in recent decades. The National Health and Community Care Act 1990 laid the groundwork for the marketisation of social care and radically altered the structure of local authority social services departments. The local authority role of defining and assessing adult care needs had to be organisationally separated from the provision of adult care services. In spatially separating the legal duty to assess care needs from the duty to provide care, each local authority was encouraged to procure care services from private-sector organisations based on commissioning processes. The UK became the first state in Western Europe to build a competitive market in social care (Pavolini and Ranci, 2008). Reforms were dominated by the introduction and consolidation of market-based provision in which a narrow focus on efficiency came to overshadow broader notions of public accountability (Forder et al., 1996). Where independent (mainly private-sector) organisations were considered to have the capacity to deliver services at a lower cost than the public-sector, it was expected that local authorities would enter into service-delivery contracts with them (Jaffe et al., 2008).

Several of the local authority homecare workers whom I interviewed for this book recalled how their jobs had changed in response to the introduction of market pressures. In the first instance, their laundry service work and other time-intensive tasks such as shopping and going out to collect pensions were contracted out to private providers. The plan in their local authority area was to enable 'in-house' homecare workers to dedicate themselves to personal care and a more intense and demanding work rota. Eager to retain homecare as a public-sector service, Michelle and her colleagues had negotiated through their trade unions to change hours of work and they entered into new split-shift patterns which concentrated their working time in the peak demand periods of early mornings, weekends and late evenings. As the pressure to prove their economic competitiveness increased, homecare workers were expected to perform more of the work which had previously been carried out by district nurses, and demands for efficiency and value for money seemed unending. Caring for people with increasingly complex medical conditions presented homecare workers with an opportunity for 'up-skilling' and many engaged positively with that prospect because they wanted to be recognised as care professionals.

Service-users began to see changes too. Local authority commissioners found ways to purchase homecare on a 'time and task' basis, defining the care needs of individual service-users on the basis of tight time allocations. In towns and cities across the UK, the private sector's share of the market grew much faster than had been initially expected (Knapp et al., 2005, pp. 4–5). As early as 1996, research began to show that privatisation did not improve care quality and that the marketised system resulted in shorter visit times and a lack of continuity of caregiver (Lewis and Glennerster, 1996). However, its attraction lay in cost savings and the opportunity for short-term cost cutting was 'irresistible' to the state (Rhodes, 2005, p. 146).

In addition, there were concerns about workforce training. A scheme of national minimum standards laid down via the Care Standards Act 2000 required that at least 50 per cent of workers in any organisation providing homecare services were qualified to NVQ Level 2 in social care. The standards also introduced mandatory induction training for all new staff as well as a requirement for employment references and criminal record checks prior to recruitment. Assuming that care quality would flow from a combination of light-touch regulation and market forces, the Labour governments of 1997–2010 gave insufficient priority to the planning, regulation and training of the care workforce (Lewis and West, 2014). Consequently, local authority homecare services, where a majority of trained workers were employed, were competing with private-sector organisations that appeared reluctant to comply with the standards. Seven years after the standards became a legal requirement, over 20 per cent of homecare organisations remained in breach (Rubery et al., 2011). In 2010, and under a new Conservative-led coalition government, plans to make homecare a registered profession based on national minimum qualifications were abandoned altogether. By 2015, industry regulators reported that a third of care workers lacked any basic on the job induction training at all (Boffey, 2015) and a 2016 study of homecare workers engaged in the independent sector in Wales reported that, despite the claims and assertions of managers and local authority commissioners, homecare workers complained of having no access to training at all (Atkinson et al., 2016).

Given the industry-wide and aggressive emphasis on cost reduction, as well as the lack of formal accreditation of skills, the fundamental flaw in the cheap nurse approach to the management of local authority homecare services was that Cheap Nurse could never be cheap enough. The industrial issues most likely to give rise to discriminatory pay were given free rein. These included, the absence of collective bargaining in the private sector, the concentration of care in domestic settings, the segregation of women into all-female workgroups with contracting organisations, the commodification of care, non-standard hours of work, intense labour cost competition, disregard for issues of public service, invisible labour within contracting chains, the shaping of work practices on the basis of gendered norms, non-enforcement of legal standards and the degradation of women's skills. In such circumstances, it was inevitable that Michelle and her coworkers would be replaced by a lower cost, contracted workforce.

Sex discrimination and marketisation

Cost pressures formed the backdrop to an equal pay claim heard in 2008 which concerned local authority-employed care workers in Coventry. The case of *Coventry City Council* v. *Nicholls* exemplifies the impact of marketisation on local authorities across the UK ([2009] IRLR 345 EAT). On behalf of homecare workers it was argued that, contrary to their entitlements under the Equal Pay Act 1970, they had been paid less than was paid to men in equal work in other council departments. The employer submitted in its defence that the difference in pay was not because of sex discrimination but because the men were paid a bonus for enhanced productivity and delivered efficiency savings. However, this explanation was not accepted by the Employment Appeal Tribunal. In a judgment which supported the women's claim, Justice Elias reasoned that efficiency savings in departments employing workers in traditionally male jobs were only possible because departmental budgets were more generous to begin with than in social services. He found that the pay differences were tainted by sex and reflected a sex-based bias in the practice of paying bonuses to the men. Social services budgets had been stripped back to the bone on the basis of pay structures which 'under-rewarded jobs occupied almost exclusively by women' (Justice Elias [48], confirmed in *Coventry City Council* v. *Nicholls* [2009] EWCA Civ 1449). The processes of marketisation to which homecare workers at Coventry had been exposed followed long-standing and sexist conventions which kept pay low within an almost exclusively female workgroup.

Since the National Health and Community Care Act 1990, successive governments have chosen to place state responsibilities within an environment characterised by the 'relentless extension' of market relations (Lawson, 2007). Services are continuously subject to reorganisation so as to become conducive to trade, and they remain transitory and transportable. Reorganisation alters the geographic dimensions of care because market forces facilitate the move of state-funded care into lower cost places such as service-users' own homes and away from more expensive places such as hospitals and residential care homes. Under a market-based system of social care provision, a large number of people who would previously have been admitted to residential care institutions are alternatively provided with an intensive homecare service, to include personal care and several visits by care workers to their home each day. Marketisation impacts on the scale of homecare too, as services are parcelled into quantifiable packages, which meet some of the needs, of some of the people, while leaving others unaddressed. This fluidity of supply, however, is not mirrored by a fluidity of care needs across the population. With more people living longer, considerable growth in demand for care has been both foreseeable and consistent with predictions (Mullan, 2000). Where state-funded care services are either insufficient or unavailable, people with care needs have little choice but to rely on the unpaid labour of family (wives and daughters), the generosity of neighbours, or else they are faced with enduring the mental and physical consequences of neglect.

Despite the huge cost savings which have accrued from shifting care directly into people's own homes, the turn towards homecare provision has been grounded in 'considerable pressure to reduce costs', almost from day one (Knapp et al., 2005, pp. 4–5). As a political strategy, marketisation means that the state no longer directly *provides* care to *recipient* citizens; instead, care is bought and sold as a commodity by the state, by commercial organisations and by service-users. Throughout the UK, the marketisation of homecare has coincided with reduced expenditure on care services by the state. State-funded homecare has been exposed to competitive pressures, which include structural pressures to set wages at levels which are discriminatory on the basis of sex. The cost difference between services purchased from the private sector and those provided by the public-sector are stark. In 2009, private and voluntary sector providers were charging an average of £15.10 an hour while public-sector costs were on average £30.85 an hour (UKHCA, 2012). It would appear that the effect of privatisation was to cut the price of homecare by half. However, these figures overlook the impact and injustice of discriminatory rates of pay consequently imposed on women providing hands-on care, the loss of skills and competencies to redundancy, the reduction in care quality and the aspects of homecare delivery lost in the contracting process.

Through marketisation, new forms of caring relations arise in older and disabled people's own homes yet they draw on time-worn sexist assumptions about women's propensity for care work in domestic spaces, as well as on the social stereotyping through which jobs intended for working-class women are designed to offer poor-quality employment. A contemporary innovation, however, has been to capture these classed and gendered devices of domination within a marketised system, and exploit them as a competitive resource. 'Marketisation' names the political and organisational environment in which 'Cheap Nurse' is required. Every aspect of homecare provision is regarded as a cost and, as I will now discuss, this includes the basic right of homecare workers to be protected from sex discrimination in pay.

The issue of equal pay in public-sector homecare

Until the mid 1990s equal pay issues in local authorities were dealt with by negotiations between trade unions and employers. Only a handful of cases were ever presented to the tribunals or courts and, in those instances, it was the existence of workplace collective bargaining which made it possible for women to connect their pay to potential comparators (*Leverton* v. *Clywd County Council; British Coal* v. *Smith and North Yorkshire County Council* v. *Ratcliffe* [1994] IRLR 342 CA). Yet the ruling of the European Court of Justice in *Enderby* v. *Frenchay Health Authority* ushered in a radical step-change in equal pay litigation (C127/92 [1993] ECR 1-5535). It determined that in circumstances of indirect discrimination, a case could proceed when there was strong statistical evidence of a pay difference between comparable men and women but no identified provision, criterion or practice with which the pay difference corresponded. It was significant for trade unions because discrimination could now be inferred between men and women who had their pay determined by entirely separate collective bargaining processes, so long as they worked within the same establishment. Previously, the law had identified common collective bargaining as a provision, criterion or practice through which indirect discrimination might arise and legal interest lay in ensuring that the terms of any resultant collective agreements were free from discrimination. Following *Enderby*, however, the law was open to exploring discrimination which might be hidden within or between different collective bargaining processes.

In local government, there were known pay disparities where groups of either predominantly male or predominantly female workers were covered by separate collective bargaining processes and there were also large bonus payments available to workers in traditionally 'male' manual occupations (National Joint Council for Local Government, 1998). Aware of their potential exposure to equal pay claims in the courts, public-sector employers responded to the *Enderby* development by integrating bargaining arrangements and committing to harmonise terms and conditions (Hastings, 2003; UNISON, 2005). In 1997, local authorities signed a landmark national agreement to introduce non-discriminatory pay within a decade. Known as 'Single Status', this was a commitment to harmonise hours and place all workers on the same single pay spine based on local job evaluation assessments. However, neither central nor local government was willing to increase their overall wage bill in order to correct historic pay discrimination (Thornley, 2006). As a consequence, achieving the aim of pay equality depended upon cutting pay in several male dominated and mixed-sex workgroups in order to offset the costs of levelling up the wages of underpaid women (TUC, 2013). Owing to the complexity of negotiations which needed to take place, and in the absence of a national plan to finance equal pay, the implementation of Single Status proved painfully slow in many parts of the country and non-existent in others (Local Government Employers Association, 2006).

The largest group of workers who stood to gain from the Single Status process were local authority care workers. They had been subjected to discriminatory rates of pay ever since the post-war foundation of the welfare state (Thornley, 2006). When the jobs of homecare workers were graded in job evaluation exercises alongside the jobs of men in traditionally 'male' occupations, homecare work was rated as a 'skilled' job. For example, it was graded well above the work of cleaners and as being equal to the skilled operation of refuse collection lorries by HGV drivers. However, throughout the UK the take-home pay of (female) homecare workers employed by local authorities was dramatically lower than the take-home pay of (male) drivers in the refuse collection service. Indeed, the annual earnings of many homecare workers was even less than that of men employed to work in lower-graded jobs such as grounds maintenance (see *Redcar and Cleveland Borough Council* v. *Bainbridge* [2007] EWCA Civ 929). Such widespread pay differences were a consequence of productivity bonus schemes –predominantly available in 'men's work' and unavailable to women in homecare. Nevertheless, as the law stood at the time, local authority employers seeking to defend potential equal pay claims could proffer the reason of greater productivity as a genuine material factor defence, and even if that strategy failed, they could rely on greater productivity as a justification for any indirect discrimination – or so it was thought.

Equal pay and privatisation

In 2003, and in response to an earlier ruling by the European Court of Justice, the existing statutory limit on financial awards in successful equal pay claims was increased from two to six years' worth of compensatory back pay.[4] This made formal legal claims in the UK a more worthwhile economic prospect for women in low-waged or part-time employment. However, it was the equal pay claim of homecare workers in the case of *Redcar and Cleveland Borough Council* v. *Degnan* that provided a watershed moment. The ruling paved the way for tens of thousands of women to be able to claim equal wages with men on higher pay ([2005] EWCA Civ 726). The Court of Appeal accepted that the payment of bonuses in work predominantly carried out by men was to the detriment of women in traditionally female occupations and the result of indirect discrimination. Therefore, unless local authorities were able to prove that bonus payments were genuinely linked to productivity improvements, bonuses could not be justified and the pay differences between claimants and their comparators would be unlawful. The law would treat men's extra money as being part of their basic wages and female claimants would be entitled to compensatory back pay to cover their losses.

Bonuses had been the centrepiece of locally negotiated productivity settlements since the 1960s. The cumulative effect of bonus increases over several decades had been to secure take-home pay in jobs carried out by men that was between 30 and 100 per cent higher than that paid to women in equal work (National Joint Council for Local Government, 1998). The task of justifying bonuses was complicated and many local authorities had neither the paperwork nor the managerial evidence to link payments to ongoing productivity improvements. In truth, local authorities had awarded bonus payments as a matter of routine and this created widespread differentials between male and female rates of pay (see, for example, *South Tyneside Metropolitan Council* v. *Anderson* [2007] EWCA 654; *Barker* v. *Birmingham City Council* [2010] unreported 3921 23/04/2010 ET). Rectifying the legacy of public-sector sex discrimination would prove to be hugely costly and following *Degnan,* over 200,000 individual claims for equal pay proceeded at an estimated settlement cost of £5 billion (TUC, 2013).

Three-quarters of local authorities failed to implement Single Status by the 2007 deadline (Local Government Employers Association, 2006). In response to the sheer scale of the collective liabilities they faced, local authorities tried to protect themselves from claims. One obvious strategy was to focus on the time limits that governed women's ability to claim, another was to reconfigure relations of employment to ensure that women would not be able to make valid comparisons to higher paid men. Hence

---

4   The Equal Pay Act 1970 (Amendment) Regulations 2003 followed *Levez* v. *TH Jennings* [1999] IRLR 36 to bring equal pay remedies in line with those generally available for breach of contract.

employer priority shifted from rectifying pay inequality towards outsourcing jobs. A particular focus was the privatisation of care work (potential equal pay liabilities were greatest among the local authority care workforce). While awaiting the implementation of non-discriminatory pay in the period 1997–2007, almost half of the eligible local authority social care workforce was shifted into private-sector employment with contractor companies, either through transfer or by redundancy and rehire with a new employer (see Rubery and Urwin, 2011, pp. 123–4). The benefit to local authorities was twofold. Firstly, since equal pay claims are subject to time limitations which require submission to a tribunal within six months of the end of employment, their exposure to claims became time-limited (cf. *Abdulla* v. *Birmingham City Council* – see note 2 in this chapter). Secondly, once outside of the public-sector, homecare workers were occupationally isolated, working in exclusively female settings, without access to the benefits of public-sector collective bargaining or trade union negotiated agreements. In addition, they were no longer employed by the same employer as the male local authority workers with whom they had previously been able to make comparison, and consequently homecare workers lost their legal entitlement to pay equality within local authority pay schemes.

In 2010, the Equal Pay Act was repealed and replaced by Part 5 of the Equality Act. As this new legislation passed through the House of Lords, peers with a lifetime of knowledge about the weaknesses of equal pay law were critical of continuing with its minimalist approach, its lack of fit with the organisation of labour in the contemporary economy and its focus on individual claims-making in the face of systematic pay discrimination (see, for example, Lord Lester, Equal Pay and Flexible Working Debate, Hansard, cols. 1890–4, 23 January 2009; Lord Lester, Equality Debate, Hansard, cols. 939–44, 19 January 2010). Indeed, Baroness Prosser described the legislative framework as 'a busted flush, it does not work' and called for 'root and branch change' (Hansard, col. 1887, 23 January 2009). Nevertheless, the structure of equal pay law remained largely unchanged – a review undertaken by the Government Equalities Office in 2015 noted that equal pay measures from the 1970s were 'essentially recreated' 40 years later under the Equality Act 2010 (see Post-legislative Review of the Equality Act, para 2.71). As a consequence, equal pay law continues to support the segregated and low-wage employment of women in female-dominated occupations. In the discussion in the section that follows I argue that privatisation strategies have been incentivised by the ability of local authorities to lawfully shift women's jobs into a private-sector, cost-competitive environment, where sex discrimination in pay-setting is effectively permissible in law.

An invisible right to equal pay?

The privatisation of homecare services has transferred resources, including public money, the labour of homecare workers and their expertise, experience and skill, from the public-sector to non-public (mainly private-sector) organisations. What has been 'privatised' is both the state's responsibility to provide care and its wherewithal to deliver. It is a political project with two faces: one economic and one social. With the first, the state has divested of its own care provision, and with the second, the state has reconfigured care needs as private responsibilities which ought to be met by family or individuals. While this chapter has given primary attention to privatisation's economic face and the transfer of service provision to commercial organisations, the social face of increased individual responsibility is ever-present in the privatisation processes under examination (see, for example, the speech *Personal Responsibility* given by Health Minister Rt. Hon. Jeremy Hunt MP, Local Government Association, 1 July 2015, Harrogate).

Private-sector organisations now dominate the UK homecare landscape, but on occasions local authorities have awarded commercial contracts to voluntary organisations or to 'not-for-profit' social enterprises. Such diversification has given rise to the use of the term 'independent sector' (rather than private sector) to identify the group of organisations holding homecare provision contracts. By drawing attention to the 'independence' of non-public-sector care provision, the term deflects attention from the 'private' economic interests served when public services are contracted out. Labelling the organisations with homecare delivery contracts as 'independent' suggests that, in the hands of these purportedly autonomous and free-thinking providers, services are liberated. Yet 'independent' is a strange word to attach to enterprises that exist solely through their receipt of billions of pounds of state funding. While the ethos of charitable and not-for-profit organisations is not the same as the ethos of private-sector organisations, in relation to privatisation they bear fundamental symmetries. As holders of commercial contracts, all must operate on a commercial basis, all are concerned with profit (they do not anticipate financial loss on the contracts they enter into) and all engage in competitive tendering. Private sector, social enterprise and charitable organisations populate an 'independent sector' which has been strategically positioned by successive governments to compete with the 'public-sector'.

Homecare is a labour-intensive activity and it seems unlikely that productivity can be improved by replacing people with machines or technology. Therefore, competition for contracts is essentially a competition over labour costs, and it is one which the independent sector has won hands down. Significantly, the 'independence' of the independent sector rests in its legal capacity to locate the employment of homecare workers outside of local authorities. Its distinguishing feature is a *legal independence* to employ homecare workers on lower pay and according to lesser terms and conditions. Independence in pay-setting is a major driver of homecare privatisation and, as my discussion of legal authority from the UK and EU courts will demonstrate, this independence eliminates the cost of protecting homecare workers from the economic impact of sex discrimination.

In *Ratcliffe v. North Yorkshire County Council* the House of Lords considered equal pay claims brought by school meals assistants who worked for a local authority that was under pressure, indeed required by the Local Government Act 1988, to provide services at the lowest possible cost ([1995] IRLR 439). Because the local authority wanted to continue employing these female workers directly, it dismissed and re-engaged them on lower pay. Their wages were then reduced below the level commensurate with an earlier job evaluation exercise, which had graded the school meals jobs as being of equal value to that of male council employees working in gardening services. These pay reductions meant that the local authority could run its own school meals service at a similar cost to services offered by the private sector, but the claimants argued that this was a breach of their right to equal pay. When the *Ratcliffe* case had come before the Court of Appeal, it was determined that the employers' 'need to compete with a rival bid' was a satisfactory material factor defence based on a reason that was 'genuinely' owing to market forces and responded to statutory demands (p. 838). The Court of Appeal decision was based on a prior ruling of the House of Lords which found that the law allowed employers to successfully defend the payment of higher wages to male comparators on the basis of 'market forces' if the explanation was genuinely based on reasons of sound administrative and economic efficiency (*Rainey v. Greater Glasgow Health Board* [1987] IRLR 26). However, when the *Ratcliffe* case reached the House of Lords, their lordships took a novel approach. Instead of focusing on whether market forces made it acceptable to pay men a higher wage, they focused on the question of whether it was lawful to allow a 'market forces' explanation for the lower pay of women. In overturning the earlier judgment of the Court of Appeal, they ruled that by substituting a lower rate of pay in order to make the school meals service commercially competitive, North Yorkshire County Council had engaged in unlawful sex discrimination. Lord Slynn advised, 'though conscious of the difficult problem facing the council in seeking to compete with a rival tenderer, I am satisfied that to reduce the women's wages below that of their male comparators was the very kind of discrimination in relation to pay which [equal pay law] sought to remove' (p. 841).

However, while the legal action in *Ratcliffe* was still in progress, North Yorkshire County Council privatised its school meals service and made the claimants redundant. The private-sector provider that won the contract then employed these same women at even lower rates of pay than the reduced rates previously introduced by the local authority. In response to this second attack on their terms and conditions of work, the women took an equal pay claim to the European Court of Justice, but were unsuccessful. The judgment in their second case, *Lawrence* v. *Regent Office Cleaning*, ruled that because the claimants were now employed independently of the local authority they were no longer able to argue that the local authority had discriminated against them (C–320/00 [2002] ECR I-7325). In addition, they were unable to argue that their new employer had set discriminatory rates of pay because that employer was not responsible for the employment of men in equal work. Without a 'single source' of discrimination, women could not bring equal pay claims in the context of contracting arrangements.

The third source of authority on equal pay in relation to privatisation is *Allonby* v. *Accrington and Rossendale College* (C–251/01 [2004] ECR I-873). Mrs Allonby was a part-time lecturer at a further education college and she was paid less per hour than full-time lecturers. The part-time workforce at the college was predominantly female and the full-time lecturers exclusively male. Fearing an equal pay claim, and also encouraged by opportunities for further wage cuts, the employer made all its part-time lecturers redundant and contracted out the work on an hourly paid basis to a labour agency. The rate at which the college contracted with the agency meant that wages were necessarily reduced and when Mrs Allonby took up a position with the agency, she taught the same courses, in the same lecture rooms as she had previously, but now she was paid a lower wage. Recalling my earlier discussion of equal pay rights, EU law differs from UK law in that it does not explicitly require a woman and her comparator to work for the same employer. In *Allonby,* the Court of Justice of the European Union was tasked with deciding if Mrs Allonby had a right in EU law to be paid equally to the men that she lectured alongside (since she and they were in equal work at the same establishment). In its judgment, the Court affirmed that for the purposes of equal pay claims, pay differences between workers performing equal work in the same establishment or location must be attributable to a 'single source'. Since the college employed the comparator men, and the agency employed Mrs Allonby, neither could be held responsible for the pay inequality between them. The single source requirement held, even though the agency arrangement had been explicitly implemented to remove equal pay rights (see comments of the Attorney General in *Allonby* [AG43]).

The doctrinal positions established in *Ratcliffe, Lawrence* and *Allonby* have permitted the continuation of women's economic inequality, an injustice that equal pay law purports to address. From the perspective of the homecare workforce, the right to equal pay has proven capable of offering some protection from sex discrimination, but only where homecare workers are directly employed by local authorities. When employed by 'independent-sector' contracting organisations, equal pay law offers no effective legal protection from low pay on grounds of sex, because women are prevented from making relevant comparisons with higher paid men. In the context of privatisation, equal pay has become an 'invisible' right. Consequently, the economic disadvantage to which a homecare worker may be subject is rendered invisible by the law. It would appear that privatisation creates circumstances in which legal rights, alongside resources of money, labour and skill, are reconfigured as they transfer from public to non-public spheres of economic activity. The right to equal pay has been tempered by legal accommodation of sexist assumptions that the value of women's work is only worthy of legal protection in relation to the work of comparable men, and of consequent restrictions on the ability of women to participate in a labour market free from sex discrimination.

Historically, the UK courts have considered the public functions of local authorities and their obligation to spend taxpayers' money wisely as a reason to limit their employment powers (Davis and Freedland, 1997; Poole, 2000). The judgment in *Ratcliffe* is arguably a contemporary example. Albeit in the name of equal pay, the courts removed the power of a public-sector employer to bring wages in line with market rates and effectively forced it to privatise a public service. The practical outcome of the decision was to expose the women affected to even greater levels of pay detriment on grounds of sex. There was no scope in law for privatisation to be prevented, and the House of Lords had no legal tools with which to implement a fair rate of pay for the job, even if it had so desired.

The *Ratcliffe* decision carries echoes of a 1925 ruling by the House of Lords in the case of *Roberts* v. *Hopwood* in which Poplar Borough Council's attempt to implement equal pay in wage-setting was declared unlawful ([1925] AC 587). Poplar had proposed to pay its female employees equally with men but the House of Lords found that the council had failed to act 'reasonably' (and there was no statutory right to equal pay at that time). In the judgment of Lord Atkinson, Poplar Council had no legal authority to pay women according to 'some eccentric principles of socialist philanthropy, or by a feminist ambition to secure the equality of the sexes in the matter of wages in the world of labour' (p. 594). To twenty-first-century ears this may sound like a dreadfully old-fashioned and sexist view. Yet my review of the line of authority stemming from *Ratcliffe* shows that legal developments in both EU and UK courts have severely undermined progress towards economic equality for women. Despite the introduction of statutory protection against sex discrimination in pay-setting, the message communicated by the House of Lords in *Hopwood* remains little changed; discrimination in pay setting is regarded as a necessary means to secure value for money in the delivery of public services. What has changed over the decades, however, is the mechanisms by which the state has maintained the ability to satisfy its demand for cheap female labour in public services.

In my discussion of equal pay law and public policy, I have positioned the Cheap Nurse character narrative within its legal and historical context. At a local level, wage costs have been held down by management practices which reflect the long-standing misrecognition of caregiving skills. In addition, strategies of privatisation have sought to resist the introduction of non-discriminatory pay for homecare workers in local authority employment. Meanwhile, at a national level, the government has marketised care provision in order to stimulate competition, focus on 'efficiency' and extract long-term labour cost reductions. In the final section of this chapter, I consider the impact of privatisation on caregiving relationships between homecare workers and the older and disabled people for whom they care. I draw on a specific account by a local authority homecare worker, Sophie. It exemplifies how privatisation is experienced in practice, and its impact on day-to-day customs, routines and expectations.

Caregiving relations as market relations

When I spoke with Sophie she told me that despite being able to take a redeployment opportunity elsewhere in the local authority, she was devastated at the loss of her homecare job. She had a service-user named Mavis, of whom she was very fond and had been visiting as part of her work schedule for over ten years. Mavis had dementia and she was also now suffering from lung cancer. Each morning, Sophie visited Mavis at 8.45 a.m. Their relationship was close. It had become apparent that Mavis's confusion was reduced if she was woken by classical music prior to Sophie's arrival. Sophie had programmed a clock radio to play soothing tracks from 8 a.m. and had set it by Mavis's bedside to reassure her that Sophie would arrive before the music finished. Sophie and her colleagues also kept a journal for Mavis. Each new day warranted a fresh page entry with a schedule detailing how Mavis's care visits would be arranged and who was coming to visit her. The journal was kept next to a television magazine in her lounge so that Mavis could try and understand where she was in the day, according to what was on the TV.

When homecare was privatised, the work of looking after Mavis was part of a package contracted out to a care agency. However, in the week prior to the switch, Sophie was responsible for showing an agency worker how she had cared for Mavis. Sophie explained:

> the management turned round to us and said that because [Mavis] was privatised then basically we had got to work with the agency in Mavis's home to show the new homecares what needs to be done. As soon as we had told the new girls what they are doing, we are out of the door! We have had to train them, showing them how to do our jobs and then we are gone. It's not fair. But then at the end of the day we have to do it for the families and for the service-users because it's them that will suffer if the new workers don't know how to look after them.

Despite her feelings of indignation, deep sadness and loss, Sophie turned up at Mavis's house at 8.45 a.m. on the day the handover was to happen. She put on a brave face, acted as though it was nothing but an ordinary day, and she waited for the agency worker to arrive so she could show her the ropes. When no agency worker turned up, Mavis began to get agitated because her routine was not running as she was accustomed. In the circumstances, Sophie decided it was best to begin bathing Mavis on her own, to make her bed, to put her make-up on for her as she usually did, to brush her hair, give her medication, make a cup of tea and help her eat breakfast. By 9.45 a.m., and still with no agency worker in sight, Sophie was getting very worried on Mavis's behalf because today was the last time she was employed to care for her. Sophie telephoned the agency directly. She said, 'look, I'm a homecare with the council, I've been waiting for over an hour for one of your agency girls to turn up and she hasn't'. They replied, 'Oh yes, sorry about that but the person who was supposed to come has phoned in sick this morning'. Sophie was so cross that she found it hard to contain her feelings. No one had phoned to let Mavis know she was not forgotten; no one had let Mavis know that they cared. To Sophie, the experience indicated that her caregiving relationships, however fundamental they were for her service-users, were utterly invisible within the privatisation process.

The collective dimensions of homecare labour

Much academic writing focuses on care as an individualised practice, as an individual experience and as an individuated relation between caregiver and care-receiver. For example, care has been defined as, 'feelings of affection and responsibility combined with actions that provide responsively for an individual's personal needs or wellbeing in a face-to-face relation' (Cancian and Oliker, 2000, p. 2). The nature, extent and substance of caregiving relationships are affected by *where* they take place. In contrast to ideas of institutionalised care, an assessment of homecare work by sociologists Kim

England and Isabel Dyck (2011) conceives of a service-users' individual physical body as a 'place' of work. In industrial relations literature, homecare workers are typically discussed as individuals performing intimate personal tasks in a relationship with individual service-users (see Bolton and Wibberley, 2013; McGrath and DeFilippis, 2009).

Such individualised understandings also show up in judicial comments about homecare work. For example, in *Cumbria County Council* v. *Dow* Justice Elias decided that a homecare worker claimant could not make a valid equal pay comparison with a male worker in receipt of productivity bonus ([2008] IRLR 91 EAT). His reasoning suggested that homecare workers were not 'productive' because they lacked control over their work rate. He said:

> a care worker who works properly is subject to the demands and requirements of the patient and cannot sensibly dictate the speed of working. ([145])

Justice Elias's formulation of what it means to be a paid care worker lacks the presence of an employer controlling her work rate or requiring her to take responsibility for deadlines and a schedule. In this picture, the claimant's relations of employment are obscured and her legal status as a paid worker is rendered barely visible. The ease with which the employee–employer relationship is overlooked in social policy-making about care services has been previously explored in research seeking to understand the regulation of homecare quality as a human resources issue (Rubery and Unwin, 2011). However, the appearance of the same phenomenon in this example of legal doctrine sheds light on the sexist stereotyping brought into play when paid care work is assumed to be individualised and unproductive. It is claimed that a homecare worker works 'properly' when she has no control over her own work rate. The use of the word 'sensibly' suggests it would be folly for a homecare worker to try and influence her rate of work at all. The image of a homecare worker properly subject to the demands of the 'patient' invokes notions of women's subservience and gendered expectations of women as 'selfless' carers in a domestic context. There is a significant distance between this judicial view and what we know about the homecare industry's heavy reliance on time restraint, cost control and its obsession with productivity measurement (a point upon which I expand in Chapter 2). It offers an important example of how 'judicial imagination' can transform legal doctrine through a subtle, yet complex, reliance on reductive myths about women in paid work.

In Sophie's story about Mavis it is clear that caregiving is based on a personal relationship and it is 'personalised'. Nevertheless, perceptions of homecare workers as isolated caregivers are gendered, reflecting a sexist impulse to align them with the idea that women best belong in private domestic spaces where their interests are subordinate to the personal needs of others. This is not to deny the reality that homecare workers are a distinctive occupational group, different from factory or retail workers, for example, because they lack a central or regular place of work in which to interact. Indeed, a homecare worker with 25 service-users to see in a week has 25 different workplaces, and might work with no one else but those service-users. This does not mean, however, that those relationships are free-standing or individually contingent. Social care provision relies upon management, coordination and cooperation between large numbers of actors, a continuity of resources, the predictability of organisational order and timely access to knowledge, equipment and personnel. In our conversations, local authority-employed homecare workers frequently referred to caregiving as 'the only link to the outside world' for their service-users. This offers an important rejoinder to images of isolation. Homecare workers represent the *outside world* as they deliver the state's responsibilities for ensuring welfare and well-being.

An excessive focus on caregiving relationships as individualised encounters denies the communal 'being-ness' of homecare work and fails to appreciate its collective coordination. Individualising the substance of homecare work relies upon sexist conventions which assert that what goes on 'behind closed doors' is 'private'. It misreads 'home' as a privately owned domain in which service-users are conceived as proprietary actors. It also echoes illusory aspects of the marketisation agenda which presumes to credit vulnerable, socially excluded and often politically powerless older and disabled people with the benefit of having a market 'choice' about the care which is provided to them at home (service-user choice and control is the subject of discussion in Chapter 4). However, through the lens of the Cheap Nurse narrative we can see that the relationship between a homecare worker and service-user is not private, and does not rest on a one-to-one connection. Caregiving activities are a basis of community, in the sense that communities are 'forged' in the social and cultural reproduction of what it means to be a human-being in a particular time and place (Anderson, 2000, p. 14). It is people, rather than places which are central to understanding how care expresses solidarity. Communities are not sterile geographic locations but exist within social relationships, through intergenerational linkages, and they are experienced as mental frameworks of imagination and emotional sensation (Anderson, 1983; Pahl, 2005; Studdert, 2006). It was amply described in the research I undertook for this book that homecare work transported meanings of 'community' from home to home. Some of these meanings are undoubtedly local, in the sense that they reflect a shared local history and knowledge of customs, local traditions or an appreciation of local dialect or food preferences. However, the work of Cheap Nurse, as a state-funded caregiver, also transmits meanings of national community and is profoundly rooted in understandings of public duty. Through the Cheap Nurse narrative, we gain an important insight into the difference between state-funded homecare and unpaid family caregiving: homecare workers, whether employed by local authorities or contracting organisations, carry public priorities, public duties and public policy into domestic environments.[5]

As marketisation has changed the delivery of care, meanings of community and public duty have changed in accordance with revised public priorities. The contact that service-users have with homecare workers represents the relation of service-users to the state – not only as the subjects of the state's welfare provision but also as citizens to whom the state is accountable. The social, legal and organisational changes which have characterised homecare workers as cheap nurses have facilitated marketisation. However, while marketisation has denied homecare workers a communal or public service status, privatisation has reasserted that caregiving is built on individualised, and sexist, relations of gender. By reconstituting relations of employment, privatisation is the state's signal that caring relationships and notions of community are no longer a public policy priority. Indeed, they are crafted as excessive, unvalued by-products of caregiving in domestic settings, and when care is reduced to an individuated commercial exchange, they are rendered invisible. Through privatisation, established forms of community have been ruptured and social difference based on sex, in which the 'domestic' domain is set apart from the wider labour market, is reaffirmed. Both workers and service-users have faced the consequential dismantling of caregiving relationships which had offered continuity and communal security in otherwise uncertain, insecure and socially excluded lives.

Privatisation as community trauma

I spoke with many homecare workers who expressed the fear and anxiety which is exemplified in Sophie's concern for Mavis as a 'forgotten about' person. They also shared in Sophie's realisation that privatisation treated their presence in service-users' lives as insignificant. Sophie's story powerfully illustrates the need for researchers to adopt a wide-angled lens approach because paid caregiving is so much more than an individual interaction between a worker and a service-user (Milligan and Wiles, 2010, p. 738). The social and economic relations through which homecare work

---

5 While the work and function of unpaid carers will also be shaped by public policy, I believe they act as a conduit of private, rather than public duties.

is organised are also the ingredients from which state-funded care is produced, and any resulting injustice or inequality reflects the political priorities of a much wider welfare regime. Sophie's experience of privatisation heralded a world in which she sensed all certainties had collapsed, and her intense fear of the future was shared by others. The threat which privatisation presented to their way of life, and to that of their service-users, drew on a collective knowledge grounded in the experience of everyday sexism – that homecare workers weren't worth much in economic terms to the outside world. As the discussion in this chapter has evidenced, the impoverishment of women as caregivers has a history which stretches back decades. It has fuelled anxiety about the annihilation of the homecare service and the perils to which service-users would be exposed. From the perspective of the local authority homecare workforce, privatisation was and is the antithesis of care. As public servants, the women whose voices echo throughout this book have physically represented the community foundations of the service in which they worked. Privatisation inflicted community trauma and was understood by them as a finality which warranted grief.

Such sentiments and concerns about a loss of community values, and the discontinuation of historic patterns of social life, social relationships and behavioural routines are typically attached to narratives of deindustrialisation, such as those that chart the loss of male manual work in heavy industries such as mining, steel production and motor manufacturing (see, for example, Walkerdine, 2010). When we think of large-scale redundancies and of industries that have closed down, we tend to think of men losing jobs they have lived and breathed for decades, and of the decimation of communities and the associated loss of pride and tradition. However, Sophie's story testifies that the loss of homecare work to the private sector has blighted the lives of individuals and inflicted community harms which are just as 'real' as those born of deindustrialisation. Sophie said that being expected to show a rival worker how to do her job made her feel, 'like I'd been slung in the trash'. In her realisation that caring relationships are considered a drain on public expenditure, Sophie contributed to the Cheap Nurse narrative an understanding of care as a commodity to be preprogrammed, processed, decommissioned, repackaged, transposed and traded.

Conclusion

When homecare workers are presented as, or recall feeling like, cheap nurses they experience the undervaluing of their skills, the belittling of their economic contribution and a marginalisation of their economic needs as working women. In this chapter, I have linked the character narrative of Cheap Nurse to a historical account of homecare work. I have also subjected the relationship between equal pay law and the marketisation of homecare services to critique. This has highlighted the parameters of inclusion and exclusion which assign the benefit of legal protection to some people, while denying them to others.

Considerations of homecare as 'invisible' work help to explain the place of sexism in creating and maintaining a low-cost homecare workforce. Equal pay law provides that the only legitimate way to identify low pay as a product of sexism is to identify individual pay disparities between men and women in relation to the legal construct of sex discrimination. It fashions a right to equal pay which is of dubious benefit to women who work in places where men do not. For women in female-dominated workplaces, the Equal Pay Act 1970 was designed to offer little in the way of remunerative improvement. Its repeal and replacement by provisions in the Equality Act 2010 has merely affirmed the state's lack of interest in protecting women's pay from the impact of sexism. Indeed, the framing of equal pay law reinforces male economic dominance over women by ensuring that the right to be free from sex discrimination in pay is contingent on the proximity of a woman's work to the work of men. It is perhaps paradoxical that legal provisions purporting to establish equal pay give ideological support to discriminatory attitudes and sex-based hierarchies through which women's caring labour is undervalued. In my assessment, equal pay law is a woefully inadequate mechanism with which to protect homecare workers from the economic injustice of sexism. By incentivising privatisation, equal pay law has facilitated the transition of homecare work away from the public-sector. In an 'independent-sector' homecare industry, women may be lawfully employed at rates of pay diminished by sexist subordination. They are denied the economic benefit of access to public-sector collective bargaining and their ability to advance a legal claim for equal pay is effectively rendered invisible. If women work in homecare, it seems that they now have little choice but to accept discriminatory rates of pay en masse. This testifies to the performative power of law – to its capacity to shape experiences of work and social relations.

It is evident that sexism puts homecare workers at an economic disadvantage as a collective group. Indeed, the character narrative of Cheap Nurse provides a counter to reductive and isolating assumptions about the private and familial qualities of caregiving. It represents the idea that state-funded homecare work communicates notions of 'community' which transform private homes into accessible places of welfare and open up the domestic sphere to caregiving as a matter of public urgency and priority. However, in social policy, in judicial commentary and in some strands of academic debate, there is an inclination to conceptualise paid care work on the basis of individual relations between care workers and service-users. In my view, this reflects a conceptual flaw which closes down our capacity to understand how the legal treatment of sex discrimination relates to the organisation of the homecare industry. Indeed, it dissuades us from thinking about caregiving as a matter of 'industry' at all. Denied a collective industrial identity, and without the credit of public service, the location of homecare work within the domestic sphere is wrongly taken to confirm the separation of homecare labour from the mainstream world of work. This is a sexist representation in which 'home' symbolises a lack of economic worth and the notion of a 'private' realm is used to justify the absence, removal or ineffectuality of legal rights.

The early employment protection statutes of the 1960s to the 1980s contained provisions which expressed the intention of the British state to use its legislative powers in ways which distinguished men from women in the labour market. However, the example of equal pay law reveals that law at work performs a social-sorting function which is rather more sophisticated. Women who work in mixed-sex workplaces, or in occupations which are also widely performed by men, are more likely to have access to an effective right to equal pay yet they are less likely to experience sex-based pay detriment than are women who work in female segregated sectors. The right to equal pay does not straightforwardly sort men from women so much as it sorts some women from other women, on the basis of their relations to men. The impact of law is not only to distinguish between social groups at work, but also to *create* them. Equal pay law has helped to shape the privatisation of the public-sector-employed workforce because its deficiencies have facilitated a rapid rise in private-sector contracting. As I explore in the next chapter, experiences of working life have therefore become markedly different and homecare workers are far less resilient to sex-based subordination in the labour market. Legal entitlements have the capacity to shape society beyond the courtroom or tribunal. The working futures of women represented in this book have been configured through the prism of the legal right to equal pay – futures in which their continued underpayment and collective devaluation are required, made possible and technically justified through the limitations of equal pay law. These limitations are part of the sexist foundations upon which the homecare industry has been built.

2
Two-a-Penny

Out there, we are two-a-penny. On a zero-hours contract you can either have too many hours, or they give you hardly any work and offer up whatever old cock and bull story they want. There is no pension plan for our old age; no sickness benefits when we need care. Nothing. Even when we have diarrhoea and vomiting, we still work.

I saw an ad in a shop window, walked in the door and said, 'I'm looking for a job.' I did my so-called 'training' and didn't get paid while doing it. They gave me a uniform and said, 'Here is a piece of paper showing where you have to go.' There was no introduction to the clients and very little shadowing time to learn who you would be working with. It was scary at first. Dead scary; I was shitting myself. I was like, 'Oh my God! What have I got to do with you then?' You know deep down that clients all have different routines, and ways, and different needs, but it's not till you actually get to the house and look at the care plans that you think, 'Have I really got to do all that, in the time that I have got?' Seeing it on paper, and then working out how to actually do it, is a bit daunting.

I had to sign to say I would accept a zero-hours contract. That was the very first thing, before I did anything else, that had to be agreed. They said we will try and give you all the hours that you want, but you need to be flexible. I agreed to work every day apart from two weekends in a month, to be with my family. I had to buy shoes and trousers for the uniform, the only thing they gave me for free was a tunic top, and if I wanted another I had to pay £15 to the firm. I didn't know if the job would last, so I just had the one and washed it every night when I got in from work.

Each day without fail there were extra service-users to be seen and the office would cram more in on you. We have to keep our mobile phones with us. They can ring at any time and say, 'Get to Mrs So-and-so, she needs to use the bathroom.' Some of our clients will easily spend half an hour on the loo, so you are late for the next call and its ongoing then. With back-to-back calls you are rushing all day ... inside, you feel like you want to cry and you need a break, but you can't take one. I was running around like a headless chicken. It is manic, dangerous driving actually, and the poor clients! Sometime you are talking about working over 30 hours in two days. No wonder people get burnt out under those conditions.

When I saw my payslip I couldn't believe it! They pay only while you're in the house; but nobody explained it when I was interviewed. If you work from 6.45 a.m. till 10 p.m. at night it sounds like you will be getting a good day's pay. But when you actually get your pay you are getting five hours, sometimes eight hours' money, from up to 15 hours' work. They assume that you will know, but unless you have worked in homecare before, there is no way you do. I can't think of another job where if you had your uniform on and were available, that you wouldn't actually be paid. It put a panic on me: 'What am I going to do?' I had to borrow money.

When you are in a client's house you are constantly looking at the time. Sometimes you are going to see people, who to be honest are complete strangers. You haven't got time to sit there and read their care plans because by the time you do it, you've wasted 10–15 minutes. You've got 15 minutes left then to do everything and it's diabolical. All that is going through my mind is, 'Right, I've got half an hour to get out of here because I am not paid if I go over my time.' It's like saying to yourself, 'Right Ethel, I've got to get you in here; washed, dressed, out again; put drugs in you, whip the hoover round and get out.' When you start rushing a job you can make mistakes. If mistakes happen when you are looking after someone, then it will all come down on you. You are so worried about all that, you forget that Nelly hasn't had no dinner. Rushing around you are bound to forget things sometimes because you've got so much on. You're meant to empty bins, do their beds and all that, but you have to cut corners. You can't hang around and have to say, 'look, I'm in a rush'.

You can get stuck in traffic and be 20 minutes late. Then you have to find somewhere to park. Lots of older people live in flats, you have to get into the building, through all the security doors, and then go up and it hits you, 'Oh no! poor old Mrs So-and-so is really slow this morning!' I tell myself I can only do my best, but already I am an hour late for my next call. You are against the clock; it's on your mind the whole time thinking, I should be at the next house right now but I can't even leave yet. There is never any travelling time put in our work programmes.

I went to another agency, I explained all the whole scenario of no travelling time, too many calls and the things that upset me. They said, 'We guarantee you, we promise that won't happen with us. You will get ten minutes of travelling time for each call. If you start at seven and finish at two in the afternoon, you get paid £7.80 for all those hours, each and every single hour.' The training period was for two whole weeks, with no payment for that, but I took the job. I even had to pay for my own criminal record check. So, a lesson for anyone who is skint: you have to find that money up front. I borrowed again.

When I got the rota through, it was ridiculous! I was supposed to be in two places at the same time. I tried it for a week and two days, but I had to say, 'I can't do this, sorry.' It was only once I'd started working for them that I realised how bad it was. Even though you were on the rota in one block, and paid from client to client, they were stupid hours. So instead of actually finishing work at two o'clock, you were finishing at five o'clock but only getting paid till two o'clock.

I went to work for Bestcare. I signed what they said was a 32 hours a week guaranteed hours contract. They never honoured that contact. Imagine the worry when you've got your bills to pay; one week you'd have 8 hours, the next its 40 because some other homecare has walked out on the job. If you complained, they said, 'Well, go to another area and work.' Apparently other people had caused a fuss about it. I don't know legally how they stand, but I didn't want to upset the office so I decided to look for a second job instead of complaining. To earn enough to survive, I started part-time with Tesco; because at least working in a shop I was paid for the whole time I was there.

At Bestcare, the amount of calls for quarter of an hour was absolutely ridiculous. In quarter of an hour you are supposed to assist them to the commode or toilet, freshen up, welfare check and make sure they have taken their tablets. If you find you've got to cream someone's legs, the call will take longer. There is no time for travelling to the next one, so you have even less time to spend with them;

it's so stressful. A 15-minute call is not fair to us, because by the time I've driven there to make sure she's taken her tablets, it's two quid of pay. It's not worth it because then you have to come all the way back, and you're paying out for petrol. But if you moaned about not having enough travelling time, they would just take those clients off you and then you would have a big gap, a huge hole of no work in your programme. And with big gaps, you can't even go home because you can't afford the petrol to drive home. So many times, I was just sat in the car in the pouring rain listening to the radio.

My hours were all over the show. Sometimes they would run a guilt-trip on me and say, 'We can't find anybody to work tonight can you do it?' If you said, 'sorry I have a doctor's appointment', or 'my daughter is in a school play', they would tell you to cancel it because, 'we need you' and 'Mrs So-and-so can't be left alone'. They would really tug at your heart strings. Saying no meant they put it on me to phone round and find someone else to work. Even at eleven o'clock at night. Because the other girls would refuse to answer their phone if they knew it was the office calling. Then they would cut my hours again. They were up and down with hours. If you did what they asked, when they asked and how they asked, you would get the clients. They just see it that they are giving you hours and you should be grateful; not the fact that you've got to pay bills and that. If you do moan about the job – like you say what a hard day you have had, you're fed up with this and that – they cut your hours down. They say they are short staffed, but they employ so many new people. If you do just one thing wrong, they get rid of you.

Bestcare started employing more and more carers because they were saying we were short. But whether we were or not, I'll never know. For maybe a couple of weeks I'd have enough work, and then the rest of the time they would have too many carers. I was doing 6.45 a.m. to 2.30 p.m. but only taking home between £125 and £160 a week. To get extra shifts you would have to work on your days off or go to a different area, travel for longer, but I couldn't because I would have to start my shift with Tesco. So I was just continually working and trying my best at surviving. But the pressure of rushing around to two different jobs – I've got to take both uniforms with me because I haven't got time to get changed at home. I have to try and fit in walking the dogs. I have to make sure I'm not late for Tesco. Say you get to somebody, if they are slow, if something is wrong, it invariably takes longer than it says on the rota. When we are late to the next call, the person will kick off. Some of them can go really mad. I cried more than once because a client had a right go at me. Then I was worrying about losing my Tesco job.

It got so bad, my blood pressure was sky-high and I had to go to the doctor's because I wasn't well; my health was really suffering. I was having panic attacks and went on antidepressants, which made my sleep go haywire. I was late to work and told I'd be sacked if it happened again. So the next time I overslept I panicked like you would not believe. My early morning call, I had missed her. I got there as soon as I could and did all of her personal care, breakfast and everything and then I filled out the paperwork to say I'd been there earlier. I know I shouldn't have done it, but I was really concerned for my job and truly, the lady was fine, no harm done. I carried on working for the rest of the day like there wasn't a problem but I got reported for turning up late. I was in the shit; lying on a legal document. I was out of work literally the same day and I don't remember anything then until I got home and thought to myself, 'What the hell?' It was just totally out of the blue and when you take a knock like this, you get knocked 100 per cent.

The company I applied to for the next job said I would have calls in the northern part of the city where I live. So I done everything, all the training, paid the criminal record check and was going out to shadow another worker. Next thing, I find out they lied; there was no work in the north. I had to work on the south side, and there was never no apology. I don't have a choice about it and I know they are doing us out of mileage too; it's all about pennies. We used to put our own mileage calculation in from one client to another. Now it's all done from the office by Google. I used to do 50 miles a week and get £20 for petrol. Now I am doing the same 50 miles but I am lucky to get £6. The company are permanently after new staff, and there is always an advert in the paper. You see 20 new girls coming in for training. They get trained up, get their uniforms on and then our hours go down to like 6 hours a week. No one can survive on 6 hours a week, ever. Where are all my clients? Where are the people I have been seeing for months? Every time I get a new job I think, 'It is going to get better ... I feel a new lease of life instead of feeling down ... Yes! this time it will get better'; but it never does.

Two-a-Penny and the protection of employment

'Two-a-penny' is how Lucy said it felt to be working in a 'terrible' job, for a company that paid very low wages yet had access to a plentiful supply of labour. I built the narrative of Two-a-Penny to capture the stories of homecare workers who were employed in the independent sector. It characterises their experience of employment insecurity and financial hardship. Before a job offer has even been made, the character of Two-a-Penny has foregone wages for the duration of her induction training, has paid upfront for a police records check about her past and bought clothes for her uniform. She is already in personal debt by the time she meets her first service-user. Although Two-a-Penny desperately wants a secure job she feels frightened at her lack of control over her income and inability to plan from one day to the next. Previous experience tells her that employers don't play fair, but Two-a-Penny is determined to try and make things work out. She kids herself that she can avoid the risk of not being given enough paid hours by agreeing to do whatever work is offered, wherever or whenever she is asked. Yet as the weeks unfold, she finds herself under so much pressure that she is regularly in tears; her life is now dominated by worries about work and she feels ground down at constantly being late for appointments and having to cut corners with caregiving. The harsh reality of her employment insecurity kicks in when service-users' visits are removed from her schedule and her paid hours of work reallocated to others; when she realises she has been short-changed over petrol; or when she cannot work because she is sick and has no guarantee of work to which she can return.

As homecare workers spoke to me about their terms and conditions of employment it became clear that many had experience of chronic employment insecurity and were vulnerable to unlawfully low pay. Their accounts were consistent with those detailed in reports by think tanks, trade unions, parliamentary groups and charitable organisations who have all engaged in recent research. Collectively, these reports have linked concerns about worker exploitation to concerns about falling care standards and a lack of regard for the human rights of older and disabled people. Terms and conditions of work in homecare have been described as 'among the worst of any', 'illegal' and 'shoddy' (Kingsmill, 2014, p. 3; Koehler, 2014, p. 5). However, the arguments I develop in this chapter move discussions beyond a descriptive picture of what is happening. I use the Two-a-Penny character narrative to contextually consider *how* homecare workers are so persistently degraded by the organisation and conditions of their work. My focus is the under-protection of homecare employment in law.

Through privatisation, a workforce, whose skills had been devalued and historically overlooked in the public-sector, has been denied access to non-discriminatory terms and conditions of work. However, the inadequacies of equal pay law are not the sole foundation of poor-quality homecare jobs. The character narrative of Two-a-Penny provides a perspective from which to explore the relationship between employment insecurity and legal provisions intended to defend or uphold an employment contract in the face of adversity. Central to this discussion is my assertion that the availability and impact of employment protection law shapes homecare workers' experiences of work and the quality of their jobs. By way of contrast to legal rights based on the characteristics of an individual (for example, anti-discrimination rights, equal pay and rights available to parents and carers), employment protection rights are predicated upon the contractual relationship between an individual and their employer (for example, rights which depend on the type of contract, the length of time it has been in operation and the nature of the commitments between parties). Employment protection law is a cornerstone of employment security and reflects the extent to which the state recognises that stable employment relations are fundamental to economic well-being and cohesive communities.[1]

The analysis in this chapter highlights that employment protection law offers stronger protection in some parts of the labour market than in others. In the homecare industry, it is especially weak. This suggests that the state is unwilling to protect the type of employment relationships in which homecare workers are now most often engaged. In legal adjudications over employment protection rights, some work activities and forms of employment are interpreted as being 'different' from those which attract protection in law. Empirical evidence suggests that the poor working conditions which prevail in these jobs reflect the 'social location' of the workers who typically participate in them (and by implication, their legal status, see Fudge, 2012, p. 4; Pratt, 1997). Across the UK labour market, a large majority of insecure and 'undesirable' jobs are filled by women (Gregg and Gardiner, 2015). Sex-based subordination is embedded in low-waged industries and the composition of the contemporary working-class is largely female. Nevertheless, women are not the only people impacted by poor-quality employment. Increasingly, terms and conditions deemed historically appropriate for women (as a subordinated class) are found in labour-intensive sectors such as logistics where young, working-class men with few qualifications are often employed. It is not simply paradoxical that workers in good-quality jobs have access to stronger legal protection than workers who are most likely to be exploited or badly treated; it exemplifies the subordinations of gender and class which are perpetuated in law.

In the previous chapter, I explained that Parliament historically chose to exclude women from the benefit of statutory employment rights. I also drew attention to the fact that statutory provisions could be designed in ways which give legitimacy to sexist ideas, even when those provisions are presented as being of benefit to women in the labour market. What is of

---

1 As Baroness Turner of Camden noted in a House of Lords debate about employment protection law 'employees should continue to feel that protection exists. Job insecurity is not helpful in any industry or commercial environment', col. 536, 3 May 2006.

benefit to some women will not necessarily be of benefit to all, since other women are purposefully excluded by the architecture of legal provisions. I suggested that traditional notions of male and female spheres of social activity were reflected and reproduced in the carving out of well-regulated and poorly regulated areas of the labour market. In this chapter, I explore ways in which legal principles established by judges, judicial doctrine, can affirm deep-seated gender stereotypes and sexist ideas about women's social inferiority.

Judicial doctrine focuses protection on forms of employment in which men have been, and continue to be, typically engaged. The legal reasoning upon which this doctrine is based offers justification for under-protecting forms of employment which do not satisfy standards set against a benchmark of male participation in the labour market. Excluded forms of labour market activity are typified as those most likely to be undertaken by working-class women. I focus on two examples. Firstly, the doctrine of mutuality of obligation upon which protection in the event of unfair dismissal is contingent. Secondly, the impact of so-called 'fragmented TUPE', which negates the application of employment protection law when work transfers from the public to the private sector and gives rise to what I have termed a doctrine of displacement. These examples help us to understand that the Two-a-Penny character narrative expresses homecare workers' subjective experience within a system of employment protection law that rests on gendered legal principles. A lack of employment protection sets the stage for insecure and precarious employment, extremely low wages and a workforce which is inadequately trained, ill-equipped and under-prepared. The experiences outlined in the Two-a-Penny character narrative – those of stress, financial hardship, anxiety and corner-cutting – are widely shared by women working in homecare throughout the UK. I argue that these material outcomes are connected to their exclusion, and perceived exclusion, from employment protection in law. The stark contrast between the character narrative of Cheap Nurse and that of Two-a-Penny indicates that the impact of sexism in the labour market is not fixed but fluid. Subordinations of sex and class are expressed in dynamic ways and the Two-a-Penny narrative offers a very different perspective on homecare work to that of Cheap Nurse. While Cheap Nurse put matters of skill and sexism centre stage, the character narrative of Two-a-Penny highlights the economic position in which homecare workers find themselves: the resources required of them in order to secure work; the physical routines that the job demands; and the challenges of moving between one job and another in search of decent treatment.

My assessment of the judicial doctrines of mutuality of obligation and of displacement provides an explanation for the gendered distribution of employment protection rights across the labour market. Social prejudice about the needs, capabilities and interests of working-class women is bound together with the legal principles that determine the availability of employment protection. In conclusion, I suggest that the gendering of employment protection law offers justification for day-to-day management practices which affirm the inferior status of homecare workers. Hence, the diminution of the needs and interests of working-class women expressed in law, is experienced by homecare workers as the active performance of social disregard for their needs and interests in their relations of employment.

Social inferiority and gendering of law

According to medical historian Thomas Lacquer, prior to the eighteenth century, women's bodies were understood to be versions of male bodies, albeit inferior, problematic and unstable in comparison (Laqueur, 1990, pp. 4–11, 22). For example, it was thought women's sexual organs were the internal replicate of male sexual organs, that the vagina was an inside-out penis and that ovulation was a female form of male ejaculation which occurred as a consequence of orgasm. The physiology of a woman was that of a man, but differently ordered. This is exemplified in the biblical story about God taking Adam's rib to craft Eve from his biological matter and create the first woman as a supplementary reflection of the first man. With a 'one-sex' version of human bodies, the social hierarchy through which men were regarded as superior to women was necessarily vertical. The experience of 'being' a man or a woman was rooted in the supposedly natural sociological order of gender that attributed a secondary rank and place in society to women. It was not until much later, that gendered hierarchy was linked biologically to a horizontal separation of men from women on the basis of their 'being' two sexes. While in the earlier period, women's inferior social position reflected their presumed lesser biological perfection as human beings, later understandings of biological difference used the male body as the default standard and plotted the physical 'differences' of the female body as scientific justifications for women's social inferiority. This one-sex to two-sex historical trajectory of gender is reflected in contemporary sexist thinking that interchangeably draws on notions of women as both the horizontally 'opposite' and vertically 'weaker' sex.

The idea of women as an inferior social group is reproduced in the gendered organisation of the labour market. Women working part-time earn on average 37 per cent less per hour than their full-time male counterparts (Office of National Statistics, 2016). However, men and women typically participate in the labour market in distinct ways. In contrast to men, women's working lives are punctuated by their changing social identities – as single women, wives, mothers and unpaid carers of elderly relatives. Generally speaking, it is the gendered experiences of women that lead them towards periods of absence from the labour market and periods of return; it is women who are likely to take part-time paid work when they experience the heaviest burdens of unpaid work; it is women's experiences, socialisation and education which lead them towards employment in personal service work rather than work with machinery. In fact, over 75 per cent of women's paid employment falls within the five occupational categories of cleaning, caring, catering, cashiering and secretarial work (Benetto, 2009) – occupations which are aligned with experience gathered as the social subordinates of men and the facilitators of male interests and activities. Whenever women's lesser pay or conditions of work are explained within a frame of reference that foregrounds women's work/family commitments, the 'unskilled' character of their accomplishments, their 'natural' suitability in secondary or supportive roles, their lesser utility to employers or their weaker economic interests, the idea of female inferiority is invoked.

When examined in respect of law, the 'social inferiority' model of gendered hierarchy communicates women's inability to conform to standards associated with men – to assume, on the one hand, that men and women are 'equal', in order to show that, on the other hand, women are inferior (Conaghan, 2013, p. 96). Legal reasoning purports to treat both men and women 'equally', but in so doing often puts women at a disadvantage. Such 'equal yet inferior' positioning is not a matter of bad fortune or coincidence, it is an outcome of being judged against standards imagined and imposed by men, to advance male interests (MacKinnon, 2007). The ability to produce 'difference' as inequality on the basis of sex is primarily an ability to generate power on the basis of sex. This power finds expression through social institutions such as religion, education, science, politics and law. Each contributes to the social rules and expectations which govern and shape relations between men and women (Scott, 1986).

My discussion in this chapter builds on prior scholarship which has shown how employment protection law implies a primary male subject as its intended beneficiary (Fudge, 1996; Fudge and Vosko, 2001; Morris and O'Donnell, 1999). Employment protection law does not use explicit male/female categories to establish legal entitlement; rather, it sets out generic rules which act as a sex-based 'code'. For example, up until the mid 1990s, employment protection rights were either unavailable or else heavily restricted for those working a minimum of either 8, 16 or 21 hours a week (see *EOC* v. *Secretary of State for Employment* [1994] 1 All ER 910 HL). Although both male and female claimants were equally subject to the law, the use of part-time working as an entitlement rule served as a code for the exclusion of women. Part-time work is a symbol of women's participation in the labour market and minimum-hour thresholds purposefully put women at a disadvantage in law. Although these have long been abolished, sex-based hierarchies of entitlement continue. The fact that many employment protections are not available unless an individual has worked continuously in the same employment for an extended period also acts as a sex-based code to the disadvantage of women (see *R* v. *Sec. of State for Employment* v. *ex p. Seymour Smith* [2000] 1 All ER 857 HL). The social expectation that women will bear children and raise them is manifest in working lives characterised by cycles of entering and leaving the labour market. Nevertheless, it is these gendered patterns of discontinuous working that have been selected by the legislature to serve as justification for the unequal distribution of legal protections across the labour force.

In the sections of this chapter which follow, I explain how rights to protection in relation to unfair dismissal and business transfers fail to benefit the women whose voices this book represents. Judicial doctrine gives normative regard to contractual features which typify male forms of engagement within the labour market and uses these to distinguish people who have access to employment protection, from those who do not. Consequently, when homecare workers are subject to judicial preferences and tests established in doctrine, the ensuing interpretations of their work activities, work patterns and contractual relationships are especially likely to position them outside of the boundaries of employment protection law. The Two-a-Penny narrative strongly suggests that homecare workers do not choose the forms of employment by which they are excluded from legal protection; in particular, they do not actively seek out zero-hours contracts, discontinuous employment and wage irregularity. Rather, they face the material disadvantage of these terms and conditions of work because the labour market is structured by laws that protect employment according to male standards.

Zero-hours contracts and financial uncertainty

The use of zero-hours contracts in low-waged work has been rising rapidly across the UK labour market since the financial crisis of 2008 (Gardiner, 2015; Office of National Statistics, 2015b). Economic downturn, low productivity, public spending cuts and new conditions placed on claims for welfare support have each contributed to the rise in 'undesirable', casualised, and insecure forms of employment (Gregg and Gardiner, 2015). A zero-hours contract defines an employment relationship in which an employer makes no guarantee to provide paid work and, on paper at least, a worker makes no commitment to accept work if it is offered. Workers on zero-hours contracts are more likely to be women than men, and about 40 per cent of them want to be working more hours than are made available (Office of National Statistics, 2015). While zero-hours arrangements are increasingly found in the catering, hospitality and retail industry, the situation facing homecare workers remains distinctive (Alkeson and D'Arcy, 2014).

Zero-hours contracts are so common as to represent a norm within the homecare industry (Atkinson et al., 2016, p. 2; Bessa et al., 2013; Rubery et al., 2011, pp. 15–18; Skills for Care, 2015b, p. 33). However, as the Two-a-Penny character narrative attests, a further distinctive aspect of homecare employment is to pay only for time in which workers are in 'contact' with service-users. This is because contractual terms dictate that a large proportion of working time is unpaid. Planned visits to service-users are scheduled within limits of between 15 and 60 minutes and despite official guidance that short visiting times are inappropriate for personal care, three-quarters of local authorities commission visits of 15 minutes or less (UNISON, 2016, p. 5). There are considerable impacts upon the take-home pay of homecare workers. Paid caregivers feel compelled to work on an unpaid basis to complete personal care tasks (Bolton and Wibberley, 2013). In addition, the time between each visit is unpaid. Employers across the UK have formally acknowledged that 19 per cent of homecare workers' recorded working time is unpaid time spent travelling between visits (UKHCA, 2014). Training time is also often unpaid, as is time spent waiting for coworkers to arrive, supervision time and staff meetings. Wage insecurity associated with the use of zero-hours contracts in homecare is exacerbated by the electronic monitoring of working time in service-users' homes (Hayes and Moore, 2017; Rubery et al., 2015). Often at the insistence of local authority commissioners, homecare workers employed by care providers are required to operate telephone-based technology to record the start and end times of their visits. The result is that invoices from the care provider to the local authority are automatically generated and workers are paid by their employer on a minute-by-minute basis. Systems of electronic monitoring provide direct evidence of the extent to which local authorities exercise control over the working time of individual homecare workers whom they do not themselves employ. It is because paid working time has been squeezed into an unstable allocation of 'contact time', that breaches of minimum wage law have become commonplace across the industry's 9,800 providers (an issue I explore in detail in the next chapter).

Among the women who participated in the research for this book, it was only those working in supervisory roles who were recognised as employees on contracts with regular hours of work, a stable income and pay during time spent training. The vast majority of hands-on homecare workers in the independent sector were on zero-hours contracts; they did not have any commitment from their employer about the availability or amount of work required of them. As a consequence, the job tied them to a written agreement which failed to offer any security about their earnings from one day to the next. Another drawback was that they were expected to be available for work whenever asked. This could lead to large periods of a working day being spent wearing a uniform but without any paid work to undertake. Last-minute changes of plan or new requirements by employers could either disrupt family life or even prevent workers from sleeping soundly. Heather was in her late 50s and working for a homecare agency. She told me about her attempts to cope with the insecurity of her income by becoming an extremely 'flexible' worker, available on demand, 24 hours a day.

> It is disconcerting that you might not get so many shifts from one week to the next you know. It is a bit tough ... I am so flexible that what happens is Tempco might phone me and I'll be in bed and they'll say 'can you get to this place as soon as possible', and I just say 'well, yeah give me chance to get dressed' ... I have literally jumped up, got dressed and zoomed over to somewhere.

Like many others, Heather did not feel in control of her own life because it was impossible to predict the hours that she would be required to work; she could not make reliable commitments to her family or friends and faced the uncertainty of being unable to plan time-off, even if just to get a haircut. On top of this were layered the continual economic hardships associated with surviving on little money, or worse, low wages which were also irregular. Income irregularities did not need to be large to make a huge difference; the consequences of being up or down just £30 a week could be life changing.

The trade union UNISON has claimed that it is not uncommon for employers to lend money to workers at extortionate rates of interest to cover petrol costs in lieu of expense payments (Koehler, 2014). Examples of this particular practice did not arise in the context of my research but getting into personal debt with payday loans or credit cards, sometimes over petrol expenses, was a factor which workers said prevented them from switching to a new employer. Other debt triggers included getting into a finance agreement when buying a car for work, borrowing money from friends or family to bridge unexpected income shortfalls, or taking out a loan to cover family emergencies. There seemed no easy way out of debt for women struggling to keep up with repayments. They were frightened to take an alternative job because of a high risk it would prove to be even worse. In any event, their emotional resources were depleted, they had absolutely no money with which to pay for the police check that each new employer required in advance of a job offer, and they could not manage to live without pay during lengthy induction training. For many workers, debt was structurally factored into their working practices as an established norm of the organisations they worked within. A practice described to me by several women, involved employers failing to reimburse them for the money they paid upfront for a criminal records check. Unless they worked a qualifying period of between three and six months they would not get this 'deposit' returned. The practice was specifically designed to dissuade new workers from walking out on the job in the first few weeks, and such fears were well founded. The homecare industry has the highest incidence of annual staff turnover of any sector of the UK labour market (Koehler, 2014). On average, one in three homecare workers leave their jobs each year (Skills for Care, 2015b, p. 52), and for fresh faces, the figures are staggeringly high, with some reports suggesting half of new recruits last for less than a year (Rubery et al., 2011).

Unfair dismissal and questions of obligation

Among the women who participated in my research, it was taken for granted that homecare workers risked being dismissed at will by employers when working in the independent sector. If they had not personally been subject to the experience of instantly losing a job, they all knew of someone to whom it had happened. In one story I was told of a transgender woman employed by a homecare agency. The employer insisted that service-users were made aware of her transgender identity in order to ascertain their consent before she was assigned to care for them. Many service-users declined her care. The agency found this troublesome but nevertheless was conscious that it would be 'wrong' to dismiss her, and unlawful to refuse her employment on grounds of her transgender status. Other homecare workers recognised that the transgender worker was particularly good at her work, she was 'very kind' and one service-user in particular liked her very much. This service-user invited her and her boyfriend to bring fish and chips over to the house one evening so they could eat supper together and watch TV. When 'the office' found out that she had visited a service-user without their permission, in her own time and with her boyfriend, all her clients were removed from her work programme. In an instant she was rendered automatically unemployed.

This story is memorable because the protagonist is transgender, but in its telling and retelling, the story communicates the understandings of homecare workers in two important regards. Firstly, the respect that employers afford to service-user choice as a guiding principle of service delivery only extends so far as it reinforces employer control. When service-users make choices in pursuit of closer or more stable relationships with homecare workers, those choices are largely disregarded by employers. Secondly, the story communicates homecare workers' fear of an arbitrary decision to put them out of work being taken by 'the office'. As Heather explained it to me, 'if the office decides you are too much trouble, if you are in their bad books, you will be out on your ear with no chance to put right mistakes or defend yourself.' This profound sense of insecurity felt by homecare workers, in which their experiences of work are set against a constant background fear of unemployment, has been reported in other studies as a perpetual feeling of being 'threatened' (Kingsmill, 2014, p. 13; Koehler, 2014, p. 20).

In my data, homecare workers described forms of management behaviour that suggested workers were considered to be utterly dispensable. Supervisor Ann was particularly candid when she explained to me that zero-hours contracts enabled her firm to easily dispense with workers as soon as they became unwanted. If she so chose, she would simply refuse to allocate a particular worker any more visits. She said that experience had taught her that after no paid hours for a week or so, it would 'sink in' with the homecare worker concerned that it was time to 'move on'. Ann recalled that it could be a bit embarrassing for her if she bumped into a disgruntled worker at the local supermarket; but, nevertheless, this was the way the industry generally functioned and she regarded it as an efficient means to avoid her firm the time and trouble of following policy and procedures:

> [if we decide to] we just don't use someone ... and then basically they leave because they've got no money coming in and they have to go ... It works in our favour that way. It might seem underhand and it's not great but I can see why it's done ... Can you imagine trying to pull somebody out to investigate stuff and you've got them suspended on full pay? It's just not going to happen ... with most people its misdemeanour stuff and we just decide not use them.

In the previous section of discussion, I explained that zero-hours contracts structure employment insecurity in ways which increase homecare workers' economic dependence. The above quote illustrates how zero-hours contracts give rise to a form of instant dismissal in which women are not even provided with notification that they have been dismissed. As I will now discuss, judicial doctrine in relation to employment protection rights enables employers to largely determine the scope of legal protection. On the basis of an assumption that it is legitimate for homecare workers to work in insecure employment, employers craft contractual relationships in ways which deny homecare workers the benefit of employment protection rights.

Contractual relations and the protection of employment

The extent to which individuals are entitled to employment protection depends upon the type of contract under which they work and their consequent identification in law as either employees, workers or independent contractors. In Chapter 4 of this book, I focus on the experiences of homecare workers at the intersection of employment and self-employment; there, I also consider how paid caregivers with worker status are treated differently from independent contractors in the regulation of care standards. However, in this chapter my interest lies in the availability of employment protection to homecare workers with contracts that position them at the legal intersection of employee and worker status. Since rules of statutory entitlement are articulated using different terms, according to different provisions, across a range of legislation, judicial interpretation of contractual status is contingent upon the particular rights which claimants seek to exercise. The legal availability of a right to protection from unfair dismissal is of especial relevance to the character narrative of Two-a-Penny and I use it as the focus of my discussion of contractual status in this section.

The unfair dismissal rights set out at s 94 of the Employment Rights Act 1996 (ERA) offer protection in relation to the procedure applied by an employer in the lead-up to a decision to dismiss, as well as to the fairness of the decision. However, this protection is available only to 'employees'. While s 230(1) of the ERA defines an employee by the presence of a 'contract of employment', the statute does not itself define the meaning of such a contract. Decisions about contractual status are based in common law. The legal award of employee status, and by implication the right to protection from unfair dismissal, is based on jurisprudence which is embedded in the historic development of the labour market and concerns the characteristics of a 'contract of service' – the traditional term for what is now understood as a contract of employment (see *Ready Mixed Concrete (SE)* v. *Minister of Pensions and National Insurance* [1968] 2 QB 497; *Cotswold Developments Construction Ltd* v. *Williams* [2006] IRLR 181 EAT). Generally speaking, employment under a contract of service is identified by a regular arrangement to perform work under the control of an employer, according to a minimum number of hours. Additionally, the individual concerned is typically subject to the employers' disciplinary and grievance procedures, uses employers' equipment or wears their uniform, follows employers' instructions and must personally perform work. Individuals with employee status are entitled to protection in the event of unfair dismissal as well as to a raft of other legal entitlements which include the right to redundancy pay, the right to protection in the event of a business transfer, the right to request flexible working, the right to maternity leave, the right to time off in the event of family emergencies and the right to statutory sick pay when ill.

As I discussed in the previous section, the women taking part in my research who worked in the independent sector were largely engaged on zero-hours contracts. Their recognition in law as employees was unlikely where the arrangement to work was irregular and the written contract did not specify a minimum number of hours (see *Carmichael* v. *National Power* [2000] IRLR 43 HL; *Autoclenz* v. *Belcher* [2011] UKSC 41). However, they were not without some basic legal entitlements as a result of being recognised as 'workers'. Individuals with a contract of employment have a dual legal status as both 'workers' and 'employees'. However, individuals who are not engaged under a contract of employment have worker status if, 'the individual undertakes to do or perform personally any work or services for another party to the contract whose status is not by virtue of the contract that of a client or customer of any profession or business undertaking carried on by the individual' (s 230(3) ERA). It is highly relevant to homecare workers engaged on zero-hours contracts that case law has established worker status in situations where there is no contractual obligation on an employer to provide work, and no obligation on the individual to accept work when offered, so long as the individual is paid on the basis of time, undertakes the work personally and does not work as 'part of any profession or business undertaking' (*Byrne Brothers (Farmwork)* v. *Baird* [2002] IRLR 96 EAT). Individuals with worker status qualify for legal rights such as the right to be paid no less than the national minimum wage, to take rest breaks and holidays, to protection in the event of dismissal for 'whistleblowing' and to protection from unlawful deductions being made from their wages.

However, there can be no blanket assertions about contractual status since legal interpretations are complex and are especially so for homecare workers engaged on a zero-hours basis. Employment tribunals are legally required to give consideration to the particularity of each individual employment relationship (*O'Kelly* v. *Trusthouse Forte* [1984] QB 90 CA). Nevertheless, the women who participated in my research were of the opinion, based on their experience of working life, that employment with a local authority gave rise to unfair dismissal protection, while employment in the independent sector generally did not. It was apparent that privatisation had moved the homecare workforce from a position in which their legal entitlements were clear, to one in which their employment protection rights were, at best, opaque. Where employment status is uncertain in law, four categories of doctrinal test are relevant. The first is the extent of employer control over work activities (*Secretary of State for Justice* v. *Windle* [2016] EWCA Civ 495; *Cotswold Developments; Halawi* v. *WDFG UK* [2014] EWCA Civ 1387 [2015] 1 CMLR 31). The second is the integration of the individual into the business (*Westwood* v. *Hospital Medical Group* [2012] EWCA Civ 1005). The third is the economic reality of an individual's dealing with the employer in matters such as the payment of wages, supply of equipment, coverage of holiday breaks and so on (*Ready Mixed Concrete* v. *Minister of Pensions; Quashie* v. *Stringfellow Restaurants*

[2012] EWCA Civ 1735). The fourth category of doctrinal test is that of mutuality of obligation, in which it is established if the employer is obliged to provide work and the claimant is obliged to perform work (*Ready Mixed Concrete* v. *Minister of Pensions*; *Carmichael* v. *National Power*; *Woods* v. *Somerset CC* [2014] unreported UKEAT/0121/14/DA). The written terms of an employment contract are key to judicial determinations and are typically taken at face value (*Stevedoring and Haulage Services* v. *Fuller* [2001] EWCA Civ 651). However, since employment status is determined on a case-by-case basis, written contractual terms can be considered in the light of all the surrounding circumstances (*Carmichael* v. *National Power*). It is possible for written terms to be legally disregarded if they are found to be inaccurate or do not represent the true intentions of the parties (*Autoclenz* v. *Belcher*). Increasingly, claims based on statutory rights depend upon the test of mutuality of obligation to determine contractual status and the focus of tribunals and courts frequently rests in finding the true contractual requirements of obligation on both parties (*Nethermere (St Neots)* v. *Gardiner* [1984] ICR 612).

The doctrine of mutuality of obligation

Mutuality of obligation has become a bellwether of employee status and effectively excludes casual forms of work from the coverage of protective legislation (Deakin, 2001, p. 6). It emerged as a specific consideration in employment law during the late 1970s (*Airfix Footware* v. *Cope* [1978] ICR 1210 EAT) and drew together assumptions about control, choice and risk at a time which coincided with women's increased participation in the labour market and the exercise of statutory employment protection rights for employees. In employment law, mutuality of obligation is a two-way street in which there is an 'obligation on the employee to attend, and upon the employer to provide work' (*Melhuish* v. *Redbridge CAB* [2005] IRLR 419 EAT). When applied in circumstances of zero-hours contracting, the test of mutuality of obligation places questions about control over working hours at the forefront of determining whether claimants are entitled to protection from unfair dismissal. This is well illustrated in the case of *Saha* v. *Viewpoint Field Services* [2014] (unreported UKEAT /0116/13/DM). Saha had a contract which committed her to work at least two shifts a week. However, in practice, she worked whatever shifts were offered and her working hours varied considerably. As was expected of many of the homecare workers with whom I spoke, Saha informed her employer at the beginning of each week about the times when she was available and, most often, her employer would arrange work in those periods (although in some weeks there was no work at all). Saha was able to change her mind about whether to take shifts or not. After five years, her employer abruptly ended the arrangement and told Saha that if she wanted any further shifts she would need to ask for work on a self-employed basis.

Saha regarded the removal of her work as an unfair dismissal. When she lodged a claim with an employment tribunal her employer replied that she did not have employee status and therefore did not have the legal standing to assert a right to protection. However, Saha felt her claim was justified because her written contract tied her to a minimum allocation of shifts, she had regularly worked for the employer for a lengthy period of time, it was her only job and she had always been referred to as an 'employee' in her work. The task before the tribunal was to establish her employment status and the doctrine of mutuality of obligation was the focus of its determination. Although her written contract stated that she would take at least two shifts a week, emphasis was placed on the fact that these shifts had not always been offered to her. Saha argued that the agreement to work two shifts a week represented a relationship of mutual obligation and the failure of her employer to abide by the contract should not mean that she lost the ability to claim unfair dismissal. Nevertheless, the tribunal found she was not an employee but a worker, and this left her without a right to claim any compensation when her contract was unfairly ended. A lack of mutuality of obligation, and the finding of worker status which followed from it, was upheld on appeal because there were no grounds on which to overturn the tribunal's finding of fact. Judge Shanks for the Employment Appeal Tribunal (EAT) observed that although the law was badly in need of revision, legal change would require an intervention from Parliament passing new legislation because statutory measures continue to rely on common law understandings of contract and put responsibility for interpreting contractual status with the judiciary.[2]

Although questions of contractual status are a matter of both fact and law (*O'Kelly* v. *Trusthouse Forte*), the application of the judicial doctrine of mutuality of obligation in individual cases is heavily dependent on findings of fact (*Nethermere (St Neots)* v. *Gardiner*). Hence the potential outcome in a claim for employee status by a worker on a zero-hours contract is subject to a great deal of uncertainty. If workers with zero-hours contracts are to establish the existence of a contract of service, a tribunal will have to set aside the written terms of the contract and investigate whether the performance of the contract in practice suggests that the true obligations of the parties accord with a contract of service (for example *Cornwall County Council* v. *Prater* [2006] EWCA Civ 102). The case of *Saha* provides an example in which the EAT preferred to construe the nature of the contractual relationship from established practice. In doing so, the case makes plain the extent to which the judicial doctrine of mutuality of obligation is influenced by, and respectful

---

2 Following reviews of the law relating to employment status in 2002 and most recently in 2014, governments have declined the opportunity to introduce change in the reliance upon common law tests for determining entitlement to statutory rights.

of, the power of the employer to create the relations of obligation which define the contract in practice. Employer power to choose whether or not to offer work at any particular time is a cornerstone of competitive advantage in labour-intensive sectors of the economy, yet employer freedom to engage labour on demand is regarded in law as merely the equal counterpoint of a worker's freedom to choose whether to accept work on each occasion (Fredman, 2004, p. 311).

Furthermore, mutuality of obligation is central to establishing whether individuals working under contractual arrangements which appear to fall short of judicial benchmarks of male participation in the labour market are entitled to employment protection (see, for example, *Secretary of State for Justice* v. *Windle*). Despite the ability of tribunals to recognise employee status where individuals with zero-hours contracts bring appropriate claims, the doctrine of mutuality of obligation signals that turbulent work scheduling, so extreme as to produce periods of time without any work at all, can reduce employers' legal responsibilities to a bare minimum. Like Saha, many homecare workers accept poor treatment in the course of their employment, either because their written contractual terms do not assure them of regular work or because their written terms are breached in ways which are unfavourable to their employment status. As a consequence of the judicial reading of their circumstances, the law gives normative endorsement to their arbitrary 'disposal' rather than to the protection of their employment.

From a legal perspective, precarious employment is viewed as a contractual issue rather than as a public policy or a social justice concern. When individuals are not tied to definite hours and an employer does not guarantee them work, their position at common law is to be regarded as 'not wholly at the disposal of the employer' (Fredman, 2006, p. 187). As we have observed in *Saha*, legal reasoning is typically disinclined to establish employer responsibility. The classical legal explanation for the lesser protection of individuals who do not have employee status is the assumption that non-standard workers are autonomous and are not economically dependent on their employer (Stewart, 2011, p. 77). Common law understandings developed from nineteenth-century deliberations about the contractual circumstances in which masters might owe a duty to their servants and the corresponding obligation of servants to their masters. The historic weight which the courts have placed on establishing an individual's dependence on their master is well illustrated by the Court of Appeal in *Simmons* v. *Heath Laundry Co*: 'a workman [the traditional term for a modern-day 'employee'] is treated by the legislature as being in a position of dependence on the employer and in fact as a kind of animated machine' ([1910] 1 KB 543). In a contemporary legal context, employees are not considered to be so wholly lacking in intelligence and independence as is suggested by their depiction as an 'animated machine'. Nevertheless, the image helps us to understand the legal roots of the doctrine of mutuality of obligation and legal relevance of contemporary questions such as whether individuals are able to turn down shifts, or if employers have committed to regularly provide individuals with work. The answers serve to either confirm or deny a relation of dependence which, a century before, would have been used in the courts to depict an employee as an appendage of the employer with a latent capacity for work and lack of personal autonomy synonymous with that of a machine.

The gendering of labour market autonomy

In contrast to the dependent relationship between an employee and their employer, the law assumes that individuals with worker status exercise personal autonomy in the labour market. Autonomy is identified as an individual's capacity to take paid work from several sources, or to choose to engage in unpaid work. For women, this latter explanation of labour market autonomy has corresponded with their assumed dependence on either a (male) 'breadwinner' wage or (where the breadwinner's wage is insufficient or unavailable) on state benefits. One need look no further than the 'objective inference' about women working under zero-hours-type contracting arrangements made by Lord Irvine of Lairg in *Carmichael* v. *National Power* that 'this flexibility of approach was well suited to their family needs. Just as the need [of the employer] was unpredictable, so were their domestic commitments' (p. 1231). Here, women's family responsibilities are factored into the judicial equation in order to create the impression of an equivalence of bargaining power between the parties to an employment relationship. Such equivalence is only possible if the imperative of the workers' economic dependency is assumed to lie outside of the employment relationship. Lord Irvine used his 'inference' about the weight of family responsibilities to justify an interpretation of the contractual obligations arising under the contract as being insufficient to establish employment protection rights. This judgment of the House of Lords in *Carmichael* is authority on the interpretation of zero-hours contracts and lays bare the gendered assumptions which lie behind the doctrine of mutuality of obligation. It also illustrates that unpredictable work scheduling, which a non-legal observer might think of as evidence of insecurity and de facto dependence, is assumed in common law to establish personal autonomy. Legal perceptions of autonomy are grounded in a presumption that both parties are equal and have freely entered into a contractual agreement. This presumption is gendered. For men, the presumption is that they do not have caring responsibilities and are 'naturally' free to contract on an autonomous basis. For women, however, a presumed burden of caring responsibilities means that freedom to contract can only arise in circumstances where their immediate economic needs are considered to be met outside of the labour market.

It would seem that, in a contemporary context, mutuality of obligation is a legal vehicle which translates perceptions of male/female forms of labour market participation into an employee/worker differentiation and justifies the distribution of the economic advantage of employment security towards men. Here it is worth recalling my earlier discussion of how women are constructed as inferior when measured by standards intended for men, as well as of the meaning I attach to sexism as an institutionalised subordination that disadvantages women and prioritises the meeting of male needs. For homecare workers, worker status reflects sexist legal reasoning and presumes that their participation in the labour market is not also a signal of economic dependence within the labour market. Legal regard for autonomy suggests that homecare workers' economic dependence is assumed to lie within an alternative home/family space to which they are considered best aligned.

However, establishing employee status is only a first step in establishing eligibility to claim a right to protection in the event of unfair dismissal. Unfair dismissal rights are subject to length of service criteria (except in respect of automatic unfair dismissals).[3] While s 108 of the ERA previously required employees to have a year of continuous service with their current employer, it was amended in 2012 to introduce a two-year continuous service qualification (Employment Rights (increase of limits) Order 2011 SI 11/3006). The Beecroft report, commissioned as part of an Employment Law Review by the Coalition government in 2011, supported an extension of the qualification period and claimed this could be of assistance to the health of the labour market because, under the 12-month rule, employers 'dismiss employees about whom they are uncertain after eleven months because they don't want to face the hassle of the process of dismissing someone after the unfair dismissal rules come into play' (Beecroft, 2011). The irony of this argument is to suggest that making workers less secure in law would make them more secure in practice. In the section 'Social inferiority and gendering of law' earlier in this chapter I described a continuous service criterion as a sex-based code of entitlement. By doubling the length of the entitlement period, we can observe that Parliament has recently drawn firmer demarcations of entitlement between men and women and has done so in the context of falling wages and living standards across the economy since the financial crisis of 2008. It is a legislative intervention which serves to realign protections more firmly in favour of male interests.

---

3 Some reasons for dismissal are automatically unfair and include those relating to union membership, exercising statutory rights such as the right to flexible working, enforcing the national minimum wage and being a part-time or fixed-term worker (see Deakin and Morris, 2009, pp. 429–30).

When we consider that 42 per cent of all homecare workers have been in their current job for less than 12 months (Skills for Care, 2015b, pp. 48–9), we can immediately appreciate the deepening of their employment insecurity which follows from these extended barriers of time served in a job. Yet if we layer on top of this the realisation that a large proportion of new starters with one homecare provider will have come straight from employment with a rival homecare provider within the same local authority area, we can question qualification periods as a systemic injustice. By denying protection of employment on the basis of non-continuous working, the law provides justification for practices within the homecare industry which result in a high turnover of labour. Employment protection law plays a role in creating the material circumstances through which homecare workers are unable to meet the criteria necessary to gain the benefits of employment protection. The contractual basis of work typically available within the homecare sector, marks out homecare workers as being the legal inferiors of those to whom employment protection is supposed to apply. This stratification occurs as a consequence of legal indicators of dependence *within the labour market* imagined and imposed by men (i.e. length of service, regular patterns of work, uninterrupted commitment to an employing enterprise). Such indicators are not innocuous, but rather they serve as a sex-based code which does not fit well with the contractual relations in which homecare workers are often engaged.

Determinations of employment status fail to recognise that legal notions of autonomy in the labour market are highly gendered. They do not acknowledge that women are genuinely dependent within relations of paid employment, and neither do they acknowledge the legitimacy of that dependence. Although questions of contractual status and length of service requirements in relation to unfair dismissal protection appear to draw on distinct and separate rules, each establishes that the ability of employers to disrupt and dictate working arrangements takes priority over the needs of women for stability and security of employment. When homecare workers are judged by male standards of dependence in the labour market, they may be denied statutory employment protection by common law reasoning which assumes their dependence is rooted within the social space of home/family where they rely on a husband and/or the state for sustenance. The Two-a-Penny character narrative establishes that homecare workers' experience of economic dependence and extreme economic insecurity is substantially at odds with judicial interpretations of dependence and autonomy in the labour market. Worker status can rightly be regarded as a gendered legal category since it serves as a marker of women's attachment to their homes and families (despite their reliance on paid work), as well as being a legal category which embeds women's inferiority in the labour market through its influence over behaviour and the shaping of expectations. My assessment of the gendered dynamics of decisions about employment status is further supported by evidence that Parliament has developed the statutory category of 'worker' as a tool with which to specifically include women within the scope of provisions. The examples set out in the section that follows suggest that the term 'worker' serves as a sex-based code in relation to employment protection – identifying women as the intended beneficiaries of minimum labour standards while excluding them from employment protection rights.

Worker status and second-class protection in law

Historically, casual and non-continuous working has been so closely connected with 'female' working that women were unable to secure mortgages in their own name without the signature of a male guarantor and did not acquire an effective right to independently access loans or credit until 1980 (Clisby and Holdsworth, 2014, pp. 32–3). Throughout the twentieth century, the state had established and supported collective bargaining between trade unions and employers as a preferred mechanism for the regulation of terms and conditions of work (Howell, 2005). However, successive governments required Wages Councils to operate in industries where collective bargaining was historically weak, either because of a lack of trade union membership or because employer support for joining employers' associations to enable sector-wide collective bargaining was absent. It was working women who were the primary beneficiaries of Wages Councils (Ewing, 1988). Up until their eventual abolition in 1993, it was primarily women who relied upon Wage Councils to set legally binding minimum pay rates in low-waged industries where collective bargaining was otherwise absent. The category 'worker' was used in the enabling statutes to ensure that working women were included within the scope of the Wages Councils (for example, Employment Protection Act 1975, Schedule 7, s 9(6)). Similarly, rights to protection from sex discrimination, which Parliament clearly intended to be of benefit to women, were not restricted to employees but designed for legal application to anyone with a 'personal contract to execute work' (Equal Pay Act 1970 s 1(6)a). A further example of women being specifically accommodated within statutory provisions by the term 'worker' arises in health and safety protection. For instance, the category 'worker' was used in the Working Time Regulations 1998 and legal minimum provisions for paid holiday were intended to primarily benefit working women with children (Department for Business, 2014; Lourie, 1998), a social group more than twice as likely as others to be otherwise without access to paid holiday. The Public Interest Disclosure Act 1998 offered limited protection from dismissal to individuals who disclosed information about malpractice by an employer and is applicable to an especially broad definition of 'workers' (ERA, s 43K). As is suggested by its introduction to the House of Commons by the Minister for Health, it was a measure which explicitly targeted individuals working in the National Health Service, a majority of whom are women (Rt. Hon. Alan Milburn, Health Minister, House of Commons debate, *NHS (Freedom of Speech)*, 5 November 1997). Indeed, under Tony Blair's 1997 Labour government the general strengthening of worker status was a cornerstone of a political mission to secure a flexible labour market underpinned by minimum standards. It is exemplified in the introduction of the UK's first ever national minimum wage as statutory protection for all 'workers', yet three-quarters of its intended beneficiaries were women (Lourie, 1999).

In the previous discussion I considered Parliament's preference for common law standards associated with male patterns of paid employment being used in judicial determinations of entitlement to statutory employment protection. In this discussion I have briefly illustrated how the statutory category of worker status reflects Parliament's intention to entrench the pre-existing social and legal status of women as inferior labour market participants. The statutory category of worker status signals how Parliament wishes women to be accommodated within the contemporary labour market. It is used to offer access to minimal labour standards rather than to extend to women forms of legal protection which defend the integrity and existence of an employment contract. In January 2016, the then Prime Minister, David Cameron, announced to the House of Commons that a record number of women were in paid work. He failed to also acknowledge that a record number of women were in precarious, part-time, temporary, insecure or otherwise poor-quality jobs (TUC, January 2015). The uneven distribution of the benefits of employment protection law across the labour market is co-implicated with the gendered legal development of worker status. Employers are able to avoid the statutory responsibilities of employment protection because of gendered assumptions in common law about economic dependence and autonomy. Meanwhile, worker status provides neither stability nor security of employment. In the absence of recognition as an employee, the state does not extend the benefits of protection from unfair dismissal, it does not insist that a job is sufficiently important to require a redundancy pay award on termination, fails to uphold the integrity of the contract during enforced absence because of childbirth or family emergencies, and it does not give explicit legal backing to individuals who request contractual changes to meet a need for flexible working. It is to the legal mechanisms with which the state determines the existence of contractual employment arrangements worth preserving in the event of a business transfer that I turn in the next section.

Understanding low pay in homecare as an employment protection problem

Official sources of information, including the Low Pay Commission, the Parliamentary Public Accounts Committee, the Parliamentary Audit Committee, the House of Commons Scottish Affairs Committee and the minimum wage regulator Her Majesty's Revenue and Customs (HMRC), have each asserted that hundreds of thousands of homecare workers are paid less than the minimum amount for which the law provides (the focus of discussion in Chapter 3). This problem has prompted a recent flurry of social policy-oriented research about unlawfully low wages for homecare workers (for example, Bessa et al., 2013; Gardiner and Hussein, 2015; Koehler, 2014; UNISON, 2014). It has drawn attention to the inadequacy of the national minimum wage scheme and asserted that in its stead, homecare workers deserve to be paid a living wage, that is, a wage calculated independently of government which is sufficient to maintain a safe, decent standard of living within the community.[4] Public-sector trade union Unison has campaigned for the implementation of an 'Ethical Care Charter' on the basis that local authorities should use their commissioning powers to build the payment of a living wage into the contract price for care services. The case for a living wage is morally persuasive, although it would seem that such moral persuasion is not enough to secure industry change.[5] From a market-oriented perspective it is unclear why homecare workers deserve better pay than other workers currently paid at or around the rate of the national minimum wage – workers in 6 million jobs are paid less than a genuine living wage (Office for National Statistics, October 2015). Indeed, there appears to be no shortage of workers willing to work at very low rates of pay. One strand of argument links low pay in homecare to high labour turnover and, consequently, low pay is framed as a problem of poor service quality. While evidence set out in the Two-a-Penny narrative would support these assertions, it appears to me that serious consideration of the paucity of employment protection and the absence of effective employment protection law, is largely missing from debates about low wages for homecare workers.

---

4 Not to be confused with the 2016 introduction by government of a National Living Wage, which is a higher rate minimum wage for adults aged over 25 years. The National Living Wage rate is not linked to living costs and is less generous than a genuine living wage.
5 UNISON began campaigning for its ethical care charter in 2012. As of January 2016, nine local authorities have committed to localised versions of the charter and it is unclear whether they have yet delivered on the aspiration of paying a living wage which extends to all working hours for all homecare workers and personal assistants providing state-funded care within their geographic area. See www.savecarenow.org.uk/who-has-signed-up-already

The homecare workforce has sustained very heavy pay losses since privatisation and on comparison with rates in the public-sector it is apparent that pay in the independent sector is considerably inferior. For example, in 2013/14 the average hourly rate of homecare workers employed by local authorities (albeit there were few remaining) was £10.61 (Local Government Association, 2014). This rate was well below the UK average hourly pay of £15.15 for all jobs in the same period (Office for National Statistics, 2013c) but it was based upon the implementation of 'equality proofed' systems of job evaluation. Meanwhile, the average advertised pay rate for homecare workers across both the public and the independent sectors was £7.36 an hour (Skills for Care, 2015b, p. 64). This rate fell well below the relevant living wage calculation (£7.65 an hour outside of London and £8.80 in London) and many workers in the independent sector would have actually been paid at, near, or even below the £6.50 hourly rate of the national minimum wage in 2013. However, when considered in the round, the comparison between local authority-employed homecare workers and their independent-sector counterparts is especially stark. The £10.61 hourly rate in local authorities is derived from an annual salary of £19,312 in 2013/14, based on a guaranteed 35-hour working week, which is enhanced by an occupational pension, an occupational sick pay scheme, occupational paid holiday, and paid time for travelling, training and supervision meetings; none of which is available in the independent sector.

The decimation of the remunerative benefits of homecare work is the result of employers' ability to disregard legal standards which must be observed elsewhere in the labour market. In the previous chapter, I discussed legal freedoms to pay women at discriminatory rates as a consequence of the outsourcing of the employment relationships upon which public-service delivery depends. In the next section of discussion, I will show that contractual protections which are supposed to shield employees from contractual detriment fail to adequately protect homecare workers. I shall argue that employment protection law interprets homecare work as an inferior form of employment and does so on the basis of gendered doctrine. The vast differences in economic and social benefits which exist between local authority-employed and independent-sector-employed homecare workers are traced directly to the sexist assumptions which lie behind the construction of employment protection law.

Parity of terms and statutory employment protection

Public-sector trade unions have previously advanced claims for parity of terms through processes of collective bargaining, not specifically for homecare workers, but on behalf of all local authority workers. Indeed, from 2005 there was a non-binding code of practice agreed between local government employers and trade unions. Where services were contracted out, the 2003 Code of Practice on Workforce Matters in Public-sector Contracts required that if 'new staff work on a public-sector contract alongside staff transferred from a public authority, the service provider will offer employment on fair and reasonable terms and conditions which are, overall, no less favourable than those of transferred employees'. It built on an assumption that, in the event of work being transferred to a contractor, statutory protection would ensure that local authority staff would be able to transfer their employment contracts and preserve terms and conditions. Such protection has been available in the UK since the early 1980s (see Council Directive 77/187/EEC and Transfer of Undertakings (Protection of Employment) Regulations 1981). The current EU directive upon which this protection is based came into effect in 2001 and the UK further widened the scope of its statutory protection with the Transfer of Undertakings (Protection of Employment) Regulations 2006 (known as TUPE). TUPE serves to protect employees from losing their jobs when a business takeover occurs, when a business is sold to a new owner or when services are outsourced or re-tendered by a client. The impact is to ensure that affected employees can retain their employment and benefit from statutory protection of their contractual terms, which cannot be diminished as a direct consequence of a change in ownership or transfer of service provision.

Against this legislative backdrop, trade unions had negotiated the code of practice to give local authority employees further protection from aggressive wage competition. It required each local authority and its contractors to ensure that new recruits were engaged on terms equivalent to those of ex-local authority staff. However, in 2010, the incoming Conservative-led coalition government issued a notification to abolish the code in order to 'facilitate greater competitiveness and to drive value for money for the taxpayer'. Although the statutory protections upon which the code was predicated remained in place, the abolition of the code paved the way for labour cost reductions to be pursued more brazenly by potential contractors.

As is highlighted in the Two-a-Penny narrative, homecare workers whom I interviewed for this book reported terms and conditions in the independent sector which deviated dramatically from those they had previously enjoyed as local authority employees. Although statutory protection under TUPE is available to all employees, these women had not been able to continue their employment when external organisations won service delivery contracts. Instead, their jobs had been made redundant by the local authority. I learned from them that their opportunity of employment protection under TUPE had been circumvented by the way in which contracts had been distributed between service providers. This was later confirmed in a conversation I had with a senior legal advisor dealing with homecare privatisation. As the discussion below illustrates, employment protection in relation to TUPE is subject to judicial doctrine which has set homecare workers in such circumstances outside of its protective scope. By explaining in detail the legal reasoning which applies in the event of service provision changes, I show how activities most likely to be undertaken by women come to be regarded as different from other employment activities, and hence are judged to be less suited to contractual protection in law.

Protecting employment in the event of a service provision change

The TUPE Regulations protect employees from a default legal position in which their employment contract would otherwise automatically terminate when the identity of their employer changes (*Nokes* v. *Doncaster Amalgamated Collieries* [1940] AC 1014 HL). According to the definitions at regulation 2, an employee is 'an individual who works for another person whether under a contract of service or apprenticeship or otherwise but does not include anyone who provides services under a contract for services'. TUPE regulations ensure continuity of employment without a loss of rights or privileges to the employee. Regulation 4 requires that all the transferor's duties and liabilities under the contract are transferred to the new employer and that the employment contract must continue 'as if originally made between the person so employed and the transferee'. In addition, it also protects the employee from a worsening of their pay or other contractual terms if 'the sole or principal reason' is 'the transfer itself', expressed by the Court of Justice of the European Union as meaning, 'on the occasion of and because of the transfer' (C-108/10 *Scattolon* v. *Ministero dell'Istruzione, dell'Universita e della Ricerca* [2012] 1 CMLR 17) (see also McMullen, 2012).

Prior to 31 January 2014, the protection of employment offered by TUPE also made void any contractual changes subsequently introduced by the transferee employer which were for 'a reason connected with the transfer' that is not an 'economic, technical, or organisational reason' (Regulation 4(4)(b)). Following the introduction of a legislative amendment in 2014, contract variations in respect of transfers occurring after this time may be made where the 'sole or principal reason for the variation is an economic, technical, or organisational reason entailing changes in the workforce, provided the employer and employee agree that variation' (Collective Redundancies and Transfer of Undertakings (Protection of Employment (Amendment) Regulations 6(1)). The extent to which TUPE offers protection from contractual variation is a complex legal issue which has generated a substantial volume of case law and commentary. In broad terms, TUPE provides that a transferee employer has no greater legal power to impose contractual changes than a transferor employer and, as a matter of legal principle, an employee is not put in a weaker employment position as a consequence of transfer. In the discussion which follows, I do not embark on a critique of the benefit of TUPE where it applies but rather I seek to illustrate how the homecare workforce has been impacted and shaped by the potential of their exclusion from TUPE protection. I will argue that gendered legal reasoning regards homecare as an inferior form of work.

Since the introduction of the 2006 Regulations there are two separate 'gateways' through which TUPE protection is available (Justice David Richardson, *Aguebor* v. *PCL Whitehall Security Group* unreported UKEAT/0078/14/JOJ, [23]). The original and first gateway is available when an economic entity changes hands, a situation defined at regulation 3(1)(a) as:

> a transfer of an undertaking, business or part of a business situated immediately before the transfer in the United Kingdom to another person where there is a transfer of an economic entity which retains its identity.

The phrase 'economic entity' is clarified at regulation 3(2) as,

> an organised grouping of resources which has the objective of pursuing an economic activity, whether or not that activity is central or ancillary.

The more recent, second gateway to TUPE protection is available where responsibility for the delivery of a service changes hands. This is known as a 'service provision change' and is defined at regulation 3(1)(b) as a situation in which,

(i) activities cease to be carried out by a person ('a client') on his own behalf and are carried out instead by another person on the client's behalf ('a contractor');

(ii) activities cease to be carried out by a contractor on a client's behalf (whether or not those activities had previously been carried out by the client on his own behalf) and are carried out instead by another person ('a subsequent contractor') on the client's behalf; or

(iii) activities cease to be carried out by a contractor or a subsequent contractor on a client's behalf (whether or not those activities had previously been carried out by the client on his own behalf) and are carried out instead by the client on his own behalf,

This is subject to qualification at regulation 3(3). Immediately prior to the service provision change, there must be,

i) An organised grouping of employees situated in Great Britain which has as its principal purpose the carrying out of the activities concerned on behalf of the client.

ii) The client intends that the activities will, following the service provision change, be carried out by the transferee other than in connection with a single specific event or task of short-term duration

So, to summarise, TUPE applies through gateway one when the transfer of an economic entity occurs in relation to an organised grouping of resources which pursues an economic activity. TUPE applies through gateway two when a service provision change occurs in relation to activities carried out on a client's behalf (whether subcontracted or re-contracted) if there is an organised grouping of employees carrying out activities on behalf of the client immediately before the transfer. The outsourcing of homecare work would seem to fall squarely for consideration as a 'service provision change' through gateway two, with the client in question being a relevant local authority.

The potential for local authority jobs to be protected under TUPE existed long before the 2006 regulations were passed. Since the 1990s, and under previous TUPE provisions, on some occasions when local authorities contracted out services the courts had found that labour-intensive services could constitute 'an organised grouping of resources' and had applied protection through the original gateway one (*Wren* v. *Eastbourne Borough Council* [1993] 3 CMLR 955; *Dines* v. *Initial Healthcare Services* [1995] ICR 11 CA). However, the case law was inconsistent, particularly in relation to second-generation contracting (see C-13/95 *Suzen* v. *Zehnacker Gebaudereinigung* [1997] CMLR 768), and therefore contract-bidding processes were often overshadowed by legal uncertainty about potential liabilities (Keter and Jarrett, 2011, pp. 3–4). Parliament recognised that fresh regulatory clarity could restore confidence in public service contracting and in 2006 a Labour government introduced the new 'service provision change' measures to make it certain that TUPE applied to labour-intensive activities such as the outsourcing and re-tendering of public-sector services. As Baroness Turner of Camden told the House of Lords, the new regulations were worthy of widespread support because they would 'value and improve protection for employees' (Hansard, col. 536, 3 May 2006). A consequence of the 2006 regulations is that TUPE clearly applies where a service is contracted out; when a service contract is relet to a new contractor; and when a local authority decides to take back in-house a service that it had previously contracted out (McMullen, 2006).

The first opportunity for judges to interpret the impact of TUPE in the circumstance of a service provision change came in the case of *Kimberley* v. *Hambley* ([2008] IRLR 682 EAT). Here, an organisation lost a service provision contract during a re-tendering exercise when the client awarded it instead to two rival contractors, splitting the contract geographically. The lion's share of contract activities (providing accommodation and support services to refugees) went to one organisation, and a much smaller element to another. The parties questioned the proper application of TUPE in such circumstances. Justice Langstaff framed the issue before the EAT as follows: 'which of those two (contractors), if any, should take responsibility for any employee who had been engaged in performing the service previously and on what principled basis?' (*Kimberly* [1]). It was not in dispute that the relevant transfer under consideration fell within the service provision change second gateway, and did not qualify on first gateway grounds as an economic entity. However, since there was no existing legal authority about what should happen in the event of a 'service provision change' split between different contractors, the EAT looked to the most senior source of guidance in relation to the transfer of an 'economic entity': that of a 1985 decision of the European Court of Justice addressing the application of employment protection when only part of a business was to be transferred (C-186/83 *Botzen* v. *Rotterdamsche Droogdok Maatschappij* [1985] ECR 519). It had ruled:

> the only decisive criterion regarding the transfer of employees rights and obligations is whether or not a transfer takes place of the department to which [claimants] were assigned and which formed the organisational framework within which their employment relationship took effect. (*Botzen* [14])

This ruling required that courts in all EU member states question how employees may be linked to the fabric of a transferring department or section of an organisation. They were mandated to recognise that an employment relationship physically materialised in the organisational locations to which their employees were 'assigned'. Consequently, it was only if an employee was assigned to a transferring part of the organisation that employment would also transfer. The decision was summarised by the European Court of Justice thus: 'an employment relationship is essentially characterised by the link existing between the employee and the part of the undertaking or business to which he is assigned to carry out his duties'(*Botzen* [15]). It was applied by UK judges in *Gale* v. *Northern General Hospital Trust* where it was suggested that an employee might be identified for the purposes of transfer as being 'part of the ... human resources of the part transferred' ([1994] ICT 426). Similarly, in *Duncan Web Offset (Maidstone)* v. *Cooper,* a case in which only a section of a business had been transferred to a contractor and it was unclear whether certain employees would remain or transfer, the EAT questioned which employees were 'assigned to the part [of the business] transferred?' ([1995] IRLR 633 [15]). These examples establish a doctrine of 'assignment', which determines employer obligations in the event of the partial transfer of an economic entity.

Returning to the issues before it in *Kimberly* v. *Hambley*, the EAT considered how to apply the 'assignment' doctrine in the circumstances of a second gateway 'service provision change'. The EAT saw 'no principled reason for there being any different approach'. It was argued and accepted that, since the transfer of an economic entity might, in some circumstances, also qualify as a service provision change, gateway one and gateway two claims were not 'mutually exclusive' (*Kimberly* [42]) (recall that since the 1990s, TUPE applied on occasions through the first gateway when local authorities contracted out services). Accordingly, the EAT ruled, 'no difference of approach *should* be taken' (my emphasis). Having decided to adhere to the assignment doctrine, the EAT swiftly found a resolution to the dilemma before it. Justice Langstaff summarised that the correct approach was to determine 'to which aspect of the activities involved in service provision the employee is assigned' (*Kimberly* [47]).

Kimberly had proceeded on appeal from a first-instance tribunal which had attempted to split liabilities between the two different contractors according to the volume of each contract. Justice Langstaff for the EAT argued, however, that there was no legal basis for the tribunal to make an order of proportional liabilities. He relied upon a long-standing principle in common law which establishes that a single employee cannot be the servant of two masters at the same time (*Fitzpatrick* v. *Evans & Co* [1901] 1 QB 756). In a situation where the activities of an individual employee are split between two service providers, the correct position at common law is that neither their employment nor liabilities in respect of it can be split proportionally. The EAT's ruling determined that responsibility to an individual must be found to fall in full to one or the other of the new service providers, and that tribunals should decide which service provider inherits which employees by tracing where the activities concerned have been assigned.

Hence the application of the 'assignment' doctrine in the context of a new gateway resulted in a small, but significant legal development. What had begun with the European Court of Justice identifying the link between an employee and the 'part of the undertaking or business to which he is assigned' (in the pre-transfer employment relationship), was now applied to identify 'the link between the employee and the work or activities which are performed' (in the post-transfer situation of a split contract see *Kimberly* [47]). Although the EAT saw the overlapping scope of the two gateways as reason for a singular scheme of determination, it set the 'assignment' doctrine in a new context. The doctrine was unmoored from its 'economic entity' associations and charted new 'service provision' waters. Judicial understanding shifted from a past-tense examination of where or how employees '*were* assigned' with the transferor, to instead examine the activities *to which* the employee is assigned in the context of a contractual split of services (see also *Duncan Web Offset* [46]).

In establishing this approach, the EAT in *Kimberly* noted the possibility of circumstances in which is it too difficult to determine who should take responsibility for an employee because the contracting arrangements between different organisations are 'so fragmented that nothing which one can properly determine as a service provision change has taken place' (Justice Langstaff [35]). Hence the decision to apply the doctrine of assignment within the context of service provision changes gave rise to a new doctrine of displacement, through which affected employees could be denied the protection of TUPE should a decision by their employer to split a contract into many different fragments serve to displace an otherwise clear connection between the employee and their work.

Understanding the doctrine of displacement

The more complex the division of activities between service providers, the greater the risk 'of employees falling outside the protective scope of the service provision change regime' because they are unable to show their work has been 'assigned' anywhere in particular (Wynn-Evans, 2008). Such a situation arose when Cornwall County Council re-tendered the contracts for a telephone advice service. It reduced the number of contractors from 17 to 9 organisations and shared the existing work between them. When a tribunal was asked to consider how the jobs of workers in the 17 organisations should transfer to the 9 successful bidders, it could not identify the specific functions that had transferred to each service provider and therefore held there was no relevant service provision change (*Thomas-James* v. *Cornwall County Council* [2007] Unreported ET 1701021-22/07). As the tribunal put it, there was 'no nexus between any of the transferors and any particular transferee'. The EAT agreed; telephone calls were allocated randomly between the contractors, the percentage of the service provided pre-and post-transfer could not be compared directly because the number of providers had changed, and the allocation of hours was varied and subject to fluctuation. It was the requirement to consider the assignment of activities after those activities had been split that necessitated a doctrine of displacement to operate alongside a doctrine of assignment to explain why some workers would now fall outside the boundaries of TUPE protection. Hence the doctrine of displacement provides incentive for client organisations to fragment work between multiple service providers in order to obstruct the potential claims of employees for employment protection and to secure labour cost savings for both the client and the contractor. The legitimacy of circumventing TUPE protection by fragmenting work has been affirmed in subsequent EAT decisions and it forms part of the statutory guidance offered from 2014 by the Advisory, Conciliation and Arbitration Service (ACAS), a non-departmental public body which sits within the remit of the Department for Business to advise on employment relations (for example *Enterprise Management Services* v. *Connect-Up* [2012] IRLR 190 EAT; *Metropolitan Resources* v. *Churchill Dulwich* [2009] IRLR 700 EAT; *Clearsprings Management* v. *Ankers* [2008] Unreported UKEAT/0054/08/LA. See also ACAS, 2014, p. 5).

There are other ways in which clients can organise contracts so as to circumvent TUPE protection. As a consequence of the decision in *Metropolitan Resources*, and its subsequent introduction as a statutory amendment, qualifying activities are now required to be 'fundamentally the same' as those in which the employees were previously engaged. We also know from case law that if a contract is subject to the removal of just 15 per cent of the activities performed prior to transfer, TUPE protection may not apply (*Enterprise Management*). Similarly, TUPE has been circumvented where the location of care services transferred from an institutional setting to individual domestic homes, even though the service provision change concerned the care of exactly the same group of disabled people (*Nottinghamshire Healthcare NHS Trust* v. *Hamshaw* [2011] Unreported UKEAT/0037/11/JOJ). Nevertheless, my discussion of judicial doctrine in relation to assignment and displacement has explained how the homecare workers whom I interviewed had ended up in a situation where their employment was not protected under TUPE law. In their local authority area, homecare services had been privatised in a way which meant individual service-users were randomly distributed between contractors, both through the contracting process and in the ongoing performance of the contract.

The ability to identify and effectively pin down the specific activities that are transferred, and to link those activities with the jobs of individual claimants, is crucial for establishing whether TUPE protection applies (*Eddie Stobart* v. *Moreman* [2012] IRLR 365 EAT). While the transfer of an economic entity may appear to be interchangeable with a service provision change from a legal perspective, in practice they are not analogous with one another. It is pertinent to the argument upon which I now embark that a majority of workers employed in service provision occupations in the UK are women. I will suggest that the idea of 'fragmented work' is gendered, that it serves as a sex-based code of entitlement, and that the legal reasoning which underpins it points to the subordination of women within the labour market.

A gendered difference of human interaction?

In a case about workers who had been wrongly laid off prior to a transfer, Judge Serota QC summed up the purpose of TUPE. He observed that redundancy compensation payments are 'not a substitute for continued employment' and that TUPE serves to 'protect employment and avoid redundancy' (*Inex Home Improvements* v. *Hodgkinson* [2016] ICR 71). The protection of employment available under TUPE is of particular importance to women in the UK, because women are more densely concentrated in sectors most affected by TUPE than elsewhere in the UK economy.[6] A lack of employment protection in the event of employment transfer is a key indicator of women's unequal status in employment law and it gives rise to sex-based economic inequality in the labour market. The public services contracting industry is larger in the UK than anywhere else in the world outside the USA (Julius, 2008). Therefore, it is unsurprising that women's employment in service provision is a type of employment most likely to transfer between a succession of contractors.

In addition, it seems that employees in service occupations based on one-to-one human interaction are most likely to be excluded from the benefit of statutory protection. Such services are tailored to meet the personal demands of a transient, individualised and changing cohort of service-users. Hence employees in this situation are particularly susceptible to being allocated between contractors in an ad hoc fashion. The doctrine of displacement provides justification for differentiating their work from activities which TUPE is apparently better designed to fit (in particular see *Clearsprings Management v. Ankers* [18]). For example, in services where employee activity attends to specific machinery or to physical property rather than human beings, the doctrine of displacement presents little impediment to the application of TUPE protection. One might think of bus services where a driver occupies a vehicle on an established route (*Abellio v. Musse* [2012] IRLR 360), building workers assigned to a specific construction project (*Inex Home Improvements*), property management, prison or security services located in fixed physical spaces and places (*Rynda (UK) v. Rhijnsburger* [2015] EWCA 75; *Aguebor v. PCL Whitehall Security Group*; *Ottimo Property Services v. Duncan* [2015] ICR 895; see Ludlow, 2015). These forms of work activity are typically found in areas of the service sector synonymous with 'male' employment and they support a raft of case law in which TUPE protection is found to apply in service provision change situations. Meanwhile, work activities based on human interaction/personal service work are an indicator of 'female' forms of engagement in the labour market and these predominate the case law in which judges decide that the scope of contractual protection has been exceeded.

The legal reasoning which supports the doctrine of displacement gives regard to, and bolsters, the prerogative of local authorities to fragment public service contracts without first ensuring that employment contracts will be protected in the process. It enables service activity to be regarded

---

6 These sectors are: health & social care, retail, catering, administration and facilities management (including cleaning) see Department for Business (2013) *Revision of the Transfer of Undertakings (Protection of Employment) Regulations 2006*, Equality Impact Assessment.

separately from the activity of the workforce that produces those services. It overlooks the fact that there *is* no service without employee activity and assumes employees are replaceable.[7] Legal reasoning permits agreements to be made between client and contractor about the ad hoc or highly fragmented exchange of services without giving primary regard to the protection of employment. In particular, it is in relation to services based on one-to-one human interactions that legal reasoning creates a fiction that service activity can exist in the absence of the active performance of those services by employees. Those employees set at a disadvantage under the doctrine of displacement, most likely women, are accordingly disqualified from the benefit of employment protection under TUPE. Its underpinning legal reasoning communicates that work activities associated with women are less deserving of protection because women can more readily be disconnected from their work than men, and it also reproduces the sexist justification that women's engagement in the labour market is more transient, and their tenure less secure, than that of men.

The doctrine of displacement acts as a sex-based code in employment protection law. It explains why the homecare workers with whom I spoke were being made redundant from local authority employment rather than being transferred to any one of the 50 independent sector providers which had been awarded service delivery contracts. It also explains why the only alternative homecare jobs, in which they would be providing much the same service, were those available at far inferior terms and conditions, under entirely new contractual arrangements, in the independent sector. The doctrine of displacement assumes special significance in relation to local authority contracting of homecare services because local authorities have a legal duty to establish a 'market' in service provision (Care Act 2014, s 5, as discussed in Chapter 4). It is therefore axiomatic that a fragmentation of activities will occur as the work of caring for thousands of local authority service-users is shared within a multiorganisational market.

While TUPE protection cannot prevent pay reductions after a transfer (because an employee has no greater guarantee about their future than they did when working for the transferor), it does provide continuity of service instead of redundancy. TUPE protects those things we might think of as employee's immediate concerns; such as wage levels, trade union recognition and hours of work. A further benefit is to secure ongoing recognition of the conditions by which an individual had acquired legal status *as an employee*. Where TUPE has failed to apply in the context of privatisation, the homecare workforce as a whole has suffered a general degradation in

---

7 An inclusive approach to interpretation is explicitly rejected by Justice Underhill in *Eddie Stobart v. Moreman*.

legal status: from employee status when working directly for local authorities to worker status contracts in the independent sector. The doctrine of displacement, through which homecare workers have been denied legal protection of their employment, places them in an inferior labour market position. Being excluded from TUPE protection is a significant factor in both the deterioration of contractual conditions *and* the loss of employment protection rights across the homecare sector.

Insecurity of employment made visible

When I visited the homes of women participating in my research, it occurred to me that their living spaces could be considered to materially represent the importance of employment protection. Workers accustomed to employment via local authority terms and conditions generally lived in modest terraced houses which were spotlessly clean and very carefully furnished. I noticed design features on lounge rugs, which complemented the patterns on scatter cushions placed at intervals down each sofa, and observed that towels in the bathroom would be of the same colour and match the bath mat, or even the housing case of the toilet brush. Homes were coordinated and well-organised spaces. Meanwhile, in the homes of women who worked in the independent sector, I saw signs that they had far less time to dedicate to their living spaces and less money with which to do it. Most were in rented accommodation, either flats or houses; only two owned their own homes.

It is not hard to imagine that a job characterised by large periods without pay, income insecurity and irregular hours, might leave workers with little opportunity to spend time and money on decor and furniture. It was also quite possible that many of these women had other priorities. Nevertheless, I observed that in contrast to the homes of local authority workers, the lounge/sitting rooms of women who worked in the independent sector were not decked out with recently bought accessories. Different techniques had been used to make living spaces comfortable and welcoming. In some homes, large multipattern throws and blankets were laid out over outdated or ripped sofa fabric and there were no extraneous cushions. Where there were insufficient cupboards or shelf space, the area between the back of the sofa and the wall behind was deployed as a storage area. Numerous school photographs of children, grandchildren, nieces and nephews were used as vibrant wall decoration.

During the time I spent with homecare workers, invariably I asked to use the bathroom. In some homes there was no carpet on the stairs and the wallpaper had long ago been stripped in the hall or stairwell in preparation for a moment when sufficient time and money might come together for redecorating. In others, the bathroom was in a particular state of disrepair:

leaking taps, mouldy walls, stained baths. In two homes, the toilet flushing mechanism was broken; one woman was so kind as to go upstairs first to fill a bucket of water so I could pour it into the toilet bowl as a manual flush; another gave me a Marigold washing-up glove so as not to get my hand wet when I reached down into the cistern to pull up the flushing mechanism because the handle was broken.

I do not want to imply that all the homes of women working in the independent sector were in need of maintenance; they were not. Indeed, in one home I was shown around a newly decorated hallway, dining room *and* kitchen while being regaled with stories about the shops from which various wallpaper had been chosen, and why. In another, a homecare worker lived with her friend in a tiny fully furnished flat which was as smart and stylish as a business-class hotel suite. However, when I spent time with research participants in their own homes I was able to 'see', as well as to listen. This was an inevitable part of the research process and I was struck by my realisation that the absence of employment protection was visually apparent in living spaces. The homes of local authority workers looked like permanent and secure spaces in which women had time and other resources to invest. The homes of independent sector workers looked somewhat transient, reflective of function and necessity, and rather more unsettled in their organisation. In my own mind, matching towels, scatter cushions and broken toilets were symbols of employment protection or its absence, made viscerally 'real' in the mundane artefacts of daily living.

Two-a-Penny, insecurity and the gendering of employment protection law

The character narrative of Two-a-Penny vividly illustrates that poor-quality employment is enmeshed with poor-quality care. Homecare workers identify themselves as two-a-penny workers: under extraordinary time pressures, aware of their inability to provide good care and fearful of dismissal. Being unable to meet the needs of service-users leads to feelings of guilt and inadequacy but homecare workers are also frustrated that their own needs (whether economic, physical or psychological) are disrespected. The impact on homecare workers' personal confidence and health is readily apparent.

Before they begin work, many homecare workers have made a financial investment in buying their uniform, spent up to two weeks of unpaid time in training, paid petrol costs upfront and found the money to cover fees charged for a criminal records check. Their practical, emotional and ideological commitment to the job locks them into a cycle of low pay and erratic working hours, maintained by routine management practices of over-staffing and pervasive threats about the withdrawal of paid work. In an atmosphere of intense labour competition, homecare workers are deceived by their employers; contractual guarantees of hours of work are not honoured, verbal agreements about the location of work are broken, mileage expenses are not fully reimbursed and there are large periods of working time which do not attract pay. The experiences highlighted in the Two-a-Penny narrative are supported by findings from other studies and appear to be so commonplace as to represent systemic failures in the organisation of employment in the UK's homecare industry. The purpose of this chapter has been to build on this supporting evidence by exploring how poor working conditions are institutionalised by the influence of deep-seated social stereotypes and sexist ideas of women's social inferiority which circulate in law.

The Two-a-Penny narrative has provided a perspective from which to question the degradation of homecare employment in relation to employment protection law. The discussion centred on two examples of judicial doctrine and the legal principles by which access to employment protection is distributed across the labour market. I have shown how the doctrine of mutuality of obligation and the doctrine of displacement associate legal protections of employment with male standards of labour market participation. I have indicated how homecare workers are likely to be denied access to the benefits of employment protection because of judicial reasoning which focuses on the structuring of their employment. With a focus on judicial doctrine, I have also suggested that the employment of homecare workers is organised so as to signal its exclusion from the benefits of employment protection. The implication is that judicial doctrine, and the reasoning upon which it is based, has a social impact which extends far beyond the adjudication of individual legal claims.

Employment is a special form of contractual relationship. It is evidently different from a standard commercial contract because the relationship created by an employment contract is one to which the state is willing to extend particular protections. Hence common law and statutory provisions erect a boundary around a limited selection of employment relationships, to craft them as arrangements into which normative expectations may be imported and legally enforced. Legal reasoning which awards advantages in forms of employment typically associated with men, also serves to actively disadvantage individuals in forms of employment typically associated with women. This suggests that employment protection law communicates key messages about the inferiority of working-class women and reproduces gendered subordination in the organisation of paid work. Justifications established in law serve as wide-ranging sex-based codes which skew economic advantage towards men. The legal regulation of employment protection is based on legal reasoning which hinges on women's failure to attain male standards, and provides justification for their ensuing disadvantage.

The contract of employment is a cultural artefact, a tool used in the formulation and application of legal rules (Deakin, 2001). As has been highlighted, the interpretation of legal rules through the application of judicial doctrine establishes legal facts which are far removed from the social and economic relations to which they seek to correspond. The protection of employment depends on a blend of statutory rights and common law principles. Deference to historic precedent pulls our collective past into the future. Even if statutory rights are intended to reflect new ways of thinking about the legal regulation of the labour market, Parliament has permitted their application in the courts to be founded on the apparent rationality of common law, which preserves existing patterns of privilege. Hence, homecare workers' experiences of poor-quality employment are shaped in part by judicial doctrine which identifies differences between their work, and work which is more readily supported in common law assessments. My intention has been to demonstrate that the experience of homecare workers, expressed in the Two-a-Penny narrative, is not an incidental consequence of marketisation. Rather, what is expressed is the materiality of sex-based injustice which is engineered through the unequal distribution of employment protection law.

Judicial doctrine structures the labour market as a gendered social space in which the inferiority of women working in homecare is institutionalised. Criteria of entitlement constructed in judge-made law draw on normatively 'male' perceptions of a contract of employment to justify the uneven availability of employment protection across the labour market. In doing so, legal reasoning communicates powerful messages about the social worth of working-class women in paid employment. For example, it serves to exclude individuals from employment protection where employers casualise work opportunities on the basis that staff are regarded as being of little value (because they are perceived to lack skill and are easily replaced, as in *O'Kelly* v. *Trusthouse Forte*); or on the basis that staff are not fully committed to the enterprise (because of judicial regard for the imperative of meeting family needs, as in *Carmichael* v. *National Power*); and with the expectation that paid work is not of primary economic significance in everyday life (because women depend on male earnings and/or state welfare, as explored in Grant et al., 2006; Thornley, 2007). Sexist understandings that associate working-class women with poor-quality employment inform legal justifications that can deny employment protection in the type of employment situations typically experienced by homecare workers.

Although employment protection law applies equally to all men and women in the labour market, in the context of homecare it is particularly apparent that judicial doctrine communicates an implicit presumption that low-waged women are less capable, less committed and less deserving than other labour market participants. The lack of employment protection available to working-class women signals the institutionalised separation of homecare work from the work and forms of employment relations in which other workers are engaged. It also signals that inequalities of sex and class in the labour market have not been created by immutable economic forces but are shaped by legal rules that have been imagined, approved and largely put into operation by men.

3
Mother Superior

When I was growing up, I lived with my nan. My great-grandmother was in the house and needing care. I was only sixteen at the time. Looking back, she was a right pain to me at that age! She used to drive everybody cracked because she would have this hand-bell permanently going off. It was, Ding-ding! ... Oh God, here she goes again, and our nan used to say, 'You can go in and change her pad for her', and I would say, 'No way, I'm not doing it!', but the care was more or less forced on me. There was me and my brother Tommy, more or less the same age as me, but, well he was a boy. As the girl, I was supposed to help out. Even though I didn't do a great deal, it was enough to truly put me off care. It wasn't something I thought I would like to do when I was older. It was something that made me want to heave; do you know what I mean? My granddad, he ended up with cancer of his neck and I will never forget making him this egg and milk drink, and I used to be disgusted, 'Urgh, Grandad, how can you?' and he used to grin back to me, 'Yum, it's lovely!' Nan used to do all his personal care, but I'd be expected to help, you know? Then, as an adult, I found I would always do little bits and pieces for people. My friends all said I would be brilliant at care, but I couldn't see it in me. How my life turned out though: after my children, my divorce, hating other jobs; I thought care would be worth a try. At the job interview, they asked about my experience and, of course, I told them how much I enjoyed helping my nan!

I didn't think this would ever happen, ever, but I think it's my destiny. It is what I am going to do for the rest of my life. I have never looked back. Care should come naturally, I think with me it was bred into my genes. Once you become a mum it just comes natural; but not till you have got children. I absolutely love the job. It is in my nature to put the client's needs first – even over and above my own family. If you haven't got care in you, you will never get it, so go and work in a shop or drive a taxi instead. You can't train to get care; it's built into a person. There are two types of carers – those that really care and those who are in it for the money, you know? And those carers wouldn't care if they've upset clients. I see myself as one of the better homecares. It has been said to me, 'You're just an inspiration to care'. I believe in treating whoever I'm working with as I would want to be treated myself. If you haven't had good care before, it's a bit of a shock when good care comes along. You gotta get out there and physically give each person the care that they need, no matter what. If you can't do that, don't join the job, it's simple. You are in homecare because you care; it's not about money because you will never be paid enough. I have put in a lot of extra time; not because I wanted to, but because I had to. When we do an extra hour, which happens quite often, you don't get paid but it's your duty of care. Companies aren't worried about care; they're worried about revenue, that's all. I've been putting in my own time on a night-time too. I've been pulled up by the office about a man who had messed the bed, asking why I went there at 2 o'clock in the morning because it wasn't my time. But, hey, we've got a paraplegic here, a gentleman who is also diabetic, who has faeced the bed. Who is gonna say to him, 'Sit in it and I will get there in the morning'? By the morning it will have burned his backside which means we then get sores and infection problems. Hang on ... wash, change, clean, done, cream; no sores. That's my objective; nobody gets sores, not on my watch.

I don't think it's right for teenagers doing this job, not right at all. A young person, you take it from me, they don't want to wash an old body and an older person doesn't want them seeing them. Older women, they've got a little bit more experience in life. To the youngsters it's a job. The majority of them haven't got a clue. A lot of them are out of their depth, because they're inexperienced and they don't like to listen. You cannot do a 50-hour week and do your job properly, not in this job. There are a lot of young girls in my care company who go into people and they write they emptied and cleaned the commode. Well, it might be empty, but it certainly ain't clean! And that's disgusting to me. I've got nothing against the young girls, but the job to them, it's the money, it's the Friday night out. Whereas the older women tend to take it a bit more serious, they care that little bit more because they're at the stage in life where they're reflecting more on what's going on around them.

I get my clients little things, little treats from my own money because sometimes they haven't got talcum powder, or deodorant, or tablets to soak their teeth in. You do it; you can't help it! Sometimes it's a *basket of strawberries, or something from the butcher's. I do like looking after them – making them comfy and making them happy. Just going that extra mile can make their life ... more of a life. If a client was short of flannels one day I'd say, 'I'll pick you up some flannels, no problem', but if I told the office I was doing that, I would be told not to. Some clients have to pay privately. I remember one couple that couldn't really afford it. My care for them always took 45 minutes, but I used to log it as only 30 when we had a cold snap because I knew they struggled with the extra expense of heating. There is one lady that I take a fish pie round for; another I just call in for a cup of tea. They get to know you and they get so upset if you are leaving. It's really warming to think that I make a difference.*

I do quite a few of my shifts out of the goodness of my heart because somebody has got to be there. One evening I was sat here, it wasn't even on my shift and I had a phone call; a client had fallen and his neighbour found my number in the file on his table. I never thought about the money, I thought about nothing else except to get him off the floor and that man – very ill with dementia – they phoned me, nobody else. My job is not just my job, it's my life. It's something I have dedicated myself to. You see, I have made a commitment to them. I've got my memory candle for the special people I've been privileged to know. It might sound a bit sick to you but I've laid out quite a lot of dead bodies; I mean washing them and making them look nice for the families. I know that other people wouldn't be able to do it and I can't say I enjoy it but it does give you some sort of satisfaction because you've done it for the family. With one lady, I remember we had done what was needed on our duty, made her comfortable, but when we left that night, I just knew she was ready to pass on. Half an hour later, her daughter rang: 'Please come, for mum. I don't know what to do.' She idolised her mum, but her mum had gone. When we got there, her mum didn't look very nice, the way she was sat all stiff. We could lay her down right though, and put a nice clean nightie on, a nice scarf to match it and her favourite brooch. She looked lovely and the family could not thank us enough.

You just can't believe some people's lot. They've got so many things wrong with them, so much taken from them; some people can be in an awful situation. I find it impossible to care about people and not take an interest in them. One lady had a son who lives 10 miles away, yet he only comes once a year at Christmas. I would find that so hurtful and upsetting if it were me, I just don't understand people. I remember another; she had lost both her daughter and her son, they'd both died and she had nobody. It makes me cry when I think. In families, old people can become like a spare part. I see a lot of loneliness. Families say, 'we'll see you next week', and I have seen the person sat there looking out the window and I'm watching them watch. When the family don't turn up, it's me that gets their tears. It makes me angry; it makes me want to get on the phone and say, 'Where are you!' I know that some would come if they could, and they have families of their own, and they need to go to work themselves, and sometimes they just cannot deal with the problems. But occasionally I do get angry. One man, he was quite wealthy but he never had no visitors. When he died, his family appeared like locusts, they stripped his flat of fancy stereo equipment and his TV. When we went round the back to the bins, we found a suitcase with all his old photographs spilling out, pictures of him as a child, his clothes; this was only the day after he died; but his money and anything of any financial value they took.

Before I did this job I never realised how many lonely people there were. The basic – food, water and medicine – you can give that to people; but it's the loneliness that kills them. One morning I went to a woman who was upset. I put my arm around her and I give her a hug. She was startled. She said, 'It is so lovely; for the first time in forty years someone has cuddled me.' It broke my heart. From then I made sure, irrespective of money, I always hug or touch my clients. It's being alive, just to touch them. To gently touch their hair so they can feel the sensations through their body. That's how they know you care. That somebody out there actually cares. To be alive through touch.

I'll tell you another story. I had a gentleman, he's not with us anymore, and he was a bit of a grump. He was blind and he loved to moan. I had told my boss at the time that he was so obnoxious I didn't want to go in there anymore, but this was my last try. That morning, I decided to go in with a different attitude. Before work, I got all genned up on the news. He was an intelligent man; he wasn't nobody's fool. I went in there and said, 'good morning'. I was rather flat, rather curt. He said back, in a miserable voice, 'Hello'. I went: 'Have you heard that terrible news this morning?' and me and him hit it off straight away because all I'd done was moan about the world too. This man used to have a good job; things were fine when he was working. He paid his taxes, paid his dues, fought for his country, but now he was just completely demoralised. Anyway, I moaned every day and he got happier. But one morning, it was so sad. I went in and called him, he never answered. I rushed straight up the stairs and I found that man in his back bedroom sandwiched between a sideboard and a bed. He must have weighed about 8 stone, all his legs were cut, his head was cut, and he'd been there all night. He was so damn cold on that floor, and the reason why he was so cold was because there was no heating on. He was actually frozen.

Mother Superior and the national minimum wage

The voice of homecare workers who gave care without concern for money is represented in the Mother Superior character narrative; they said it was the best way to be. I brought together stories which highlighted their selfless devotion to service-users, the idea of care work as a vocational calling and their understanding that caring skills and competences were an expression of female identity. In these Mother Superior stories, care work was aligned with mothering, raising children, emotional strength and moral conviction. Those who shared the view that care was not a job but a way of life, included women working in the independent sector, those with long service as local authority employees and those working as personal assistants. Each was confident in the innate value of their work and the difference it made to the lives of others.

This chapter offers an extensive discussion about the Mother Superior character narrative and engages with academic literature about caring, gender and class before moving on to consider national minimum wage law. I begin by drawing on key sociological ideas about emotional labour. The first element of my argument is that stories fitting the Mother Superior narrative associate homecare work with middle-class maternal understandings of care as an unpaid activity. Experiences of gender and class shape the notions of identity and generosity through which relations between service-users and paid care workers work are presented as being 'like family'. I suggest that the Mother Superior narrative indicates how homecare workers can use story-telling as a resource with which to collectively protect themselves from being shamed by stereotypes about the worthlessness of low-waged women. In the second part of my argument I build on research suggesting that workers who believe they gain personal benefit and satisfaction from the intrinsic properties of their work are more likely to accept low pay (England, 2005; Folbre, 2001; Lucas et al., 2009). I explore the gendered and classed landscape within which homecare workers 'choose' to work without economic reward. It seems that the multifaceted character narrative of Mother Superior represents the idea that 'good' women *ought* to be happy to work without wages. Hence expectations of adequate economic compensation for caring labour are traded away in return for the opportunity to gain social respect. The implication is that when homecare workers are characterised as Mother Superior figures, or indeed cast themselves in this light, working without pay becomes a moral imperative.

By using the Mother Superior narrative to engage in an extensive discussion of caregiving literature, I am able to identify that gendered notions of female self-sacrifice and familial morality underpin homecare work. Social relations of class influence maternal understandings of 'care' which are reified within 'moral landscapes' of value. The moral landscape of 'family', in which mothering work is unpaid, is antithetical to the moral landscape of 'law' in which employment relations establish an economic contract. With this tension in mind I move on to consider the legal administration of the UK's national minimum wage scheme. In previous chapters, the methods I used to examine law at work have explored the framing of statute and considered the role of judicial doctrine in bringing common law standards to bear on decisions about employment protection. The methods used in this chapter enable me to assess the extent to which provisions in the National Minimum Wage Act 1998 and National Minimum Wage Regulations 1999 meet the intended purpose of the legislation and I also review legal interpretations of fact upon which understandings of 'work' hinge.

It is well documented that in recent years the homecare workforce has been underpaid by millions of pounds because employers have routinely flouted national minimum wage law and the state has failed to adequately enforce the minimum wage in the social-care sector (HM Revenue and Customs, 2013; Kingsmill, 2014; Koehler, 2014; National Audit Office, 2014). However, my assessment in this chapter suggests non-compliance is symptomatic of an underlying problem of sexist stereotyping in the legal mechanisms through which the UK's national minimum wage is administered. Despite public policy claims of universal benefit, the right to be paid the national minimum wage is not sufficiently inclusive to communicate that care work is as legitimate and worthy of economic regard as any other work. Findings of fact which establish that caring labour does not always count as 'work' communicate the low status of homecare workers and the people for whom they care. Legal answers to the question 'what is work for the purposes of the national minimum wage?' reveal the prejudice at the core of statutory wage protection. Working-class women are coerced to give care for free in lieu of adequate economic reward by powerful stereotypes about gender and class which are supported and reproduced in law.

Mother Superior as a collective imaginary

I chose the name for the 'Mother Superior' character narrative, inspired by Rosa's anger about employer disregard for the women she called 'the devoted carers'. Reports about poor-quality care frequently suggest that older people are put at risk by homecare workers with inadequate skills and a lack of commitment (see, for example, Cavendish, 2013; Chorley, 2014). Rosa wanted to distance herself from this negativity and explained that she was not one of these 'others' who were 'just in it for the money'. In creating a Mother Superior character narrative, I paid attention to homecare workers' accounts of the moral meaning of care. I hoped to capture Rosa's imagined community of 'devoted carers' as well as to document her inclination to exclude those with whom she did not identify. While it was Rosa who gave me inspiration, her sentiments were widely shared. Through their story-telling, many homecare workers created considerable moral distance between themselves and 'other', less reputable, care workers. These 'others' included men; younger women; women who did not have English as a first language; and managerial-class women. Conceptions of caregiving were infused with class-based social meanings. Rosa credited working-class women such as herself with being in a position to 'know' about care in ways that managerial-class women were not. She said, 'whether those women are good managers or not, they don't know the value of what we do, the real value of what we do. They have no idea at all.'

Despite economic hardship, the character narrative of Mother Superior illustrates that homecare workers draw on traditional notions of gender to distinguish themselves from demeaning and disrespectful assumptions which circulate in relation to 'poor' people. However, in separating themselves from unsuitable 'others', the accounts of homecare workers reinforced the very perceptions that they sought to challenge, namely the assumption that impoverished workers lacked sufficient emotional finesse or moral discipline to be able to do the job well. The Mother Superior character narrative expresses the 'collective imaginary' of homecare workers and represents a form of story-telling in which people portray their community through personal narrative (Hall and Lamont, 2013). Collective imaginaries link past events to the present status of a community, and link aspirations for the future to the values that bind a group together (Taylor, 2004, pp. 23–6). These are not free-floating utopias but are shaped by the social hierarchies, dominations and existing inequalities which contain and contextualise our experiences. Collective imaginaries are grounded in life experience and reveal the social power of long-standing, gendered norms which establish how men and women *ought* to behave in return for social regard (see for, example, Walkerdine and Jimenez, 2012).

As a collective imaginary, the Mother Superior character narrative communicates feelings of pride and self-esteem as a counter-balance to the stigma of low wages and repeated accusations of poor-quality care by the mainstream media. Through Mother Superior-type stories, homecare workers can articulate what it means to be a 'devoted carer' and identify who is, or is not, included in this resourceful and valued community. The dominant values expressed provide a guide as to how 'devoted carers' might be expected to behave when faced with particular challenges. In this vein, Sophie told me it was a worry to her that the profit motive of private-sector providers would encourage women working as new homecare recruits to 'just see it as a business'. Claire said she was concerned that the care provider she worked for had started to give jobs to women who were simply 'in it for the money' and she didn't want to work alongside them because they 'wouldn't care if they've upset a service-user ... and will walk-off.' According to this view, problems of high-labour turnover in the homecare industry were not caused by insecurity of employment or low pay, but conversely were the result of recruiting care workers who wrongly privileged money over care values. However, Claire's concerns also suggested that she felt threatened by these new recruits – that they would somehow adversely impact upon her reputation.

Rosa articulated very strong concerns about falling care standards: 'either you like the job and you want to do the job or you don't. You can't start to get greedy about looking after somebody.' Even though Lucy had been dismissed from several previous homecare jobs for poor timekeeping and extended sickness, she didn't hold back from telling me that she was not like 'other' homecare workers whom she said had a 'bad attitude' and were 'in the wrong job'. Lucy identified herself as one of 'the good carers' who 'do not work for the love of the money'. Accordingly, the character narrative of Mother Superior emerged from accounts of class-based and gendered self-discipline in which 'you don't even *think* about the money; the money is just the second thing when it comes to paying your bills.'

In stories that fit with the Mother Superior narrative, it seems that homecare workers communicate the value of their work by asserting that caring is a practice which centres on distinctly feminine forms of identity. In the discussions about emotional labour which begin in the next section, I use the terms 'feminine' and 'femininity' to refer to behaviour, aptitude, rituals, routines and activities which are associated with the disposition of people who have a female body. It is because caring is aligned with the female body that care work is considered to be a natural and innate performance of femininity. However, femininity is not a female condition and female bodies are not necessarily feminine bodies. Femininity is a social acknowledgment and an aspect of identity that differentiates women from men (Charlebois, 2010, pp. 5–8). Femininity is the construction of gender (Barrett, 2014 [1980], p. 196). It facilitates the employment of women in caring professions and militates against the employment of men because femininity is the benchmark against which women are trusted to provide care and men are regarded with suspicion (Huppatz, 2009, p. 53).

Emotional labour and mothers' work

The Mother Superior character narrative communicates the significance which homecare workers attached to caregiving as a mark of socio-sexual hierarchy. For most, looking after older people required skills and attributes which came from living and loving as mothers. Several talked as though care work was a destination they had arrived at on their life journey; examples of this discourse of female progress included recollecting 'how I got here', referring to care as 'my destiny' or 'what I am going to be doing for the rest of my life', and identifying a job in homecare as a point of transition from which they 'never look[ed] back'. Michelle and Sophie had taken up employment opportunities in homecare after each having a second child. They both believed that care of the elderly was not 'natural' in girlhood. Marilyn explained that generations who are 'worlds apart' could not connect with one another and said young people 'haven't got the life skills' to do the work well. She elaborated, 'it takes a certain kind of person to be able to [care]' – by which she meant that care could not be taught in abstract isolation from knowledge acquired in the course of a lifetime. Indeed, when I asked homecare workers about the characteristics which made a person suitable for care work, all referred to the increasing presence of young people in the industry, and did not regard it as a welcome development (a finding also noted in Atkinson et al., 2016, p. 3). Claire was the youngest of the women with whom I spoke. She had worked in homecare since her early twenties and, rather than justifying her own appointment, Claire said the job was inappropriate for the young because the emotional work involved was so complex. She said the job demanded total commitment and being prepared to 'take on what [service-users'] lives are, how emotional they are, and how they [struggle] dealing with their own life', and she didn't think young women could have yet acquired sufficient emotional resources.

Service-sector jobs are distinctive within the labour market because they require workers to exhibit sophisticated knowledge of the emotions which ought to be expressed in particular situations and to manage and adapt their personal emotions in interaction with other people (Hochschild, 1983). Such 'emotional labour' is vital to paid care work (James, 1992). The Mother Superior story about a homecare worker discovering that she could communicate effectively with a service-user by having a 'moan about the world' is an exemplary account of emotional labour in practice. She described how she adapted her own emotions to meet the emotional needs of another person. Sophie identified that her communication skills and the strategies she used to engage with her service-users meant she could 'reach a person at any level'. Rosa said it was her job to make 'people … feel good about themselves'. Trish, who had worked for the local authority for 23 years before taking a job with a private care company told me, 'I've found being a homecare that I've got to be five different people a day. Five different personalities … [with each service-user], you have a different mask on and you just find you have to be adaptable.' Emotional labour is gendered and women are socialised to develop the skills which underpin emotional work. In heterosexual personal relationships, the deployment of women's unpaid emotional work is thought typically to offset their financial dependence upon men (Hochschild, 1983, p. 7). However, the emotional labour of caregiving has distinctive qualities. Care workers must always go beyond what is technically required and caring labour (being distinctive within a broader category of emotional labour) requires workers to make a 'gift of the self' (Bolton, 2000). As discussed in Chapter 1, the practice of homecare produces qualities which cannot be explicitly remunerated and it is the personal gift aspects of caregiving which augment its emotional labour.

A gift of the self

The idea of giving a 'gift of the self' came into play when I asked homecare workers to discuss productivity. They struggled to reconcile the accounts they had shared with me about selfless devotion, with the reality that their work was strictly organised on the basis of timed visits (see the Two-a-Penny narrative in Chapter 2). Carol, who had worked in homecare for over 25 years, felt that the allocation of time limits to service-users failed to take account of the personal nature of the service that homecare workers provided. She explained that the same task 'might take so-and-so 15 minutes and it could take me three quarters of an hour, that all depends how you work'. For Michelle, working at a different pace from one another was an inevitable consequence of 'different lives' and 'different backgrounds'. Marilyn described her own labour as being a 'gift' to her service-users. Nevertheless, there was a general consensus that training and experience in the job improved productivity. Yet it was striking that homecare workers resisted all prompts from me to acknowledge that productivity gains were progressive. They preferred to evaluate their own work in moral, as opposed to economic, terms. Productivity was overshadowed by the greater significance of personal integrity: a good woman would know how to work productively; a bad woman would be overly concerned with 'process' and 'clock-watching' as a way to avoid proper caregiving.

In an industry which relies upon feminine skills acquired through socialisation, assessing a 'gift of the self' is, by its nature, extremely personal. Homecare workers were keen to stress that making someone feel cared for meant putting their needs centre stage as the primary concern in all interactions. Caring requires self-denial and dedicated service to the welfare of another person. Although there are massive contradictions between these assertions and the actually existing organisation of paid care work, questions about what constitutes 'good care' are often framed as moral questions about how best to express caring responsibilities (Sevenhuijsen, 2005, p. 132). Such assessments of moral conduct are primarily about how people should treat one another, but they cannot be divorced from their political context and the power relationships upon which such assessments depend (Tronto, 1993, p. 5). The Mother Superior character narrative suggests a level of resistance to the idea of paid care work as an economic exchange. It is a resistance which is based on moral assessments, but also represents a rational response to the harsh economic realities of paid care work. Homecare workers are not valued, respected or rewarded as healthcare professionals and therefore locating themselves within a framework of occupational professionalism is unlikely to provide them with a route to self-esteem or a positive story to tell (Meagher, 2006). Normative assumptions about women's role in society and the attributes of a 'good' woman are deployed by homecare workers as a moral framework through which they are able to present themselves as socially valued women.

Caring as a class issue

While caregiving is synonymous with social functions normatively assigned to women, social class shapes understandings of what the work of care actually 'is'. Working-class women and middle-class women experience the gendering of care in different ways. In particular, the character narrative of Mother Superior sheds light on the motivation of homecare workers to exhibit working-class 'respectability' (Skeggs, 1997). They discussed their work as the performance of a socially acceptable femininity in order to counter the social disrespect they routinely encountered. Values of nurturing and self-sacrifice are highly gendered and derive from the private sphere of home and family. Homecare workers relied upon them to suggest that high levels of emotional competence were required to provide good care. Yet as the earlier discussion of productivity suggests, homecare workers were as much presenting an account of how they wanted the job to be, as they were telling me how it was. As an allegorical resource, these portrayals represented an attempt to rise above their subordinated social position and make the best of being at the margins of the labour market. However, scholarship from the field of psychology suggests that emotional well-being is difficult to achieve in situations of poverty (Reay, 2004, p. 69). There is considerable tension between celebratory accounts of care as a 'gift' and the economic hardship of unpaid working time and wages blighted by sex discrimination.

In the context of paid care work, women capitalise on their femininity because caring identities can be realised in economic as well as social terms. It is commonly supposed that paid employment enables people to participate in a 'working life' which is compartmentally separate from their 'private life'. Yet this implies a degree of psychological separation which is not born out in homecare worker's experience. As I have noted above, it is a prerequisite of emotional labour that workers are able to distance themselves from their immediate feelings and make 'best-fit' choices from a range of readily available emotional options. The giving of 'good' care demands that care workers are not overwhelmed by their own emotional needs and can detach from their own self to master the intensity of their own emotions (Huppatz, 2009, p. 56). However, it has been suggested that poverty creates problems for the integrity of paid care work because 'the depleted care worker, deprived not only of fair pay but of equal voice, and of mutual relations of recognition with employers and others, cannot possibly meet the needs of care recipients' (MacDonald and Merrill, 2002, p. 75). The suggestion here is that poor women cannot care well because poverty reduces emotional reserves and self-esteem such that the desired separation of 'work life' from 'private life' is not possible.

Emotion contributes powerfully to the making of class inequalities and the need to be respected, or to be seen as respectable, is a primary motivator of human behaviour (Sayer, 2005). Some people are deprived of the social or economic resources necessary to behave and live in ways that bring the positive recognition of others. On account of the social conditions in which they are typically situated, working-class women bear the greatest psychological burdens of social inequality and may find it more difficult than middle-class women to engage in emotional labour (Reay, 1998). However, we should not accept uncritically that the economic or social conditions imposed on paid carers have a psychological impact which renders them unable to exercise the emotional skill and judgment which good care demands. The ideological desirability of a 'work life' which is separate from a 'private life' points to the persistent alignment of paid work with masculinity. Economic need and emotional capacities are common to humanity yet are too easily assumed to symbolise care workers' classed and gendered inadequacy. Indeed, it follows logically that if poor pay produces poor care at an individual level, poorly paid homecare workers ought to be benefiting from relations of economic dependence on others (typically men) if they aspire to give 'good' care. Furthermore, the perspective suggests that poor-quality care arises as a consequence of the psychological weaknesses of working-class women. Both observations serve to highlight that understandings of paid care work acquiesce to gendered and classed inequalities which are deeply embedded in social structures and thought. It is supposed that women's individual subordination to men is a qualifying requirement of 'good care' and essential for the success of homecare workers' emotional relationships with service-users.

This draws our attention to the ways in which perceptions of care, and its various social meanings, depend upon how 'care' is defined at the offset (Duffy, 2005; Duffy, 2007). Basic understandings of care are coloured by class. A middle-class romanticism about 'nurturant' care imputes to care a strong emotional dimension and establishes a way of thinking in which meaningful one-to-one relations lie at the heart of the caregiving process. Alternatively, the day-to-day tasks of 'reproductive' care (the labour needed to maintain people daily and intergenerationally: cleaning, laundry, cooking, personal care, childcare and so on) tends not to be discussed in relation to feelings or relations but is rather framed pragmatically as the unskilled domestic labour needed to reproduce (or simply get through) each day. This is the mundane flip side of care work and many middle-class women (and men) use the purchasing power they acquire by 'going out' to work to buy in the domestic labour of 'cleaning ladies', childminders, laundrette personnel and so on. Homecare labour potentially straddles both nurturant and reproductive formulations of care and the Mother Superior character narrative identifies that homecare workers seek positive associations with nurturant care in particular. Definitions of care which emphasise a labour of emotional exchange tend to reflect middle-class notions of caring. They downplay the 'dirty work' of care which is assigned 'more naturally' to the working classes and ethnic minority women (Duffy, 2011). While middle-class women are held to social account against an ideal of the nurturant (and non-labouring) mother, working-class women are stigmatised by their apparent inability to meet this bar (Boydston, 1990, p. 158). Through popular culture, working-class women are persistently confronted with middle-class conceptions of care and experience insidious pressures to compete for recognition of their femininity on the same terms as more privileged women, but without the same resources and advantages (Peacock et al., 2014).

However, the beliefs upon which behaviour is founded are more than the internalisations of values, culture or convention. They are also a rational response based on experience drawn from distinct social positions which are both classed and gendered (Baum, 2004, p. 1077). Homecare workers are concerned with making the best choices in their caregiving notwithstanding the inequality and injustice that may prevail in their lives and the lives of their service-users. Emotions and values are not the opposites of fact and reason. They are often perceptive and *reasonable* judgments about situations and processes. It is an important observation that sentiments such as pride, compassion, contempt and resentment are forms of emotional reason (Sayer, 2005).

As we have seen in previous chapters, the types of employment in which working-class women are most likely to be engaged have been degraded as a matter of state policy. It is also pertinent to note that the unpaid mothering labour of working-class women has been under attack from successive UK governments who have required poor women to find paid employment in exchange for welfare support (Paz-Fuchs, 2008). The work of mothering, particularly that of single mothers, is deeply devalued by society, and without employment, working-class women are constructed as worthless individuals (Ringrose and Walkerdine, 2008; Skeggs, 2005; Tyler, 2008). Welfare policy communicates that working-class women are obliged to 'pay their own way' and must not exhibit economic dependence on 'out of work' state benefits. This is the political context in which homecare workers mark out moral boundaries between themselves and 'others' whom they locate as being outside the community of 'dedicated carers'. Such 'distinguishing behaviour' is prominent in social groups who 'are anxious about their position in terms of how they are regarded from above and the risk of falling into the groups they despise and fear below them' (Sayer, 2005, p. 593).

The emotional experience of inequality has been explored as class shaming (Peacock et al., 2014). It seems to me that the aggressive emphasis on time rationing in the organisation of homecare services creates circumstances in which individual homecare workers are likely to feel shame. As a consequence of the commodification and under-resourcing of care they are unable to live their working lives according to their values and commitments to other people. The collective shaming of working-class women employed in situations where they do not have enough time to care is structurally generated. At an individual level, homecare workers who wish to provide care in a way which is compatible with self-respect must do so on an unpaid basis. The allegorical quality of stories which fit with the Mother Superior character narrative appears to offer homecare workers a resource with which they might protect themselves from unfavourable moral assessments. In social policy research it is not unusual for data gathered in interviews with homecare workers to draw attention to their prioritisation of love over money and emphasise the significance of intrinsic job satisfaction (for example, Lucas et al., 2009). This can lead (and has led) to the conclusion that better wages are not a pressing issue in the lives of homecare workers and hence industry-wide pay increases are dismissed as being an unnecessary remedy for the industry-wide problem of high labour turnover (see Centre for Workforce Intelligence, 2013; Rubery et al., 2015; Skills for Care, 2013).

Consequently, I hope to have drawn attention to the importance of interpretative nuance and the trade of fair pay for respectability which is a central component of Mother Superior narratives. In 2014, I attended an event organised by a political think-tank about poverty pay in the care sector. Key speakers included a care worker who spoke of her deep commitment to care and her economic hardship. She was followed by the director of a large Employers' Association. From the podium he praised her as 'one in a million' and enthused, 'we would be blessed if all care workers were as dedicated as you'. It was apparent that her toleration of economic abuse was cause for a declaration of social respect from a man who most likely lived in easeful wealth while representing an industry in which unlawful pay is rife.

Working-class caring identities

In contrast to the suggestion that caregiving by working-class women is corrupted by economic deprivation, the character narrative of Mother Superior points to a counter-suggestion: that care can emerge from a shared recognition of what it means to have little social standing and consciously experience oppression. Rosa's strong sense of care as dedication and an expression of love resonated with the views of other homecare workers who talked to me about care work as a call to serve and as the culmination of much of their life experience. For some, their experience of living 'a hard life' enhanced their personal capacity to make emotional connections with disadvantaged people and show empathy for service-users in distress or struggling with economic poverty. Heather, Abbi, Debbie and Michelle each expressed the view that they were more caring and more tolerant because they had known abuse, illness or mental pain in their own lives. They each reflected on their suffering and, positioning themselves as survivors (rather than victims), they perceived that they had gained emotional skills which they drew upon in their work. Homecare worker Katy pointed to emotion-matching and empathy as occupational competencies which grew from her experience of domestic violence at the hands of an alcoholic partner. She explained, 'it left me with a lot of care in me. I don't like people being hurt. Maybe that's because I was hurt and I didn't like that hurt.'

Caring relationships fall into two broad camps: those which involve caring for and about persons who are constructed as being more vulnerable than the one caring, and those involving caring for and about persons who are constructed as less vulnerable than the caregiver (Bowden, 2000). Focusing solely on the former is a source of much misunderstanding about what it means to care. The nurturant or maternal view of care which we discussed in the preceding section positions the cared-for as more vulnerable than the caregiver. However, as we observed, caregivers are subordinated within relations of patriarchy, economic dependence or employment subservience and this subordination is the gendered foundation and near-surroundings of care (Bowden, 1997, p. 8). As the work of legal theorist Martha Fineman (2008) exemplifies, vulnerability is a universal quality which defines our lives as human beings. The accounts of homecare workers summarised above suggest that caring relationships emerge from a perspective of solidarity and that homecare workers are able to draw on an awareness of their own vulnerabilities as a caregiving resource. By accepting the inherent yet pervasive social inequality in which homecare workers and their service-users are situated, care relationships can begin from a recognition of shared vulnerability. This stance is a rational response to homecare workers' perception of their subordinate position. The reality of their low status closes down avenues of professional standing in which homecare workers might otherwise quasi-clinically define, diagnose or assess the needs of service-users on a non-reciprocal basis (Bowden, 2000). The Mother Superior character narrative represents a highly attuned recognition by homecare workers of the dynamics of disempowerment in which they are occupationally situated. It exemplifies that the experience of gross inequality or abuse can be a resource through which care is conceived as an expression of mutuality, interconnectedness and equality with service-users as human beings who are vulnerable too. Homecare workers, despite economic and political depletion, have the potential to generate the psychological and emotional conditions for developing self-worth and expressing the value of themselves as human beings, through the care that they provide. Through their trading away of economic reward in return for greater social respect, homecare workers understand their situated capacity to work for love in lieu of money as the exercise of an empowering 'choice' to care well.

Both Rosa and Nadine described care as a 'passion' and used the term 'a call of duty' to explain their motivations. Other homecare workers also associated care work with the service of 'heroes' in the army. Sophie, for example, a single parent in her early forties, suggested her work was a reciprocal form of national service to a generation who had 'all been in the [second world] war'. These were highly gendered portrayals of the duties that men and women owe to the state: men make war and women tend to those who are wounded. However, they have something to say too about caregiving as the social power of the collective; men unite in an 'army'; women as a national caring force. An ethnographic study of homecare workers in the USA has identified that homecare workers may express their Christian religious identity through caregiving (Stacey, 2011). Earlier research focused on a community of Russian immigrant care workers (Solari, 2006). It noted that those who identified as Russian Orthodox Christians deployed a language of sainthood to discuss their work in ways that focused on a moral, rather than an occupational, hierarchy. These women rejected notions of 'worker' identity and preferred to frame their relationships with service-users in familial terms. Meanwhile, the non-Christian homecare workers tended to define themselves in a language of 'professionalism', but they had lower levels of job satisfaction than the Christian homecare workers. These insights suggest that women's attitudes towards care work are not only informed by their structural position within the labour market, but are also sensitive to pervasive cultural influences which align individual motivations to care with collective norms about appropriate regard and gendered recognition.

In the interviews I conducted with homecare workers for this book, religious motivations were not made explicit, but the cultural influence of religion was very apparent. While Rosa, Marilyn and Heather each indicated that they held religious beliefs, their discourse of duty, love and selflessness was also evident in the accounts of the larger majority of women who did not identify as holding religious beliefs. Their opinions converged through common cultural beliefs about womanhood and feminine identity. These beliefs accord with religious ideals which centre on women's capabilities and identity as mothers and, in the Christian faith, are most notably represented by the figure of Mary, mother of God. What Mary symbolises, as the chosen woman, is the centrality of motherhood to aspects of feminine identity, some of which are passive and subordinate, others of which are protective and majestic (as a protector, a brave and empowered woman, a life-giver, a mourner, and a pure and exalted being).

There is a long history of Christian tradition in which believers show their respect for the sanctity of the body by cleaning it of traces of disease or illness after death, in preparation for admission to heaven (Quigley, 2005, pp. 52–3). Three long-serving homecare workers chose to tell me that they had bathed or washed the bodies of service-users after death as a gift to families. Rosa recalled an occasion when her offer to wash a woman who had died was declined and alternatively she had sat with the body while waiting for the mortuary attendants to arrive. She said it was a comfort to the family to know that 'the shell' of their mother was not left alone and she was pleased to have been able to protect family members from seeing how roughly and disrespectfully a dead body was handled by official staff. After the body had been taken away, Rosa stripped the bed, tidied away the medical equipment, folded up the wheelchair and opened the bedroom windows so that when the family came upstairs, the room was flooded with light and fresh air. Nadine had learned about body washing when working as a nursing auxiliary and she had helped other homecare workers in washing the dead. Marilyn shared a story about how she had honoured a service-user by bathing her dead body in the same bath, and in the same way, as Marilyn had bathed her when she was alive. For homecare workers, it was both a practical act of giving comfort to others and a symbolic assertion that their involvement in a service-users' life had been meaningful. Their willingness to touch and cherish the body of a person they had known intimately was also a form of resistance to the impersonal and clinically efficient removal of a corpse by professional 'strangers'. By deciding to talk about their washing of the dead, these homecare workers chose to narrate an account of their work which invoked comparison with the historic 'wisewoman' of working-class neighbourhoods whose legacy stretches over centuries. Before the ascendance of orthodox medical practice or the development of institutions in which the sick were cared for, the 'wisewoman' was the backbone of community health care – she used herbal remedies, had midwifery skills and would lay out the dead (Moore, 2013). The story-telling voice heard in the Mother Superior character narrative suggests the continuity of class tensions between the practice of 'professionalised' care, from which poorly educated and low-waged women are excluded, and intuitive conceptions of care based on tacit feminine knowledge handed down over generations and valued as a community resource.

Feminine 'knowing'

It has been suggested elsewhere that women in highly gendered occupations emphasise a distinctly feminine group identity and celebrate their social status as 'different' and 'special' by placing high value on their gendered competencies (Bolton, 2005). In a similar vein, the character narrative of Mother Superior pursues the ideology of the 'good woman' in the apparent belief that caregiving relies upon specifically female forms of knowledge. For example, homecare worker Michelle was the main earner in her family and, irritated at traditional ideas of gender hierarchy, she told me her partner was a 'sexist' who thought that 'women should be in the home'. Yet Michelle was uncomfortable with the idea of men working in homecare. She claimed that men would not be able to do the job as well as she could, because 'only women would know [about care] on a personal basis'. Similarly, Nadine worried that I might think her a 'sexist' for asserting that care was 'best done by women', since care was what women like her 'did all the time'. Abbi, who did not have children herself, said care was natural for women and that many of those she worked with were preprogrammed to excel in homecare work since care was 'all they knew' after a lifetime of mothering. The possibility of mothering is a central constituent of women's identities whether they are actually involved in mothering practices or not, and women's lives are inevitably touched by the deep cultural and biological relations that conspire to connect them, at least indirectly, with mothering practices (Bowden, 1997, p. 23). The appeal made by homecare workers to the merits of 'natural' care is overtly gendered, yet it is also a class-specific expression of knowledge and competency shared by a social group who did not excel at school and are excluded from middle-class referents of 'intelligence' and 'cleverness' (see McCall, 1992; Reay, 2001). As homecare workers sought to protect the social value of caring identities, they were also playing an active ideological role in reinforcing as necessary the femininity of the homecare workforce. This added another dimension to the Mother Superior compact of trading respect in lieu of economic reward. Forms of knowledge which are socially regarded as 'female' are assumed to arise by nature, to be tacitly imparted and often appeal to biological notions of maternal instinct. The effect is to make low pay appear somehow natural and appropriate. When homecare workers emphasise that women are innately better suited for care work than are men, they present themselves as embodying a 'natural resource' which is ripe for exploitation. The approach accords inadvertently with a sexist disregard for caregiving as a skilled craft and promotes understandings of care work as the satisfaction of maternal instincts which extinguishes recognition of women's need for decent, secure employment.

The moral landscapes of 'family' and 'law'

Each of the homecare workers with whom I spoke was engaged in relationships of paid caregiving in which a local authority played a central role. Most were also accountable to an employing third party (even if their employer was the person for whom they provided care). Therefore, it is particularly striking that reference to employment relationships, or their sense of deference to employer control, was largely absent in the stories which built the Mother Superior character narrative. In stark contrast to the narrative of Two-a-Penny upon which the previous chapter was based, these stories framed the employment relationship as an unwelcome intrusion into caregiving relationships. Carrie, who was employed directly as a personal assistant by several older people with neurological disorders, recognised that her commitment to them as the people for whom she cared belied her own recognition that she was literally employed by them. She said, 'I am not there as a financial commodity … I am not there to judge them [as employers] … I am there for them.' Using data gathered in interviews with care workers in Southern Italy, industrial sociologist Lena Näre has argued that in paid domestic and care work, the labour contract is accompanied by a *moral contract*. Accordingly, this moral contract is based on 'normative notions of good/bad, reciprocity, shared duties and responsibilities' (Näre, 2011, p. 401). Care workers in her study aimed and hoped for employment relationships in which they felt like 'part of the family' with their service-users. Similarly, it seems that the Mother Superior character narrative stems from a perspective in which questions of employment, contractual entitlements, or effective management are perceived to lie outside the moral landscape of homecare. In this regard, Mother Superior-type stories communicated moral resistance to the idea that paid care work is based on commercialised care relationships, and railed against any suggestion that genuine feelings and family-like notions of commitment have been abandoned by homecare workers as a consequence of privatisation.

Research in other contexts has found that employers exploit the idea of a moral contract and stress that care work should be provided in return for gratitude and familial duty or affection in order to downplay worker entitlements and reduce the economic expectations of care workers (Johnson, 2015; Näre, 2011). Similarly, in the interviews I conducted, employers conjured up images of good moral conduct in order to keep labour costs low. For example, owner-manager Rebecca was scathing about new recruits to her small homecare company who 'come into it just to earn some money', accusing them of having no 'commitment' or displaying 'flippancy' should they choose to leave the job because of low pay and poor conditions. She told me that, at staff induction training, she tried to draw on women's 'better nature' and explained, 'What I say to them is that they have been given a gift. Their gift today is to go and see one of their service-users, let's call her Dorothy ... as long as we leave Dorothy with her heart lifted one inch, we know that we have lifted her for the rest of the day.' Rebecca was fully aware that low pay is a chronic problem in the homecare sector but there was no ironic intent in her describing homecare work as 'a gift'. Indeed, Rebecca saw that it was an essential part of her role as the manager, 'to let staff flow with the job, do what needs to be done and don't worry about being paid'.

Other accounts indicated how managers promoted the idea that good carers did not worry about being paid for all the time they worked by asserting that good carers were 'patient'. Claire cared for a service-user who was 'very prone to falling and you can't rush her'. Consequently, tasks always took up to half an hour longer than Claire had been allocated. She told me it was 'debatable if I get paid, so you've got to be patient'. The qualities of patience that she was supposed to exhibit when assisting a frail woman to use the bathroom were expected to dampen any expectation she may have had of being paid for all her work. Claire had tolerated the unpaid half an hour with this service-user over six mornings a week, for the past eight months and no action had been taken by the employer to reassess the visit length. When I interviewed Lucy, I shared with her my concern that wage levels at the company she worked for fell below the amount prescribed in national minimum wage law. She explained, 'The office knows for a fact the girls won't say anything to them, (a) because jobs are really hard to come by and (b) the good carers, you can't do it for love of the money, you just can't do it, because you're in the wrong job if you're after the money because there's just no money in the job. It's enough to keep you ticking over, that's your lot, basically.' My attempt to emphasise that homecare work is legally regulated through a formal contract of employment ran up against the assumption that 'good carers' do not concern themselves with money.

In stories which fit the character narrative of Mother Superior, homecare workers prioritised a moral language of family duty and affection over a language of legal understandings of employment as reflected in ideas of contract, obligation and the exchange of service in return for wages. The social institutions of 'family' and 'law' are each a background from which precepts, values and notions of moral obligation flow. The basis upon which care is exchanged within families is constituted very differently from its exchange within employment relationships. At its heart, an employment contract is mediated by money and even if payment is not referred to explicitly, an employment contract implies an agreement to pay a wage (*Stack* v. *Ajar Tee* [2015] EWCA Civ 46). Unlike the open-ended and unconditional nature of many familial commitments, legal contracts are freely entered into and specify mutually agreed duties and obligations. Social relations of family meanwhile are legally protected as private relations into which the state must not ordinarily interfere (for example, Human Rights Act 1998, article 8). Employment relations, however, are enriched by statutory obligations such as the right to a minimum wage, which are implied into the contract as a matter of public policy.

In this chapter so far I have considered ways in which the gendering of care is coloured by social class difference and I have considered how ideas about femininity and notions of the morally 'good' woman relate to ideas of what care work 'is'. I have argued that the Mother Superior character narrative negotiates social expectations to associate paid caregiving with middle-class and maternal understandings of its emotional credibility in an unpaid context. Such stories reflect an acute awareness that caregiving has integrity when it is perceived as unconditionally given, yet is judged as corrupted when explicitly exchanged for pay. I have identified that working-class understandings of care as a moral practice conceive of mutuality, interconnectedness and co-vulnerability with service-users as key values which emerge from a shared recognition of what it means to have little social standing and consciously to experience oppression.

There are important practical and conceptual tensions between the performance of care work within a family setting and its performance in the labour market. The reference I am making to 'family' is not literal but rather invokes a point of cultural reference to a moral landscape in which women provide caring labour based on norms of duty, gratitude, altruism and familial responsibility. However, social norms and associated behaviour within this moral landscape are invariably influenced by gendered relations of power and personal assessments of cost and risk, which are also classed. The significance of power and domination to the moral landscape of family must not be overlooked.[1] Indeed the institution of family is a 'powerful sociological myth' since families take many different forms (Sevenhuijsen, 2005), their constitution is heavily influenced by state policy and, if a test of 'family' is that bonds of kinship enable well-being, many are dysfunctional. The accounts of the homecare workers who have contributed to this book indicate their awareness that notions of familial love are idealised, especially since their employment sometimes fills the gap between expectations of family and its often feeble reality. In addition, the imposition of gendered,

---

[1] Andrew Sayer (2000, p. 79) goes so far as to suggest that oppressions inherent in the moral economy of traditional families means that traditional families represent an 'immoral' economy.

familial ideals of 'good care' into relations of employment fails to distinguish paid from unpaid care (Meagher, 2006). My discussion of the Mother Superior character narrative has suggested that the moral landscape of family locates caregiving within a middle-class framework of emotional bonding which serves to shame working-class women. Accordingly, the validity of care work as paid labour is suppressed, and the gendered experiences of working-class women fail scrutiny on the basis of middle-class standards. However, if the moral landscape of family is to be rejected as an appropriate referent for paid caregiving, we must model alternative ideas of 'good care' which recognise the validity of paid care work without rejecting the moral qualities of care practice within frameworks of employment. The focus of this chapter now turns to consider legal support for the payment of a national minimum wage in the UK. It is highly relevant because the national minimum wage gives legal expression to the labour market as a moral landscape (that is, one in which social values are recognised, respected and enforced in law as a matter of proper conduct). I argue that the law has a critical role to play in asserting that contractual values are compatible with the moral qualities of care practice and in validating the need and entitlement of paid care workers to realise the economic value of paid care work.

A Minimum Wage for all workers

In 2014 the parliamentary Public Accounts Committee acknowledged with 'astonishment' that over 220,000 homecare workers were being paid so little that their wages fell short of the legal minimum (Public Accounts Committee). HM Revenue and Customs is responsible for minimum wage enforcement and it acknowledged, on the basis of its own research, that half of employers in the homecare sector did not comply with minimum wage law (HM Revenue and Customs, 2013). One of the key reasons for this, as discussed in the previous chapter, is that contracts of employment common to the homecare industry do not provide pay for much of the work performed and homecare workers are typically paid only for time that they spend inside service-users' homes. The paid element of each working day is so small that when wages are averaged across the hours in a working day, they fall below the hourly rate which the law requires as a minimum.

A legally binding national minimum wage is a labour market intervention designed to benefit low-wage workers in general. However, the ground covered thus far in this chapter has identified homecare workers as a group exposed to particular social pressure to engage in unpaid labour and hence their legal rights to pay protection are of special import. A purpose of a national minimum wage is to communicate respect for human dignity and minimum wage laws reflect parliamentary intentions that a minimum price for labour set by government should kick in when the price for labour set by the market falls below a politically acceptable level (Davidov, 2008, p. 585). If legal provisions are to effectively advance this objective, each individual must be able to draw benefit from them and this is why it is so important that all workers are included within the scope of national minimum wage law.

The National Minimum Wage Act 1998 was a flagship of Tony Blair's first term in office and it introduced the UK's first ever national minimum wage. The measures had been ferociously opposed by the Conservative party on the basis that income support measures were available for low earners and business should not be burdened with wage regulation. Indeed, John Redwood MP, speaking for the opposition warned, 'a minimum wage policy will not work. We have consistently argued for a minimum income rather than a minimum wage with benefit top-ups for families that need the extra' (Hansard, col. 510, 18 June 1998). Between 2008 and 2014, and against the economic backdrop of the global financial crisis, both Labour and Conservative governments chose to reduce the relative value of the national minimum wage by applying below-inflation annual increases. One consequence was that the proportion of families relying on in-work state benefits rose steadily as wages fell. From 2011, and for the first time since records began, a majority of families living in poverty were families 'in work' (see McInnes et al., 2013).[2] In this context, the Conservative government set out proposals in its 2015 budget to make savings in public expenditure by increasing the value of the National Minimum Wage for workers aged 25 and over and reducing in-work state welfare support.

The initiative was, somewhat misleading, given the official title of a 'National Living Wage', with the intention being to phase in a higher rate minimum wage of £9.00 an hour by 2020. The policy was heavily criticised for co-opting the language of a 'living wage' while being intentionally set at a rate well below that of a genuine living wage (see Chapter 2). Other obvious flaws were to allow employers to make changes to working time, overtime rates, weekend pay and pay differentials in order to accommodate the higher hourly rate without actually increasing workers' take-home pay. Nevertheless, the first step towards the National Living Wage (NLW) began in April 2016 with the introduction of a higher rate at £7.20, representing an 11 per cent increase on the national minimum wage rate which had previously applied to everyone aged 21 and over. Government offset the higher wage burden that this placed on employers with

---

2 A trend which has continued in subsequent years; see http://www.jrf.org.uk/data/work-poverty-levels.

a reduction in corporation tax and a lessening of employer liabilities for national insurance payments. However, government offset the economic benefits to workers with the partial dismantling of in-work benefits. There are early indications of hourly wage increases in social care but rates of non-compliance are unknown (Gardiner 2016).

When the NLW policy was debated in the House of Commons the key focus of parliamentary scrutiny was its anticipated impact upon the low-waged social-care sector (Glyn Davies MP, *National Living Wage*, Hansard, col. 140, 1 December 2015). When the draft National Minimum Wage (Amendment) Regulations 2016 came before Parliament the government confirmed it would not seek to amend the National Minimum Wage Act 1998. However, problems with a 'failure to implement minimum wage legislation in the care sector' were once again highlighted (Nick Bowles MP, Minister for Skills, Hansard, col. 9, 11 January 2016). Employers in the adult social-care sector warned that the introduction of the NLW, without compensatory increases in the level of state funding for social care, would lead to business insolvency and 'market failure' (for example, UK Homecare Association, January 2016). Despite some controversy about the NLW policy of the Conservative government, the validity of minimum wage law in the UK continues to be based on its 'near universal' application (Simpson, 2009) and across the political spectrum the law is regarded as a valid form of wage protection. Nevertheless, there are systemic problems with enforcement across the homecare industry; these issues are now long-standing and, since 2010, have been formally brought to the attention of government (see Low Pay Commission, 2011).

According to the National Minimum Wage Act 1998, all 'workers' have the right to 'be remunerated ... at a rate which is not less than the national minimum wage'. The statute defines the term 'worker' to mean all those who work under a contract of employment as well as any other contract to personally perform work for another party, provided the relationship is not one of a business or an independent professional serving their customer or clients. The National Minimum Wage Regulations 1999 (NMWR) set out the detail of how the national minimum wage is calculated. The total amount of pay, less any permissible deductions, is divided across the eligible working time within a pay period.

Working time is determined in relation to four different descriptions of economic reward for work (NMWR regs 3–6): 'time-work', when a worker is paid by the hour or another unit of time; 'salaried hours work', in which a basic number of annual hours are provided in exchange for a salary to be paid by weekly or monthly instalments; 'output work' to be paid by reference to the number of pieces made or processed by a worker; and 'unmeasured work' which applies where the other three do not, and, in particular, where work is not paid in relation to a time span and the worker is required to work 'when needed or when work is available'.[3] On the basis of one of these four descriptions, working time is paid time. Across the total number of working hours, pay will be lawful if it amounts on average to at least the rate at which the national minimum wage has been set. As a matter of legal principle, the UK's national minimum wage symbolises the universal basic value of all work and all workers. The law may not have the power to lift homecare workers out of poverty, but it has the potential to communicate the value of 'care' as 'work'. There are three aspects of national minimum wage law in particular which establish its credentials as an employment protection with 'near universal' application in the British labour market. These are, firstly, its assertion that 'the home' is a place of work; secondly, its recognition that minimum wage liabilities can arise in contractual circumstances where no reference to pay is otherwise made; and, thirdly, in a wide appreciation of activities which qualify as 'work'. I will now explain each in turn.

The home as a place of work

The scope of the minimum wage is wide enough to make it distinctive in UK employment law. The National Minimum Wage Act 1998 takes the standard s 230(3) definition of an eligible worker in the Employment Rights Act 1996, and adds to it the explicit inclusion of 'agency workers' (s 32), and 'homeworkers' who work from their own home, or in the home of another person (s 35). This is legally significant because national minimum wage calculations depend upon recognising the volume of a worker's working time yet the Working Time Regulations 1999 have been characterised as upholding a principle in which 'home' is a place of 'no work at all' (Lord Justice Buxton, *British Nursing Association* v. *Inland Revenue* [2002] EWCA Civ 494 [74]).

Unlike the concern for the integrity of the labour market which is addressed by national minimum wage law, the origins of the Working Time Regulations lie in concern for the health and safety of working people across the European Union as is legally expressed in the EU Working Time Directive (2003/88/EC). The UK's Working Time Regulations 1998 define working time as time when a worker is at an 'employer's disposal and carrying out [...] activities or duties' (s 2). By accruing working time, working people are entitled to daily, weekly and annual rest breaks. The case of *Truslove* v. *Scottish Ambulance Service* exemplifies how legal interpretations of the right to 'rest' are sensitive to location and how the law preserves an understanding of 'home' that it is, by default, a place of rest ([2014]

---

3 Unmeasured work should not be confused with work under zero-hours contractual arrangements. Under zero-hours contracts workers are generally paid by time (by the hour, as the title of the contracts suggests).

ICR 1232 EAT). Claimant ambulance drivers were required to spend time 'on call' in case an emergency response was required. On some occasions, they could be 'on call' at home, while on others they were required to be 'on call' within 3 miles of the ambulance station. The question put to the Employment Appeal Tribunal (EAT) was whether they had entitlement to statutory rest breaks accrued while 'working' on call. Its answer focused on establishing the difference between 'work' and 'rest' and the need to classify activity, since that which was not 'work' was 'rest' and vice versa. Accordingly, when ambulance drivers were on call at their own homes they did not 'work', but when they were on call at a location which was not their home they did 'work'. Therefore, an activity can qualify for the right to rest if taking place away from home, and be contractually identical but disqualified if situated at home. In making this decision, Justice Langstaff reasoned that the 'quality of rest' to which workers are entitled under working time law was not available unless a worker was at home ([32]). Hence in working time law, 'home' has a symbolic quality in signifying rest.

This point can also be drawn from the case of *Lynch* v. *Bromley Arts Council* in which a man worked at a community arts centre and cinema and lived on site ([2007] Unreported UKEAT/0390/06DA). The facility was used as a wedding venue and a concert hall and he was permanently available for work during his standard and on-call hours of 9 a.m.–10.45 p.m. every day. He argued that his on-site availability should attract the right to rest within the meaning of the Working Time Regulations 1998. However, the EAT found that his workplace was also his 'home' and took note of the specific wording of this contract which stated he was required to work at least 40 hours a week 'and to be on call at all other times between 9 a.m. and 10.45 p.m. if possible'. Despite the fact that Mr Lynch *felt* obliged to work overtime because of what was accepted to be his 'diligence and sense of duty', the two words, '*if possible*', led the EAT to conclude that Mr Lynch was 'at home' and had the freedom to leave the premises or choose not to accept 'work' during that time should he wish. Taken together, the cases of *Truslove* and *Lynch* indicate that according to the Working Time Regulations, a 'home' is a place of rest where a choice not to 'work' can be freely exercised.

In contrast, minimum wage legislation is not concerned with health and safety, but with enhancing the viability of the UK labour market. The National Minimum Wage Act 1998 asserts that home can be a place of work and the National Minimum Wage Regulations 1999 ensure that regardless of location, working time is to be understood exclusively through the scheme of time work, salaried hours work, piece work or unmeasured work. For workers employed in domestic settings, national minimum wage law fulfils an important symbolic function by distinguishing the right to pay from determinations of working time made under the Working Time Regulations 1998. It establishes the value of employment situated in 'home' locations and judges have been willing to give a very broad interpretation to the word 'home'. For example, they have accepted that a delivery driver using her own car was a 'homeworker' because she was working out of personal property (*James* v. *Redcats* [2007] IRLR 296 EAT).

Recognising 'services of value'

Another important 'universalising' feature of national minimum wage law is that it can redefine a contract of employment in order to recognise that where 'services of value' are rendered within an employment relationship, the minimum wage regime must apply. The National Minimum Wage Act applies to workers under a contract of employment as well as to those under 'any other contract ... to do or perform personally any work'. When the Court of Appeal interpreted the meaning of 'work' under this s 54(3)(b) provision it required that minimum wage law should apply where a worker rendered 'services of value' to the other party (*Edmunds* v. *Lawson* [2000] QB 501 [34]).

The case of *Revenue and Customs* v. *Rinaldi-Tranter* provides an interesting example ([2006] Unreported UKEAT/0486/06/DM). A trainee hairdresser was studying with a college and placed with a hairdresser to gain practical experience. The presence of any national minimum wage entitlement depended upon whether she was personally performing work under s 54(3)(b). Even though there was no express contractual obligation between the salon and the trainee for the payment of money, the EAT found she was engaged in 'work' because her activities were of value to the salon. In doing so it established that the performance of work itself, rather than any existing contractual provision for the payment of a wage, was determinative of minimum wage rights. A contract which explicitly provided for monetary payment was unnecessary in order for the activity performed to qualify as 'work' ([13]–[16]) within the statutory scheme. Subsequently, in *Stack* v. *Ajar-Tee* the Court of Appeal established that a contract which expressly required work to be performed, but made no reference to wages, constituted an agreement to provide pay. Hence it is possible for 'work' to be found where wages are not, if a court can establish that services of value to another party have been provided.

A generous understanding of 'work'

The third aspect of minimum wage law which supports its appeal to values of universal worth is its broad appreciation of what it means to undertake 'work'. There is no necessity for an employee to prove that they are 'busy' or are performing specific contractual tasks in order for them to establish that they are 'working' for the purposes of including their time within a minimum wage calculation. Indeed, for workers who fall within the scope of minimum wage law on the basis of undertaking either 'time work' or 'salaried hours work' Regulations 15(1) and 16(1) of the National Minimum Wage Regulations 1999 establish that *in addition*, a worker has the right to minimum wage payments for time when 'available at or near a place of work, other than home, [...] and is required to be available for such work'. An exception from this provision, however, is that when workers are able to 'sleep at or near a place of work, time during the hours he is permitted to sleep shall only be treated as being time work when the worker is awake for the purpose of working'. This would seem to include forms of on-call working. However, the courts have been somewhat reluctant to rely upon these provisions, preferring instead to offer a generous interpretation of 'working' such that these extending regulations are superfluous. As a consequence, periods when workers are asleep while on shift have been taken to be periods when they are 'working' for the purpose of the national minimum wage. Take, for example, the Court of Appeal in *British Nursing Association* v. *Inland Revenue*. Although the name of the appellant suggests that the case might involve care workers, the issues raised actually concerned telephone call handlers who worked from home on a night shift. Despite their employer's claim that they were only 'working' when physically answering a call, the Court of Appeal determined that the national minimum wage should apply on the basis of 'time work' for the whole of their shift, even if they were sleeping. Lord Justice Buxton defined 'working' as 'being entitled to be remunerated' ([12]). In so doing, he deployed a particular technique of imagining the work in question was transposed out of the workers' own homes and placed into an office environment. This enabled the Court to see that waiting for a telephone to be answered was plainly a 'work' activity which took place in 'working time'. In *British Nursing*, the Court of Appeal emphasised that being 'available' to undertake a telephone answering task was 'work' and that such availability must be paid for ([13]).

British Nursing was later applied in *Scottbridge Construction* v. *Wright* to the situation of a nightwatchman who was permitted to either sleep or watch TV for 10 of the hours in his 14-hour nightshift ([2003] IRLR 21 CoS). Lord Cullen noted that Mr Wright's maintenance and security 'tasks were not onerous' ([2]), but the fact that he frequently had little or nothing to do was irrelevant to his right to be paid in accordance with national minimum wage law. Mr Wright was 'working' for the purpose of the national minimum wage, even while asleep, and the Court decided that 'the work which was paid for under his contract' was 'his attendance as a night watchman for the whole of those hours' ([11]). The pivotal concept of 'availability' was applied to the full period of Mr Wright's attendance. Both *British Nursing* and *Scottbridge Construction* support a universal value in which an employer must pay at least the rate of the national minimum wage for all the time that they require a worker to be in a particular place at a particular time. Regardless of the activities they perform or do not perform, they are at 'work' (see also *Whittlestone* v. *BJP Home support* [2014] IRLR 176).

Legal support for unpaid care work

In the remainder of this chapter I will review several significant cases in which judges have interpreted the minimum wage entitlements of care workers. It appears that both the National Minimum Wage Act 1998 and judicial interpretations of its supporting regulations communicate that homecare workers are a distinctively different and less 'worthy' group of workers. My intention is to show that the law extends ideological support to the social and contractual pressures by which homecare workers are coerced to provide work on an unpaid basis.

A 'family wage' for women?

Despite specific statutory protection for workers who work at home, the national minimum wage does not apply in family situations. This means that, for care workers in particular, living in the same house as an employer can cut off access to this most basic of employment rights. Where family members are employed to give care, and live in the same home as their relative service-user, their work does not qualify for national minimum wage coverage because of a 'family exemption' as set out at Regulation 2(4). The exemption applies even though public money may be used to pay their wages (Care and Support (Direct Payments) Regulations 2014, reg 4(2)). However, the family exemption does not only apply to actual family members, it also removes the right to claim the minimum wage from any other person who lives and works at their employer's home and is 'treated' as family (NMWR reg 2(2)). Such 'treatment' is evidenced through a statutory test which covers the provision of free meals/accommodation, the sharing of family tasks and leisure activities (NMWR reg 2(2)(a)(ii)).

In cases concerning care workers and national minimum wage rights there is a general pattern of stringent judicial readings of statutory entitlement. For example, in *Nambalat* v. *Tayer* the Court of Appeal interpreted that the 'sharing of tasks' element of the family exemption test could apply to a situation in which a live-in care worker did more than was strictly required of her under her contract: by sharing in the preparation of meals when her job required only that she clean up after meals (*Nambalat* v. *Taher* and *Udin* v. *Chamsi-Pasha* [2012] EWCA Civ 1249). Hence, the employment of a care worker was viewed through the lens of a family relation and exempt from any requirement to pay her at least as much as the national minimum wage. Nambalat was unable to proceed with her claim even though she worked under a contract of employment. Familial exemption enables the employment of care workers without regard for national minimum wage payments if it can be shown that they are 'treated' as family. Judicial interpretation of these provisions is highly subjective and the current state of law is unsatisfactory because it fails to distinguish gendered subordination based on women's traditional unpaid role in the home from subordination accruing from a relation of paid employment which sustains the family life of an employer. Judicial inability to distinguish one from another also means an inability to recognise how these two forms of subordination might collide in circumstances such as those found in homecare.

While the numbers of homecare workers covered by the family exemption are likely to be a small proportion of the workforce as a whole, their numbers will grow as the entitlement criteria by which older people can access state support are tightened and funding for care services is eroded. Increasingly, live-in care workers are employed by self-funders. With regard to state-funded services, a relaxing of the regulations governing the use of public money to directly employ care workers now permits the 'paying' of cohabiting family members where a local authority considers that it is necessary (Hayes, 2015a). As a matter of legal principle, the affirmation of 'family' as a category where basic labour rights are erased is highly significant. Earlier in this chapter we have considered that homecare workers seek relations of employment in which they are positively regarded as, and behave like, 'part of the family', despite the attendent diminution of their economic standing. It would seem particularly important for the economic well-being of homecare workers that relationships which draw on moral frameworks associated with 'family' in order to deliver 'good' care are also bolstered by the moral frameworks set out as employment standards laid down by Parliament. Statutory employment rights are created in order to apply public standards to otherwise private contractual relationships between workers and their employers. Where these private contractual relationships take root in a family-like context, the likelihood of coercion, exploitation or unpaid labour would seem to be especially high. The economic undervaluing of care work cannot be separated from the assumed 'natural' coincidence of 'women' with unpaid care work in families. By affirming 'family' as a minimum wage-free zone, the law requires that women in relations of paid employment are constructed as economic dependents inside other people's families and, since they are very low-waged, this risks deepening the existing economic subordination to which they are likely subject within their own families. National minimum wage law does not challenge either the sexist hierarchy which marks out domestic work as menial nor women's secondary status in the labour market; rather, the family exemption affirms its ongoing influence in the medium of law.

This point is firmly asserted in the minimum wage claim of two domestic workers who had fled their employment in the service of Saudi diplomat Mr Al-Malki and his wife (*Al-Malki* v. *Reyes* [2015] EWCA Civ 32). Reyes and Suryadi had each been illegally trafficked into the UK and became so frightened at the abuse they sustained in their employment that they ran away; Reyes had assistance from the police and Suryadi escaped when her employers were sleeping. Before the Court of Appeal they sought permission to bring a claim to receive at least as much as the national minimum wage for the service they had provided to the household. However, Mr and Mrs Al-Malki claimed diplomatic immunity from prosecution under article 31 of the Vienna Convention on Diplomatic Relations 1961 which provides immunity except in relation to legal 'action relating to any professional or commercial activity exercised by the diplomatic agent in the receiving state outside his official functions' (article 31(1)(c)). The Court of Appeal had to decide if, by entering into a contract of employment for the provision of domestic services, Mr Al-Malki had engaged in a commercial activity and whether he was therefore unentitled to diplomatic immunity. Lord Justice Dyson, the third most senior judge in England and Wales, pronounced in judgment that a contract for the provision of services which are incidental to family or domestic daily life is not a 'commercial activity'. Specifically in relation to non-payment of the national minimum wage, he reasoned,

> The fact that an employer derives economic benefit from paying his employees wages that are lower than the market rate does not mean he is engaging in commercial activity ... the question whether an employer is engaged in a commercial activity *depends on what the individual is employed to do.* ([34] my emphasis)

An appreciation that entering into an employment contract may only constitute a commercial activity on the basis of the type of work performed by the employee makes clear that, in this context at least, the substance and terms of the employment contract has no bearing on the right to pay protection. It is the rendering of services which are 'incidental to family and everyday life' that is regarded by the Court as non-commercial ([14]). As with family workers, and workers who are 'treated' like family, domestic workers in diplomatic households are barred from bringing an entire class of employment claims because they have no right to approach a court in respect of economic exploitation.

What these cases share in common is their power to lift the lid on legal struggles to ensure that paid work performed in the context of family is upheld as a private matter. The law plays a key role in disconnecting paid care work from the labour market and categorising it as unworthy of economic or commercial consideration. Through these judgments we can see that the values which underpin the right to be paid a national minimum wage are not universal values. They are rather values which perpetuate a fundamental injustice which arises when women are regarded as the caregiving instruments of other people and are denied recognition in law on their own merit. When it is as a direct consequence of caregiving that statutory rights fail to protect or support women as equal citizens, the state bears direct responsibility for designing law which inflicts deprivations and projects discrimination onto women as a subjugated group.

Caregiving as silent work

When judges misrecognise care work and formally classify it as unpaid labour, they craft minimum wage law as a tool for the devaluing of care work and silence attempts to gain recognition of caregiving as a labour market activity. It is likely that almost all of the homecare workers with employment contracts that I interviewed for this book would be entitled to the minimum wage on the basis of 'time work', that is, they were paid an hourly or pro rata rate for the time they spent with service-users. However, legal authority on the definition of homecare work for the purpose of national minimum wage law rests with the Court of Appeal in *Walton* v. *Independent Living Organisation* ([2003] EWCA Civ 199). In this instance homecare work was classified as 'unmeasured work' and therefore had to be either quantified as 'the total of the number of hours spent [...] during the pay reference period in carrying out the contractual duties required' or quantified through an 'average hours agreement' (NMWR reg 27). Such an agreement is made between a worker and an employer and it predetermines (and hence limits) the 'daily average number of hours the worker is likely to spend in carrying out the duties required' (NMWR reg 28). An average-hours agreement is not permissible in any minimum wage category other than 'unmeasured work' and although the law does not permit a worker to waive their right to the national minimum wage, average-hours agreements raise the possibility that workers will agree to be paid for fewer hours than they actually provide (Rodgers, 2009). In this regard, the tailor-made working time definitions which apply in the context of the UK's national minimum wage are highly significant because, if the regulations which concern working time were to apply instead, it is likely that the lawfulness of average-hours agreements would be open to challenge (C-151/02 *Landeshauptstadt Keil* v. *Jaeger* [2003] IRLR 804; C-303/98 *SIMAP* v. *Conselleria de Sanidad y Consumo de la Generalidad Valenciana* [2000] IRLR 845).

Homecare worker Miss Walton was employed at the home of a service-user with severe epilepsy for three days each week to provide a continuous service and she was paid £31.40 per day. Arguing on the basis that a day was a measurement of time, she claimed to be engaged in time work for each period of 14 hours when she was awake and providing care and supervision. Arguably, the attributes of national minimum wage law which establish its near universal application should have enabled her work in a private home to be accepted as eligible 'work' and required that her employer ought to pay her for all the hours she attended at the particular time and place demanded by her contract, regardless of her activity. Yet the Court of Appeal in *Walton* was not prepared to recognise all the aspects of her activity as being 'work'. The service-user's severe epilepsy had established the need for a round-the-clock care service but Lord Justice Aldous gave regard to the fact that this was 'a relatively easy client needing a minimum of supervision' ([2]). By way of contrast to the earlier mentioned telephone call handlers in *British Nursing* and the nightwatchman in *Scottbridge Construction*, the kind of work that Miss Walton performed, and its intensity, came under judicial scrutiny. Miss Walton's contractual attendance at the house for three consecutive 24-hour shifts was characterised as benefiting her through the provision of 'free accommodation and meals' and it was noted that when Miss Walton was not providing 'active care' she might 'please herself as to what she would do' [3]. Lord Justice Aldous said he did not 'believe' that Miss Walton worked continuously [34]. Lady Justice Smith similarly observed that Miss Walton did not have to give 'her full attention' to the service-user when she was not performing specific tasks [41]. It was never in dispute that Walton could not leave the premises and was contractually required to be in attendance [3], yet the Court of Appeal determined that she was paid on the basis of care tasks physically performed and therefore was engaged on 'unmeasured work'. In a comment echoed more recently in *Al-Malki* v. *Reyes*, the Court of Appeal considered 'the type of work involved' to be a determinative factor [31]. Its judgment silenced the unspecified caring labour that Walton provided during the time she was contractually obliged to be at work. The value of the service she provided by simply 'being there' to provide company and give attention, or being available to react to untoward situations, went entirely unrecognised.

On the basis that she engaged in 'unmeasured work', Walton's national minimum wage entitlements were limited to the hours laid down in an 'average hours agreement' (NMWR reg 28). This had been hastily drawn up after her employer was notified of a forthcoming inspection visit by HM Revenue and Customs. The agreement stated that the personal care and bathing tasks which Walton undertook with the service-user consumed only 6 hours and 50 minutes in any 24-hour period. She was not entitled to minimum wage protection for any of her time outside of this.

In the subsequent case of *South Holland* v. *Stamp* the EAT found that care wardens at a sheltered housing scheme for the elderly were also undertaking 'unmeasured work' ([2003] All ER (D)19 EAT). However, unlike the facts in *Walton*, there was no daily average agreement in place. They were required, as a matter of contract, to be continuously on-site for 103 hours from 8 a.m. on a Monday morning until 3 p.m. on a Friday afternoon and subject to discipline if they left the site without prior permission. Yet the Tribunal would not recognise that all of these hours constituted 'work'. Judge Birtles explained why it was necessary to refer to a list of Warden's duties to limit their eligible working time:

> time spent by the respondents when they are not carrying out the contractual duties required of them under their contract cannot be counted [...] thus when a warden is at home on call but sleeping, washing, entertaining or carrying out domestic chores [the time does not qualify for national minimum wage payments]. ([37])

Even though their employment contract required a continuous 103-hour service, the service was not recognised as 'work' and did not constitute a contractual duty worthy of pay. By silencing the work of caregiving; by reducing care work to the performance of tasks on a list and by misrecognising its value, national minimum wage law has supported the construction of employment contracts that require care work to be carried out without a corresponding commitment to provide pay for all the hours worked. This approach assumes that care can be stripped of the emotional labour which lies at its core since such labour is incommensurate with the idea of caring according to a predetermined list of tasks. It is possible, if not likely, that judicial assessments are influenced by concerns about the cost implications of paying in full for the working time of care workers.[4] Nevertheless, such an assessment cannot be separated from the values by which care work is socially regarded as unproductive and lacking in economic value; and it introduces the possibility that courts and tribunals see unpaid labour as a component which is inherent to care work. In effect, the courts ask care workers to work harder, or 'do more', than they ask of sleeping security guards in return for minimum wage protection. This draws on deeply engrained assumptions that the cost of caregiving should be borne individually by the women who provide care. Despite the promise

---

4 When the case of *Walton* was heard at the EAT, Justice Holland raised concerns that paying for all working time would price overnight care 'out of the market'.

of universal reach, as it currently stands national minimum wage law does not live up to the social democratic premise that women engage in paid work in return for a political willingness to publicly shoulder the economic costs of care at home (Estévez-Abe and Hobson, 2015). As a consequence, care workers are economically disadvantaged because the idea that women should care for their own families on an unpaid basis is transferred into the homes of other people through the establishment of a care market which fails to respect their economic contribution.

The care/work trap

Earlier in this chapter I discussed ways in which homecare workers distinguished themselves from other workers in order to assert their worth in moral terms. I now turn to consider how judges deploy a similar strategy when assessing the worth of care work in relation to national minimum wage entitlements. It would seem that when judges make distinctions between care work and other types of work they are prone to misinterpret the economic nature of caring labour.

In the case of *Edinburgh City Council* v. *Lauder* the minimum wage entitlements of a support worker employed at a sheltered housing facility were considered ([2012] Unreported UKEATS/0048/11/B1 EAT). Her duties included encouraging and enabling residents, and responding to emergency situations. Lauder was provided with accommodation tied to her job and her employment contract specified 36 hours of working time each week plus the provision of emergency response cover for 4 nights a week. She was responsible for staffing the emergency alarm through the night and if she was called out, was entitled to take corresponding time off in lieu or receive an overtime payment. The question considered, in the light of *British Nursing,* was whether the provision of emergency response cover constituted 'work'. Lady Smith, in delivering the judgment, distinguished *British Nursing* on the grounds that Lauder had specific 'core' daytime hours and her emergency response cover was 'in addition' to this 'normal work' ([33]). Accordingly, being available to be called on during the night was not to be regarded as 'work' and regulation 15(1) applied ([48]). Therefore, national minimum wage payments would accrue only for time when she was 'awake for the purposes of working' and not for the whole of the emergency response period.

This decision failed to recognise the ongoing responsibility of care workers towards vulnerable residents throughout the night, and workers' lack of choice in responding to needs as they arise.[5] Furthermore, it is curious that

---

5 Although not raised in case law to date, a failure to respond could result in potential prosecution for wilful neglect in criminal law under Criminal Justice and Courts Act 2015 s 20.

the presence of day working should negate the significance of night working. It gives rise to the seemingly absurd implication that employers could reduce their national minimum wage liabilities by employing a single worker on both day and night shifts. However, a more nuanced conclusion might suggest that when courts understand 'care' as work for which women are not entitled to be fully remunerated, the notion of 'availability' becomes confused. The working time of care workers is seemingly less valuable than the working time of security guards (as per *Scotbridge Construction*), or even the working time of security guards employed in care homes (*Burrow Down Support Services* v. *Rossiter* [2008] ICR 1172 EAT). Decisions about statutory entitlements which relate to specific work groups are accompanied by 'an implicit value judgement [...] about the appropriateness and efficiency of regulatory legislation' (Deakin, 2007, p. 80). It certainly seems that decisions about the calculation of eligible working time fall into a trap where 'care' is not recognised as 'work' for the purposes of the national minimum wage because of sexist expectations that women will provide their time and dedication without economic reward.

A similar pattern can be observed when the decision of the EAT in *MacCartney* v. *Oversley House Management* ([2006] IRLR 514 EAT) is considered in relation to the subsequent treatment of national minimum wage claims by care workers in *Hughes* v. *Jones* ([2008] Unreported UKEAT/0159/08MAA) and *South Manchester Abbeyfield* v. *Hopkins* ([2011] IRLR 300 EAT). In *MacCartney,* a care home manager provided an administration and organisational function, as well as on-site cover for 4 days per week of 24-hour shifts. During this 96-hour continuous shift she was required to remain within a 3-mile radius of the care home. As a manager, 'she was not to undertake care [and] not responsible for personal care' in respect of residents ([10]). MacCartney was provided with on-site living accommodation and on occasions used a cupboard area as an 'office' from which to do paperwork. The Tribunal concluded that,

> a manager or warden of sheltered accommodation who is required by her employer to remain on call to residents and for that purpose to remain on or close by her place of work is 'working' while on call even if her employer provides her with a home at her place of work. ([60])

Since all her working time was recognised as work for the purposes of pay, Regulation 16(1) did not apply. Arguably the judgment reflects an occupational expectation that the working time of a manager carries economic value throughout the 96-hour weekly period in which she is contracted. *MacCartney* was later considered in *Hughes*. This case concerned a care assistant who worked an 85-hour week, which comprised 8 hours of hands-on caregiving and 77 hours of on-site emergency cover between 9 p.m. and 8 a.m. every day. As in *MacCartney* v. *Oversley House Management,* Hughes was provided with a home at her place of work and was also found to engage in salaried hours work. Yet during the emergency cover periods she was paid only for the time when she was called out. The EAT determined that Hughes only 'actually worked' for 8 hours a week and was merely required to be on call for the remainder of the time. She was therefore not 'working' ([19]). NMWR regulation 16(1) would apply and her entitlement to payment in accordance with the national minimum wage was severely restricted. A distinction from *MacCartney* was made on the facts. Hughes' salary payment did not already include the emergency cover time and, in the event that she was actually called out, she would be paid separately. Similarly, in *South Manchester Abbeyfield* v. *Hopkins* care workers with a contract to provide care services during the day, and an obligation to remain on site for the duration of each overnight shift, were found to be subject to Regulation 15(1). The case distinguished *MacCartney* on the basis that Hopkins was contracted for a day shift but separately 'on call' at night and therefore she was not 'at work' ([30]). It appears that, for care workers at least, judges are reluctant to find 'work' during time periods in which there is not a pre-existing link to pay within the contract. This communicates an assumption that employers' contractual freedom to select the work for which they will pay is unconstrained. It diminishes the authority of workers' statutory entitlement to a national minimum wage payment. It also directly contradicts the universalising capacity of minimum wage law to recognise services of value provided under contracts which require work but make no corresponding reference to wages. Caring practices are socially enmeshed with distinctly feminine forms of identity and the femininity of caring facilitates the employment of women in homecare. National minimum wage law appears to treat care workers less favourably than workers providing different types of services. It is when care workers are denied the benefit of equal access to economic resources and legal protection that gendered subordination is entrenched and institutionalised.

The gendered assumptions of minimum wage law

Without doubt there are chronic problems with enforcing the national minimum wage in the homecare sector. However, as was discussed at the beginning of this chapter, a consideration of the Mother Superior character narrative as a form of 'collective imaginary' enables a critique of national minimum wage law based on its reinforcing of gendered understandings of work which fail to appreciate the economic interests of homecare workers. Part of the reason that the minimum wage entitlements of homecare workers are ignored, and the workforce is underpaid by millions of pounds each year, may be because the law perpetuates and undergirds some of the basic injustices that it purports to remedy.

This chapter has considered the social, industrial and contractual pressures which persuade homecare workers to provide work without pay, or at the very least to talk about unpaid work as a matter of personal, moral credibility. The discussion has shed light on a collective imaginary in which homecare workers attempt to bridge notions of 'mother' and expectations of 'worker' in order to explain the present status of a community of 'dedicated carers' by reference to long-standing and deeply entrenched conceptions of how 'good' women ought to behave. It is not only socially acceptable for women to engage in care work without pay but also appears to be expected, and, moreover, evident that women who work in homecare will expect this of themselves. As 'good women', and irrespective of pay, homecare workers narrate their lives in terms of self-sacrifice and unpaid labour as a mechanism with which to protect their personal identities from shameful characterisations of low-waged women and poor-quality care. However, the homecare workforce as a whole has been economically abused and national minimum wage law is treated with disregard by many, if not most, employers. It seems that the homecare industry draws on stereotypes about what makes for a respectable, morally wholesome, working-class woman as it requires women to give their labour for free by structuring unpaid work into the organisation of work schedules.

Very low pay is a big problem at the heart of the UK's homecare industry. It would appear that legal and political responses to widespread exploitation and unlawfully low pay, thus far, regard the problem to lie in weak enforcement and an industrial culture of non-compliance (the National Minimum Wage (Amendment) Regulations 2016 increased penalties for deliberate non-compliance; see also Department for Business, 2016). However, my analysis has suggested that non-compliance is symptomatic of sexist stereotyping and class bias. I have sought to evidence this in the structure and judicial interpretation of national minimum wage rights. National minimum wage rules appear to support the very values of self-sacrifice and family morality that lie at the heart of much of homecare workers' economic deprivation. The statutory framing of minimum wage protection is not sufficiently inclusive to communicate that care work is as valuable as any other. What counts as 'work' according to legal findings of fact testifies to harmful assumptions of gender and class that strip homecare work of value.

Prejudicial attitudes to care work put homecare workers in a position where they have little 'choice' but to trade away fair pay in return for a modicum of social respect. I have suggested that a critical role for national minimum wage law would be to support homecare workers to assert their economic worth by ensuring that contractual values and commitments are upheld and recognised as appropriate within a moral landscape of paid caregiving. Against this benchmark, I have argued that national minimum wage law in practice is aligned with gendered assumptions that society in general should not have to pay in full for the provision of care within families. The National Minimum Wage Act 1998 has extended this assumption by removing the right to pay protection when non-family care workers are treated 'like family'. I have argued that care work is not appreciated as an economic activity and is regarded as having no commercial value, despite the fact that it is an essential support for everyday life and a key site of employment. The second charge I have raised is that national minimum wage law has the effect of silencing the ability of homecare workers to pin the descriptor 'work' on much of the caring activity that they undertake. Higher standards are imposed on care workers than are imposed on workers in more traditional forms of employment. Employers are not legally expected to take remunerative responsibility for the resource of women's time that they secure when they contract for work to be provided. In this regard, national minimum wage law fails to ensure that all working time is waged time. This has provided a justificatory basis for organising homecare work around notions of productive and unproductive time. By providing succour for sex-based understandings of care work as lacking in monetary value, the impact of national minimum wage law in homecare has been to introduce new avenues through which earnings can be reduced and unpaid time constructed as legitimate.

The third issue I have raised in respect of national minimum wage law is that care workers' time is reductively compartmentalised. Selectively, and somewhat arbitrarily, courts deign to decide the activities which may, or may not, warrant classification as working time under the statutory scheme. This sends a signal to employers about the extent to which they are entitled to organise work in a manner which reduces their wage bill or diminishes their liabilities in law. The failure of the courts to show the same regard for 'attendance' and 'availability' as is shown to other workers suggests that care workers have less intrinsic worth. Since their mere presence or obedience to contractual attendance requirements is not sufficient to attract minimum wage entitlements it can be seen that the law extends support to the very ideas by which homecare workers are socially and contractually coerced to provide work on an unpaid basis. National minimum wage law should be sufficiently robust to challenge the gendered devaluing of caring labour and provide an effective wages floor to prevent sex-based exploitation. Yet legal authority and statutory provisions appear to uphold the difference of sex as a disadvantage and systematically reproduce the idea that unpaid labour is an essential component of care work. It seems that the law looks at minimum wage rights through the primary lens of family and gender, rather than looking at, and deconstructing, the exploitative tendencies of 'family' through the lens of universal minimum labour entitlements.

4
Choosy Suzy

I call myself a personal assistant-slash-carer to cover pretty much what I do. Giving people their choice has to be my first priority – whatever the client needs and wants. When people are in their own homes, more of themselves shines through; they have clout about what happens to them and independence is promoted. My work with clients comes from Gumtree and my car is like my little office; it's paramount.[1] At the moment I am self-employed on call for clients who want their hair washed or dishes done in 30-minute bites. I have one main client; he has multiple sclerosis. I get him up, showered, dressed, toileting, shaved, appointments, shopping, banking and companionship. In total, he gets direct payments money for 38 hours of care a week but he pays for 10 extra hours himself because he wants more weekend care than social services will fund. I don't know where he gets the money from, but bless him! His package doesn't allow enough hours to have a personal assistant every day, so on a Wednesday he has to go to the day centre where he just sits and does nothing, which is a bit sad.

People look for a personal assistant because agencies are so bad and they don't want their own daughter or son to be doing their personal care. When clients say they are on direct payments it's because social services have directly given them money for their care. The whole point is that direct payments put the client in charge, so they get the choice, and instead of social services buying in the care, the client does it. Some clients get an independent living charity to help them manage their money – to act like a little accountant – getting the time sheets, sorting out all the pay and holiday if the personal assistant is an employee, paying the invoices if they are self-employed. Sometimes direct payments are seen as a golden pot of money and that's wrong. One lady was going onto direct payments and she was like, 'well, I only need one

---

1 Gumtree is a large and well-known website carrying free classified advertisements.

carer'; but it doesn't work like that because personal assistants need to take days off, they get sick, they don't work 24/7. That's another way the independent living charity can help: getting clients to organise better.

Amelia was my first private client. I took her on when I was working for an agency and we came to the agreement of £10 an hour. Her son did the books for her direct payments and paid the tax and national insurance for having me. There were other girls who worked in her house too, who didn't get £10 an hour. They were 60 and 70 years old and getting cash in hand because they were happy to get some money for helping out. As the time got on and Amelia got weaker, I would help change her in the bed and give her a bed-bath whereas those other ladies didn't have that experience or anything. I looked after Amelia for more than 3 years, up until she died. During that time lots of service-users I visited through the agency told me they would have me privately, but only if I was self-employed. The responsibility of it worried me.

I feel sorry for people who are not getting the level of care they need in their assessments from social services. Personal assistants and clients can end up as just two parties put together and very much left to get on with it. If I get the right people as clients it doesn't feel like I am going to work, it feels like I am going to see a friend. But even as a friend they still have their rights to have the care done properly. It's a big responsibility when the client hasn't got much else in their life or no one else to look out for them. Who is on their side when the council cuts their money? In the last six months, the council social workers have reassessed some of my clients and just wiped over their previous needs assessments, even though their needs have not changed. A client who had 17 hours now has 12 hours, why? In actual fact, his needs have got worse since the first assessment because his eyesight is worse and he can't see to cook a meal any more, yet they have taken 5 hours off him. When I argued it, the attitude of the social worker was, 'well I've got to cut budgets'. But the council have disrespected him and taken away his dignity just like that. To them, that's okay if they save a few hundred pounds. You go into some old people's houses and they haven't got anything. They have to sleep downstairs because they can't afford a stairlift to get up to bed. And you've got other people, like a service-user up the road who actually had a proper lift installed in her house ... the council spent a fortune. Why couldn't they share it out to all the other old people that need a stairlift? I don't think it's fair how the government works. Unless you have got a bit of mouth and a bit of clout then you are not getting nothing; then you see that others have everything.

Whether you are working with older people or people with learning difficulties or whatever, they have to have genuine choices about their lives. That is my belief. I knew a woman who had a husband with Parkinson's. She had an agency to get him up in the mornings but they kept sending different homecare workers on different days and she only trusted one of them. When she rang the agency to tell them she only wanted a service on the days when the good homecare could come, they said, 'we can't guarantee you the regular person at the regular time'. That attitude made it pretty impossible to carry on with them, so the wife said 'okay, I won't have you at all!', and she asked me to come and do all the hours instead.

When two other people asked me to take them on as clients as well I was able to totally give up agency work. It looked like it was gonna be a really good opportunity. It was a disabled woman and her boyfriend; they lived separately and both had disabilities. What started as a good idea, to be their same carer, ended up being a big problem. The couple wanted to go on holiday together and I wanted them to have that dream so I took both of them away. It turned out to be an absolute nightmare and I would never ever do it again. When I got back from the holiday they refused to pay me! I queried it and said, 'You guys agreed to make up the money I was losing from cancelling clients so I could care for you for two weeks solid.' They said, 'Well we can't afford it', so I went to the independent living charity that managed their direct payments. I explained I had lost a lot of money, what with the cost of the holiday and now with an unpaid invoice. The woman from the charity looked over the paperwork and said, 'well they shouldn't be paying you £11 an hour anyway, you're not worth it; you're only worth £8 an hour and you cannot ask them for more.' I said, 'What! I have a contract with these people to pay £11 an hour, that is what they agreed, I will not work for less.' I thought, 'Pardon me? Who do you think you are to tell me what I am worth? How dare you! You give a person the freedom of choice to choose her level of care, if she comes to me and agrees with my terms she can have me. It's simple, what is your problem?' 'My problem', she said, 'is that you should only be paid £7.20 or £8.00 max.' I said, 'that is because you think I am a person who was stacking shelves in a supermarket last week, well I am not!'

I won't work for £8 an hour; there is just no way. I charge £11 an hour but it's self-employed. It's the service-user's choice to pay me what is my rate; it is their choice if they need to top up their direct payment money. Even at £11 an hour we are still actually earning less than £8 an hour because we have to take our tax and national insurance out of our money and also we are not getting holiday pay. Our professional insurance and other costs come off that too, which is terrible. For direct payment clients, if they have a package of say 17 hours a week it's a decent enough contract for me and I will take them. But if you shared the money across all the hours I actually work for them, and then take off my costs, then I am probably only working for £4–5 an hour. We are working physically and faithfully and earning this pittance. With self-funding clients the money might be better; for example I had one who didn't have any sort of care package and enough money not to need social services support. I would go in for 2–3 hours and they paid me £15 an hour. That was the deal and that rate of money is easier to take home when you think of your mortgage, bills, kids, petrol.

I don't choose to be self-employed and I would rather have it another way. I want to be employed but it's like I am being forced to be self-employed to get work. As a self-employed person I'm not entitled to holiday, I'm not entitled to sick pay, not entitled to maternity pay should I choose to have another baby, which is probably unlikely, but if I chose to have another baby I wouldn't get any maternity leave. As self-employed persons we're not protected, it might seem we have more freedom on the times we work but actually we couldn't say, 'Oh Mr Michael I can't start until 10 a.m. today because I have another client.' He would say, 'Well I don't want you then' and drop the contract. A little while ago I was introduced to a client through a charity. I was really excited about it, me and the client got on very well. He asked me, 'your partner, what's his name?' And I said, 'actually my partner is a she'. I told him her name and that we had not had our civil partnership ceremony yet. The next week I got a phone call from the charity to say that his wife did not want me to go there anymore; she said that because I am gay, my being in their house might have a negative influence on their daughter. I was devastated, I'd lost my work, and I cried for four days because of that bigot.

I desperately needed another job so I started working as a direct employee for a woman who had me for overnights; at least I got money for holidays. Anyway, it didn't last very long because I had to pack the job in when it got so she could no longer move herself. With the equipment and the space available I just found it too difficult.

When I started, I could pick her up if she fell, but it got to a point where she was too weak and I could not lift her any longer. I said I would have to stop; I made that judgment. At the end of the day the client is directing the care, but obviously it has to be in a way which is safe. Having said that, the restrictions we've got around homecare are sometimes quite unreasonable. The companies have to go along with all the health and safety, all the sort of laws and legislation and things can be quite tedious and annoying. I think people nowadays are so afraid of being sued and litigation and you know carers coming forward and saying, 'Oh I slipped and hurt my back and it's your fault because I stood on that chair', or 'I got an electric shock when I changed that light bulb'. These things frighten people but I have heard horrendous stories of clients not wanting to be hoisted and personal assistants getting hurt when they are manually lifting people. This is a problem with the system as it is, there is nothing to protect the people working for clients and they could really injure themselves. But then maybe I am just as bad; with one client I won't use the hoist because he says it makes him feel like a piece of meat and he is not a piece of meat, he is a person.

Choosy Suzy and the Care Act

The Choosy Suzy narrative captures various ways in which notions of choice are played out in the private, domestic locations where paid caregiving takes shape. The experiences of personal assistants working on a self-employed basis formed the bedrock of the Choosy Suzy narrative. I was intrigued by the twists and turns in events that foreshadowed the breakdown of agreements over pay or hours of work, difficult judgment calls made by women working alone without back-up, and stories of accidents occurring due to unsafe working practices or in the absence of specialist equipment. However, I also drew on contributions from women employed directly by the older and disabled people for whom they cared, as well as from others working in the independent sector or engaged informally on a cash-in-hand basis. In this chapter, I use the phrase 'paid caregiver' as an umbrella term to encapsulate women working in a diversity of employment situations who may interchangeably combine informal labour in private homes, with work assignments as personal assistants or care workers, and jobs with care companies. Choosy Suzy stories are those in which paid caregivers are caught between the liberatory allure of being one's own boss, and their ongoing subordination as working-class women situated and defined in relation to domestic spaces, intimacy and care. They speak of the dangers to their health and safety, their exposure to blatant discrimination and the high levels of economic risk which accompany various 'care-for-hire' style arrangements in which they are engaged.

The character narrative of Choosy Suzy represents a neoliberal epoch of enterprise in the provision of adult social care. The physical and mental impairments of Britain's ageing population are pragmatically regarded as an economic opportunity and a driver of changed relations between citizens and the state. Two facets of neoliberalism are especially germane to the arguments I present below: the exhaustive generalisation of market relations and the persistence of political anxiety about excessive state intervention throughout society (McNay, 2009, pp. 56–60). Indeed, the generalisation of enterprise in relation to social care has extended beyond the boundaries of social institutions such as local authorities, care homes and hospitals to encompass the individual lives of paid caregivers and people in need of paid care.

In this chapter, I highlight the various ways in which women participating in the research upon which this book is based made statements or told stories about personal choice in order to communicate the meaning of care. To do so, I engage in a method of discourse analysis. Discourse analysis is a technique used in social science to interpret textual data. It enables an analysis of how issues are brought to life by the construction of interconnecting written or spoken statements (Potter, 2004). The Choosy Suzy character narrative exemplifies how the work of paid caregiving is constructed in a discourse of choice and choosing. By examining this discourse we learn that choice-making by older and disabled people is of such central significance that the exercise of volition (the power to choose) is deemed to give credibility to caregiving relationships. Indeed, choice-making and caregiving are constitutive of one another.

A core purpose of discourse analysis is to uncover the flows of power which bind together social actors at the micro-level of a discreet aspect of social life (such as paid care work in the homes of care recipients). By identifying patterns within written and spoken texts, discourse analysis aims to identify the discursive capacity of language to produce the social structures which serve as conduits for such power (Holstein and Gubrium, 2005, p. 491). Readers unfamiliar with social theory might find the idea that language creates social life, a little strange. However, the purpose it serves within this chapter is to recognise that a discourse of choice automatically generates the roles of service-user/paid caregiver and constructs these roles distinctively (for example, see Armstrong, 2002; Lessa, 2006). According to its own logic, a discourse of choice also produces the necessary background condition of a market in social care. By exploring the discursive construction of paid care work, the analysis identifies social structures and power flows that shape relations between paid caregivers and their clients. Hence, this chapter is about paid caregiving as it is set in motion by a discourse of choice. I explore the extent to which conceptualisations of paid caregiving in both experience and law are synonymous with choice-making.

A discourse of choice constructs paid caregiving as a fundamentally economic enterprise which liberates care recipients by enabling them to engage as economic actors in the market for social care. While unpaid care is recognised to be bespoke and personal, the notions of love and familial duty upon which it is based are perceived to prevent care recipients from exercising a full range of choice. By way of contrast, the market exchange of care services for economic reward makes it possible for care recipients to control care. Inevitably, the Choosy Suzy character narrative sets paid caregiving in sharp contrast to the caring labour of Mother Superior in the previous chapter.

While I draw on stories told by care workers to show that understandings of caregiving are sustained by a discourse of choice, I am additionally concerned with the articulation of this discourse in the Care Act 2014. This statutory framework for adult social care promotes individual choice as an explicit objective. Although it applies only in England, the devolved legislatures of Wales and Scotland have introduced similar, albeit more nuanced, provisions. My primary focus is not with the Care Act as a whole (which runs to 167 pages), but with the impact of core provisions on employment and the treatment of those provisions in statutory guidance. Extensive new duties require local authorities to promote service-user choice and control over care, and also require them to stimulate and support local care markets. I explore what this statutory pursuit of volition means for paid caregiving and raise concerns about increased demand for low-cost labour and a step change in marketisation. By placing volition at the heart of paid caregiving, the Care Act 2014 points towards styles of care-for-hire working which refresh and renew sexist bifurcations in the labour market and deepen the gendered exclusion of working-class women from the benefits of employment rights.

The discussion is organised into three sections to reflect themes that emerge from the analysis of discourse. The first theme is of choice as a value and practice aligned with a neoliberal era of social care. Through the second theme, of care as enterprise, I consider the deregulatory impulses which find expression when a discourse of choice is cemented in statute. The third theme, set out as a conclusion, elucidates how the meaning of 'home' is reconstituted by notions of choice in social care and the ensuing consequences for understanding gender.

Choosing to care

In my research, Choosy Suzy-type stories were communicated in a distinctive discourse of choice which included core phrases such as 'promoting independence', 'enabling people' and 'support for living well'. These shed light on the experiences of a cohort of paid caregivers who expressed their motivation to give choice to people who would otherwise lack autonomy. Some acted as vocal advocates for their clients and talked about paid caregiving as a practice which gave clients the capacity to make choices about the routines around which their lives were orientated; to decide how tasks would be performed; and to ensure that their personal preferences were respected. Without choice, caregiving lacked credibility.

In addition to choice being perceived as a product of care, the experiences shared by paid caregivers suggested that choice was regarded as its necessary precondition. Consequently, valid caregiving was thought to be built upon an understanding that clients ought to determine the 'who and how' of their care by choosing the terms on which care is provided, as well as the personnel who will provide their care. This normative perspective demands that choice be exercised as a foundational condition *before* 'care' can be given or received. The pursuit of choice was the central value around which caregiving arrangements were considered desirable or correct, as well as the basis upon which relationships with clients acquired validity. In this paradigm, the paid caregivers with whom I spoke explained how they provided choices through their various interventions in the lives of their clients. For example, Carrie worked for some people on a self-employed basis and for others as a direct employee. She said that under either arrangement her role was to be 'on the side of people who want to stay in their own home'. When I asked Kim to talk about her work as a personal assistant, she said it could be best described as that of 'life manager' because she created an environment in which her clients could choose to remain living at home.

Working life as a 'care-for-hire' patchwork

There are three principal routes through which older and disabled people who receive direct payments from local authorities are able to purchase care services: to directly recruit and employ personal assistants, to purchase services from care companies, or to contract with self-employed personal care workers (ACAS, 2013). Since direct payment recipients choose between these routes; they are typically constructed in social policy discussions and academic literature as being employers, customers or clients, respectively (for an overview, see Glasby and Littlechild, 2016). Yet the classification of direct payment recipients according to these roles does not provide a basis for setting the workers providing their care and support into similar, distinct, categories. Paid caregivers are employed in an increasingly diverse array of contexts and the employment profile of the paid care workforce has shifted to reflect growing demand for personal assistants. Yet, as I learned by reviewing individual stories, the experiences of personal assistants, as a group, could not be clearly delineated from those of homecare workers. Individual women could assume various styles of care-for-hire at any one point in time – for different clients, for different establishments – within a single career.

I found that women working as personal assistants were returning intermittently to work for homecare companies as and when they needed an additional source of income. Like Carrie, many of those working as self-employed personal care workers on some assignments were working elsewhere as the direct employees of older and disabled people. Similarly, women employed in the independent sector might have additional commitments to clients for whom they cared on the basis of private, cash-in-hand agreements. Frequently, these informal work arrangements were established as a low-cost fix for the problem of otherwise unmet care needs; for example, where a service-user required a broader range of support than that for which a local authority would pay, or if service entitlements were withdrawn or reduced and the service-user was too poor to pay for additional care on a formal basis.

In other instances, women who categorised their work as self-employed explained to me that they were introduced to clients by an agency which mediated the relationship between client and care worker on an ongoing basis. I suspected that the legal status of their employment was more ambiguous than they supposed. It could be argued that the agency sought to ensure a high quality of care by directing their work and these elements of control might point to worker status (*Carter* v. *Prestige Nursing Care* [2012] unreported UKEAT/0014/12/ZT). However, many of these women had a variety of employment sources and most women who identified themselves to me as self-employed said they had not become so on the basis of a single decision. Self-employment was rather a gradual process of transition away from working for homecare companies and, for many, this transition was still in progress or they expected it to remain incomplete.

Emerging national data affirms that working for direct payment recipients indicates a significantly increased likelihood of paid caregivers holding more than one job in adult social care, at any one time (Skills for Care, 2015a, p. 33). Academic work in organisational studies has identified that the feminisation of the labour market in general is concomitant with a new norm labelled the 'portfolio career', in which workers develop a range of skills throughout their working life and expect to move from one career to another (Scott, 2004). However, the labour market position of paid caregivers in my research looked more like a patchwork of care-for-hire than a portfolio. These women had no intention, and little option, of moving outside of the social care sector. Greater experience did not widen the scope of their search for work but rather it deepened their skills, competence and confidence in the physical craft of paid caregiving. The uneven textures and bespoke patterns of their working lives were coloured by their own choices over whether to accept potential work opportunities and those of people who needed care. Just like a patchwork garment, the strength of their care-for-hire patchwork depended on their personal ability to bind one piece of work to another and to create something new from that which might have been otherwise discarded as too small, fiddly or irregular.

Here was evidence of women attempting to resolve, as best they could, problems which arose from the fragmentation of adult social care and the retrenchment of the state from its practical organisation. It is a feature of neoliberalism that working people are forced to assume responsibility, as individuals, for states of affairs for which they are not responsible (McNay, 2009, p. 65), and for governments to present this as an extension of personal choice. Care-for-hire styles of paid caregiving assumed a certain kind of entrepreneurship. The self-responsibility shown by these women was an essential response to a fragmented economic environment which offered them little choice but to bring their 'abilities and emotional resources to bear in the service of individualised projects' (see Honneth and Hartmann, 2006, p. 45).

The direct payment recipient market is relatively new and rapidly evolving (Skills for Care, 2015a, p. 16). However, as my assessment in this chapter will establish, it is not a separate labour market in paid care but an integral expansion of the 'independent sector'. Notably, the commodification of care services has begun to embrace the commodification of personal care workers *in person*. It is this development to which the homecare industry is responding, and to which the work and career expectations of paid caregivers have begun to adapt.

Caring about choice

Where caregivers drew on notions of choice in my conversations with them, they articulated concerns about care quality by considering the extent to which the autonomy and independence of service-users were promoted. Accordingly, good-quality care encouraged recipients to exercise choice by expressing their opinions, or doing and thinking for themselves.[2] On the one hand, a discourse of choice constructed the role of personal assistants in contrast to the role of homecare workers; while, on the other hand, choice discourse served to distinguish personal assistants from skilled health professionals. Albeit in different ways, both health professionals and homecare workers were constructed negatively as groups representing a deficiency of choice. The effect was to cast in sharp relief the choice-giving credentials of personal assistants and to implicitly boost the credibility of volition as a core value and practice in paid care.

---

2 There is a growing body of empirical evidence that supports this view and key indicators of care quality are increasingly identified in terms of control, choice and maintaining independence (see overview in Tod & Kennedy, 2016).

The role of homecare workers was discursively associated with a waning model of top-down welfare service provision. Stories of paid caregiving communicated criticism of the contracting function of local authorities on the grounds that it effectively prohibited personal relationships of care from developing between homecare workers and service-users. As is exemplified in the Choosy Suzy narrative, the role of homecare workers was represented in stories about the frequent, and unwelcome, intervention of institutional actors such as 'managers' and 'the office'. Such stories narrated the denial to care recipients of a regular homecare worker, at a regular time, and the stripping away of peace of mind when workers failed to arrive. The structural causes of this problem were perceived to lie with local authority commissioning strategies which compressed caregiving relationships into tradable units of time and task.

The financial efficiencies that are required of homecare providers under a welfare service provision model are predicated on achieving so much labour flexibility as to drive out the costs of non-contact time and require a high through-put of staff. Yet achieving the goal of a flexible workforce removes the prospect of being able to guarantee care recipients the services of a particular care worker at a particular time. In Choosy Suzy-type stories, the role of homecare workers was constructed so as to symbolise the Achilles' heel of time and task commissioning: an overflexibility of labour which lacked the qualities of regular commitment and duty which were necessary if care recipients were to have the opportunity of choice about care in advance of its performance. The place of choice within the contracting chain was regarded as being too dispersed, since some choices rested with local authority commissioning managers, others with care company management and the remainder with administrative staff who populated 'the office' and directed much of the day-to-day business of care delivery. Stories which accounted for the role of homecare workers did not locate the capacity for choice with either the paid caregiver herself or with the person for whom she was employed to care.

However, the situation pertaining to skilled healthcare professionals was portrayed as markedly different from the problem of over-flexible labour. A distinctive story told by Philippa illuminates that the role of skilled healthcare professionals is negatively constructed in a discourse of choice on grounds of perceived *inflexibility*. Philippa was employed directly by the family of an older woman who was terminally ill. When the woman for whom she cared approached her final few weeks of life, Philippa's ability to earn an income came under threat: 'She was coming to the end of her days and the nurses told the family to get rid of me because paying me meant they didn't have enough money to bring in proper nursing care.' Since Philippa was working directly for the family under a direct payment arrangement there was no one but Philippa to speak up for the value of her own service. The way in which she dealt with this challenge to her livelihood was to discursively construct skilled health professionals as the bearers of institutional standards, whether clinical or legal, which are alien to a home environment. In order to protect her job, Philippa was pretty blunt about the disadvantages of bringing in more skilled nurses who would, she alleged, prioritise their own health and safety over the comfort of the woman in need of care:

> So I said to the daughter, I said, 'look, do what you've got to do; it's your mum at the end of the day'. But, I said, 'I have no problem coming over three times a day and helping.' Her mum was on a double bed. I told her, 'if you get the nurses, they won't do your mum without using equipment and they will demand she has to go in a single bed because of health and safety.' I said, 'so if you go with them, you will have to make changes and have lots of different people in your house and they won't necessarily be the same people every day, they won't know your mum like I do.' I said, 'I am happy whatever way you want to do it, but I am more than happy to come over every day, three times a day and help and clean her up and settle her down for the night and that kind of thing.' So that's what I did. I did anything she needed, whatever.

Philippa perceived her unique selling point as an ability to be accountable solely to the family: to deliver a truly personal service marked by relational informality. She set this capacity in sharp contrast with the allegiance of skilled health professionals to the external authority of professional obligation and their observance of health and safety standards. As a consequence, Philippa kept the work, albeit at the cost of providing extra hours as unpaid labour and increasing her travelling costs. In the above account, Philippa does not explicitly talk about choice; rather, she appeals to the volition of her employer. She suggests that her employer can only continue to exercise choice in matters of care provision by retaining Philippa's services. Philippa presents herself as being subordinate to the wishes of the family in a way that skilled professionals cannot be.

In a discourse of choice, the role of personal assistants is constructed as a counterpoint to formal care interventions that import external standards into familial domestic environments. When combined with my earlier observation that the role of homecare workers is characterised by a lack of service-user choice over personnel and service arrangements, it seems that the discourse gives particular credibility to choice-making within informalised systems of paid care delivery. This reading of my research data is supported by other research, which I review below, that finds the employment of personal assistants to be characterised by informality and legal confusion. However, it is significant to note that a discourse of choice also prioritises the structural relations of economic exchange through which social care is financed and traded, over and above a regard for the 'craft' of caregiving (the actual physical tasks, routines and practices by which human bodies are tended, pain alleviated and disease-resisted). The privileging of concern for choice in the arrangement of care, serves to deskill care work, at the same time as it commends care-for-hire styles of paid caregiving which reflect presumptions of familial informality and locate decisions about care within the private, domestic arena. This is an observation on which I expand as the discussion in this chapter develops.

An employment model fraught with difficulty

State provision of direct payments to older and disabled people has produced considerable opportunity for care workers to be engaged as personal assistants. The take-up of direct payments is higher in England than elsewhere in the UK and, of the estimated 650,000 homecare workers in England, about a quarter are working for direct payment recipients, either through care companies or as their direct employees (Skills for Care, 2015a, pp. 23, 26). These figures, however, do not take into account those who are self-employed or working informally. Although homecare workers and personal assistants perform broadly similar tasks, the difference in job title points to the expectation of personalised relationships for direct payment recipients.

The statutory basis of direct payments originated in the Community Care (Direct Payments) Act 1996. Local authorities were given powers to make payments directly to disabled adults of working age to enable them, of their own volition, to purchase their own care (Community Care (Direct Payments) Regulations 1997, reg 2). This important reform was warmly welcomed by the disability movement since disabled people had long campaigned for social policy tools which would give them individual control over how they lived their lives, and personal choice in decisions about their care (Clark et al., 2004; Gheera, 2012). From a disability rights perspective, direct payments were conceived as an emancipatory initiative that promoted independent living and recognised the desire of disabled people for autonomy (Slasberg and Beresford, 2015). It was a significant step towards the personalisation of state-funded care, a policy agenda which ostensibly rejected the paternal instincts and language of incapacity that had characterised prior models of top-down welfare service provision (Zarb and Nadash, 1994). At the turn of the twenty-first century, older people were identified as a target user-group for direct payments and the statutory exemption of people aged 65 and over was lifted (Community Care (Direct Payments) Amendment Regulations 2000). The permissive powers of local authorities were revised and transformed into a regulatory *requirement* that direct payments be provided to all qualifying persons who consented, or for whom a prescribed person (typically a friend or family member) was identified to manage their payments (Health and Social Care Act 2001 s 57). Provisions in the Care Act 2014 require that local authorities inform individuals who qualify for state support that they may receive direct payments (s 24(1)) and set out the conditions by which local authorities must make direct payments to them (s 31–33).

Researchers have consistently found that when direct payment recipients exercise the opportunity to directly purchase their own care from personal assistants, they benefit from improved self-esteem, well-being and happiness (Clark et al., 2004). These benefits arise where people in need of care have 'total control over whom they employ' (Scourfield, 2005, p. 478). However, the Advisory, Conciliation and Arbitration Service (ACAS) – the statutory information and advice service which works alongside the employment tribunal system – regards the direct employment of personal assistants as being fraught with practical and legal complications (ACAS, 2013). Direct payments to disabled adults under the age of 65 have frequently been used to provide 'wages' to family members or friends, including those who previously acted as unpaid carers.[3] The legal identity of unpaid carers who become partly paid employees is unclear in respect of access to state support for unpaid carers such as respite breaks, advice, counselling and property adaptation (Care Act 2014 s 10(10); Carers (Equal Opportunities) Act 2004). When making determinations about entitlement in such circumstances, local authorities are expected to discern 'caring' relationships from 'commercial' ones (Law Commission, 2011, para 7.35).

It is not uncommon for friends to fall out with one another in employment disputes (ACAS, 2013) and negotiating the boundaries between friendship and employment is highly problematic (Ungerson, 1999, pp. 592–5). One study suggested that family members or friends who were engaged as personal assistants received less than half of the pay provided to others (Lakey, 1994, pp. 150–2). Even where the receivers of direct payments do not employ friends and family, their relationships with personal assistants are such that research has found that more than half regard their caregiving employees as being 'like family' (Leece, 2006, pp. 196–7). As we explored in the previous chapter, workers treated 'like family' may be ineligible for minimum wage protection.

---

3 This was confirmed in an interview I conducted in 2014 with an advice worker for an independent living organisation who helped people to manage their direct payments. For findings that friends or long-standing acquaintances are often employed under the UK direct payments scheme, see Ungerson, 2004. Three-quarters of directly employed personal assistants were relatives or friends (see Lakey, 1994).

Advisory 'scenarios' published on the ACAS website speak to the commonly held concerns of personal assistants in their relations with employers for whom they care.[4] These include being bullied by an employer, undertaking shopping for an employer who forgets how their money has been spent and being expected to walk a dog that the employer has suddenly acquired without prior discussion. It seems that the informality and domestic liberty sought by direct payment recipients limits the ability of personal care workers to be recognised as the holders of employment rights. Although direct payment relationships are designed to meet the employer's own interests, the sense of individual obligation that is generated can make it difficult for personal care workers to move on and find alternative work (Leece, 2010). Workers are at risk of exploitation where feelings of commitment to clients can push them to work beyond the boundaries of the employment contract in respect of the tasks they perform, the responsibility they assume and the number of hours they work (ACAS, 2013; Scourfield, 2005; Ungerson, 1999).

The prospect of a caregiver and the person for whom she cares engaging in a legal contest over the enforcement of employment rights seems highly discordant with the very idea of legal rights designed for workers to assert in respect of their employing organisations. Even setting aside questions of personal friendship, these are relationships in which the employer is not only a purchaser and consumer of labour but is also a coworker, in the sense of being the person with whom the 'product' of care is crafted. Another distinctive feature of jobs held with direct payment recipients is that each worker is a hands-on caregiver and the cost of management is not factored into the price of care. Indeed, under a direct payments model, the state effectively privatises management functions by reframing them as private matters and placing managerial responsibility within the confines of the private home. The greater degree of choice purportedly on offer to direct payment recipients transforms the work of management into an invisible labour and isolates the paid caregiver from any wider organisational structure or external management.

The state's interest in direct payments is strongly motivated by cost savings. Access to appropriate care and support for direct payment recipients can be 'hampered' by insufficient funding from local authorities and the low rates of pay on offer for the employment of personal assistants (Morris, 2004; Scourfield, 2005). The potential mismatch between the amount of a direct payment and the real cost of employing a suitably qualified or experienced person is encapsulated in evidence that the cost of care is calculated on the basis of nominal hourly rates which can be frozen by cash-strapped local authorities – Hasler and Marshall (2013, pp. 3, 24) found that in one

---

4 See the 'Employing personal care workers' section of the ACAS website at: www.acas.org.uk/index.aspx?articleid=3303. Accessed 1 August 2016.

area the rate had not increased for seven years. Aside from the risk of very low pay, other potential pitfalls of under-resourcing and informality are not hard to foresee. Personal assistants are often hired without being subject to vetting procedures and, as a consequence, formalities such as references from previous employers and criminal records checks are not followed. In theory, this can be explained as a consequence of care-users exercising choice. However, in practice, direct payment recipients can lack sufficient choice over who to employ, have little to offer them other than low pay and feel obliged to take potential employees at their word.

Links between the personalisation of care and the deskilling of care workers are apparent in the rejection of professionalism and lack of occupational standards training (Glendinning, 2000; Leece and Leece, 2011). Direct payment recipients who are employers typically 'choose' not to support the formal training of their employees, preferring to simply induct them in personal preferences and desired routines rather than raising the competence of personal assistants according to standards which are recognised on an occupational basis (Institute of Public Care, 2013, p. 42). A study in 2008 found that over a third of directly employed personal assistants had no prior experience of social care whatsoever (Glasby and Littlechild, 2009, p. 160). This raises questions about the interests which are served should direct payment recipients undervalue the training by which personal assistants might lever a higher market value. Direct payments arguably represent a high watermark in social policy designed to promote the independence of disabled people. In a discourse of choice, arrangements between direct payment recipients and personal assistants are presented as exhibiting values and practices of choice which give validity to paid caregiving and credibility to the service provided. However, the caregiving of personal assistants is unregulated, necessarily informalised and, as we will continue to explore in this chapter, care-for-hire style arrangements are accompanied by a high degree of economic and personal risk.

Personalisation and personal budgets

The take-up of direct payments has increased rapidly since the financial crisis of 2008. In anticipation of strong statutory support for personalisation in the Care Act 2014, direct payment take-up increased by 10 per cent in 2013 alone, covering approximately 234,000 older and disabled people (Skills for Care, 2015a, pp. 17, 19). Older people are the largest group of care-users but they are the demographic least likely to take up direct payments, evidently concerned about shouldering an associated financial/administrative burden (Gheera, 2012). Yet older people who do receive direct payments are more strongly motivated than younger recipients to use their purchasing power to maximise their hours of care contact (Age UK, 2013, p. 10; Wood, 2010, pp. 15–16). This suggests that it is especially the state's strategy of increasing direct payments to older people which increases the appetite of the market for cheap labour – driving demand for more hours at a lesser cost. Only a minority of direct payment recipients eventually choose to become a direct employer and the proportion who do so has fallen from 45 per cent in 2009 to approximately 29 per cent in 2015 (Skills for Care, 2015a, pp. 16, 18). This reduced preference for acting as a direct employer reflects the increased frequency with which direct payments are now being made to older people and the fact that many are choosing instead to use direct payments to purchase care directly from care providers. While this avoids the complexities of becoming an employer, it weakens the extent of service-users' personal control and care provision by the same care worker is not assured. Critically, there is no research evidence of better well-being outcomes when direct payments are used to purchase directly from independent sector establishments (Slasberg and Beresford, 2015, p. 481). A reluctance to directly employ, alongside the drawbacks associated with purchasing care from a company, go some way to explain why demand for self-employed personal care workers is booming (as is discussed in the section 'The case for self-employment' in this chapter). If direct payment recipients are unsure about directly employing suitable staff they may prefer the sense of control, the freedom from liabilities of tax and national insurance, and the ability to terminate agreements with ease that come from using direct payments to contract with self-employed personal care workers.

However, the social policy platform of 'personalisation' is wider than the provision of direct payments alone. Since 2008 successive UK governments have taken incremental steps to encourage local authorities to allocate personal budgets to each service-user in order to give strong impetus to the 'personalised purchasing' of care at home (Department of Health, 2006, para 23). By establishing an intermediate option between the top-down commissioning of care services by local authorities and that of direct payments, the initiative aims to encourage older people in particular to take a more proactive role in the design of their own care (Scourfield, 2005, p. 476). In 2013/14, over half a million care-users had a personal budget which they chose not to receive as a direct payment. Most asked their local authority to manage the budgets for them, albeit according to their choice and direction (Skills for Care, 2015a, p. 20). However, it is also possible for a care-user to request their personal budget be held by a third party and this presents an opportunity for market development that independent care providers are keen to exploit (Tomlinson and Livesley, 2013). The Care Act 2014 places personal budgets into law, making them the statutory norm for state support of people with care and support needs (s 26). The goal is to replace local authority led 'macro purchasing' with care-user led 'micro purchasing' (Tomlinson and Livesley, 2013). In the meantime, local authorities continue to purchase the lion's share of care even while the take-up of direct payments is evolving rapidly. Organising state-funded social care into a system of personal budgets inclines local authority intervention towards supporting individual's management of cash and promotes a culture in which increased take-up of direct payments is a primary objective (Age UK, 2013).

Formally, the choice of whether or not to take up direct payments is in the hands of each care-user. However, local authorities are placed under performance pressure by central government targets which require that they maximise take-up and align notions of effective professional practice with increasing the numbers of people who agree to direct payment arrangements (DOH, 2012; Think Local Act Personal, 2010a). Strategies of direct payment and personal budgets are consistent with a neoliberal political agenda (Ferguson, 2012). They are highly attractive to governments looking to reduce the costs of social care, and have been promoted as such (Himmelweit, 2008). The 'business case for self-directed support' is to enable people to live better lives with costs being the same or less than under previous arrangements (Think Local Act Personal, 2010b), albeit that the number of hours of care provided to each person might be considerably higher (Slasberg and Beresford, 2014). Although there are evidential difficulties in linking cost savings to demonstrable improved user outcomes (Carr, 2010), the Department of Health promotes personalisation on grounds of efficiency savings and implies that direct payments must be made to be cost-effective because increased efficiency is 'required' (Bennett and Stockton, 2010, pp. 22–4). Cost pressures in adult social care are considerable (Slasberg and Beresford, 2015), particularly in respect of the care of older people. Despite a 10 per cent increase in the population aged over 65 in four years between 2009/10 and 2013/14, public spending on adult social care provision for this age group fell by 17.4 per cent and about a third of all older people did not receive the practical care and support that would meet their needs (EHRC, 2015, p. 62). There is a belief among MPs that greater use of direct payments stimulates competition and drives down prices by promoting innovation in the care market (for example, see Chris Skidmore MP, 2012).

My review of evidence in this section of the chapter has identified that paid care workers discuss their work in a discourse of choice and draw on it to locate themselves within a neoliberal framework of personalisation in social care. Discursive invocations of choice and choosing give validity to care-for-hire arrangements and assert the credibility of paid care. I have argued that the potential for direct payments to positively secure the empowerment of older and disabled people is hampered by a state agenda in which cost savings are a constant demand. In the next section, I show how this desire for reduced public spending is expressed in a discourse of choice through statutory measures which serve to construct the work of paid caregiving as an enterprise which sits at the peripheries of the formal labour market.

Care as enterprise

Clair worked for a homecare company that paid her by the minute. She described to me how she managed each visit by deciding whether to 'stay in there for the full-time or cut your losses and carry on with the round'. It indicated the degree of discretion her job entailed and her instinct to prioritise her economic interests in order to protect herself from detriment. Even though she worked for a homecare company on a zero-hours contract, Clair took personal responsibility for organising her work in a care-for-hire style to try and make the most of her low earnings. It had taken her two years to build up a regular round of service-users: '[and] due to them being regulars I get to know the capacity for me to be able to go to them earlier or later in the day'.

The Choosy Suzy character narrative indicates various ways in which care is discussed by paid caregivers in a language of economic transaction and quantification. In discussions of paid caregiving characterised by personalisation, a language of local authority commissioning had carried over from the apparently prior era of welfare service provision, in which care 'packages' were traded between commissioning local authorities and provider care companies. Women I spoke with used the term 'package' to identify the sum of their clients' needs and entitlements. This shorthand description of the very fundamentals of human life (such as eating, drinking and toileting) revealed how care was discursively constructed by paid caregivers as being conceptually separate from the human being to whom it related. I found it striking that women engaged in the hands-on crafting of care were using the same, fundamentally economic, language of objectification to describe their relations with clients as that which was used by administrators and managers who dealt with care as a traded commodity.

The work of social geographer Doreen Massey has explained that the words we use to construct social relations as economic relations shape the way we think about the world. Her observations shed some helpful light on the question as to why paid caregivers might talk about care in a language of enterprise. She argues:

> The assumption that markets are natural is so deeply rooted in the structure of thought, certainly here in Europe, that even the fact that it is an assumption seems to have been lost to view.

> This is real hegemony. And it has effects. It removes 'the economic' from the sphere of political and ideological contestation. It turns it into a matter for experts and technocrats. It removes the economy from democratic control. (Massey, 2013, p. 16)

This suggests that marketisation in social care has not only come to be taken for granted, but that its resulting impacts, such as the trading of care, its parcelling as a product and concern for efficiency, are thought of as natural, rather than as made by politicians, lawyers and accountants. Indeed, the Choosy Suzy character narrative highlights the active role played by paid caregivers in the making of the care market. Marketisation is not 'done to' them but is rather a process in which they are centrally engaged, as both agents and objects. Our attention to discourse in this chapter requires that we acknowledge the prevalence of economic language in the accounts of paid caregivers and recognise that care is constructed as a form of enterprise which is set in motion by their everyday encounters with people for whom they care. Massey continues:

> This assumption of the naturalness of markets is crucial to the insistence that There Is No Alternative. It is one of the ghastly ironies of the present neoliberal age that we are told that much of our power and our pleasure, and our very self-identification, lies in our ability to choose (and we are indeed bombarded every day by 'choices', many of them are meaningless, others we wish we didn't have to make), while at the level that really matters – what kind of society we'd like to live in, what kind of future we'd like to build – we are told, implacably, that, give or take a few minor variations, there is no alternative – no choice at all. (Massey, 2013, p. 16)

The pursuit of choice therefore is intimately bound to the project of marketisation. The stories that are recounted in the Choosy Suzy character narrative are steeped in an aspirational language of 'opportunity', of 'having that dream' and pursuing desires (for example, a foreign holiday). They contained explicit criticism of the prior welfare service era of social care provision, for instance dismissing the value of communal day centres ('where he just sits and does nothing') and casting corporately provided services as inherently inferior and best avoided ('agencies are so bad' and have an 'attitude'). As we have seen in the preceding section of this chapter, discursive assumptions serve to construct paid caregivers as competitive agents engaged in a process of overturning that which has gone before, on grounds that choice was lacking. However, Choosy Suzy stories also point to new hierarchies of labour within the private homes of older and disabled people in which paid caregivers represent an implicit criticism of familial bonds as a caring ideal (clients 'don't want their son or daughter to be doing their personal care'). Personalisation promises to displace a familial ethic of duty, kinship and obligation with an ethic of entrepreneurial choice.

Evidently, paid caregivers are adapting to a dynamic market environment in social care and regard changes in the way that public resources are allocated to have created market opportunities for them. For example, Philippa explained: 'I have heard that some people can't have lunchtime calls from the council anymore and they have got to have microwave food, so they haven't got a choice. I can go in and cook fresh food, so I can explain to them that with me, things are better.' Hazel, a personal assistant with no previous experience before taking on her first clients, explained she was confident of her earnings potential because, 'I can find another job just like that. There's no shortage of care work, I can walk straight into it. I've just recently started working for another gentleman; I've only been with him two months, and I'm doing eight hours a week at the minute. That's self-employed and I can probably begin to push to increase the number of hours he asks me for because things are going so well.'

Most of the conversations with paid caregivers upon which the Choosy Suzy character narrative is built took place in the spring and summer of 2014. Although the Care Act had been debated and agreed by Parliament at that point, provisions in the Act relevant to the discussion in this chapter did not come into effect until April 2015. The Act as a whole is orientated around a guiding principle that local authorities must promote 'well-being' as the basis of social care provision in England. In the discussion which now follows, I will explore how the statutory principle of well-being deepens and widens the marketisation of social care in a discourse of choice. Similar measures have been introduced in Wales and Scotland where social care is a devolved matter (Social Services and Well-being (Wales) Act 2014 s 2; Social Care (Self-directed support) (Scotland) Act 2013 s 19 and relevant statutory guidance published April 2014 paras 18, 122). Although the legal project to consolidate market norms in social care is less intense the further its geographic distance from Westminster,[5] legislatures across the UK have moved social care in the same direction, supporting the extension of direct payments, personal budgets and the promotion of 'well-being' as a core objective.

The foundation of choice in adult social care law

Following the 2010 general election, in which no single political party won an overall majority, Conservative and Liberal Democrat MPs agreed to form a coalition government and their *Programme for Government* contained a

---

5 For example, the Regulation and Inspection of Social Care (Wales) Bill 2016 had proposed the prohibition of homecare visits of less than 30 minutes duration yet was amended to enable both local authority commissioned visits and those organised directly by care-users to be of shorter duration in alignment with market norms and consumer choice.

commitment to legislate to extend personal budgets and give individuals 'more control and purchasing power' (p. 30). It is the task of the Law Commission, a statutory independent body appointed by the Lord Chancellor and Secretary of State for Justice, to review the law and recommend whether reform is needed. In 2011, it undertook a major review of adult social care law and recommended the introduction of a new legal framework organised around notions of choice and well-being. However, the Law Commission made a distinction between the coalition government's aspiration of control over care and a broader goal of enabling choice about care for older and disabled people: 'it is choice rather than control that is the key principle' (Law Commission, 2011, para 4.25). Recommendation 5 of its report outlined what a new legal principle of well-being might look like. Accordingly, the government's desire for 'person-centred planning' was deemed to be an inadvisable foundation for this statutory principle because, the Law Commission reasoned, the law should be 'capable of being inhabited by different policies at different times' and 'it would be a mistake to bind our recommendations to a particular philosophy or policy' (para 4.27, paras 5.5–5.7). Furthermore, the Commission considered the idea of a 'personalisation statute' to be unsuitable and it was 'dubious' that well-being could be harnessed to an aspiration of 'active citizenship', as the government had been proposing (para 4.17, paras 5.5–5.7). In recognising the potential for policy variation across the UK, the Law Commission noted the view of the Welsh government, that 'personalisation' had 'become too closely associated with a market-led model of consumer choice' (Welsh Assembly Government, 2011, para 3.16). However, taking inspiration from the drafting of schedule 5 of the Government of Wales Act 2006, the Law Commission recommended a legislative definition of well-being in social care that would embrace six 'outcomes': health and emotional well-being; protection from harm; education and recreation; contribution to society; social and economic well-being; and the securing of legal rights (Law Commission, 2011, recommendation 28). Neither choice nor control were part of this list.

However, when the coalition government formally responded to the Law Commission's report, it insisted on 'control and freedom in every setting' and made clear its determination to boost the status of personal budgets. Personal budgets would become a statutory requirement and 'a default part of the care and support plan' so that every eligible individual could 'decide how much control they wish to exercise' (Department of Health, 2012, para 3.11, paras 8.21–8.23). Government policy was also adamantly committed to 'significantly increase direct payment take-up as part of the implementation of personal budgets for all' (Hasler and Marshall, 2013, p. 2).

From a disability rights perspective, personal budgets allow people to make personal choices about how and where they want to receive care and support. Yet the rhetoric which surrounds them points to a neoliberal, distributive assumption which is set out explicitly in a commentary by the Executive Director of employers' association the National Care Forum: putting people in control of their own care, 'makes the system fairer' (Kelly, 2013, p. 74). In 2013, the Care Bill was introduced to the House of Lords and it was based on the Government White Paper, *Caring for our Future: Reforming care and support* (2012). Critiquing state-funded care services 64 years after the National Assistance Act had first set the wheels in motion, the white paper bemoaned their piecemeal nature and argued for a new approach in which care and support was something that state intervention should prevent, postpone and minimise for as long as possible. It preferred that care and support, when necessary, should be simple to arrange and under the control of individuals. The role of the state, therefore, was to ensure the availability of information and advice, and to enable individuals to make rational market choices. This exercise of choice would force providers to 'up their game' (Diaper and Yeomans, 2016, p. 3) and the ability to choose would enable a fair distribution of services through the proper functioning of the market in social care.

Accordingly, personal budgets are a means through which the state can enable individuals to access 'a right previously available only to self-funders' (Department of Health, 2007, p. 2); that is, a right of choice. The provision of personal budgets, ideologically at least, puts state-funded care-users on a par with their wealthier self-funding counterparts. At a practical level, this has clear implications for the continuing growth of the individual employer and personal assistant market. However, a statutory focus on personal budgets also clarifies that the function of the state is to extend purchasing power to people with care needs who are eligible for state support, assisting them to engage in the social care market in a way which is comparable to wealthier others. This suggests that the relation of the state to people with care needs is to remedy a perceived disability of being otherwise unable to exercise economic agency – of being unable to provide for oneself. Hence state action in pursuit of social justice is displaced, and goals of equality and perceived fairness rest on preventing exclusion from market participation. The result is that the state casts off primary responsibility for welfare and social justice by construing them as questions of responsible self-management (McNay, 2009, p. 72).

This privileging of market relations over social justice is closely connected to the rhetoric used to justify the need for change in the relation of state to citizens, the seemingly uncontrollable advance of increased longevity. In a speech published to celebrate the Care Act 2014, Minister for Care Norman Lamb MP endorsed the need for 'a modern system that can keep up with the demands of a growing ageing population' (*Care Bill becomes Care Act*, 15 May 2014). The effect is to position government at the apex of two prevailing headwinds: market-forces and population pressure. Indeed, an ageing population is itself presented as a market component: an insatiable and relentless force of demand. Yet it is social progress and publicly available health services that created the conditions by which people have been able to live longer (Mullan, 2000, pp. 40–3). It is ironic then that these social achievements are now framed as social problems and used as reasons for discrediting the political commitments and social structures which were responsible for their creation.

The statutory principle of well-being

When the Care Bill was introduced to Parliament, it was proclaimed by Ministers to herald an historic development in adult social care provision that placed eligible individuals 'in control of their care and support for the first time' (Daniel Poulter MP, House of Commons, Hansard, col. 448, 12 May 2013; Rt. Hon. Paul Burstow, Minister for Social Care, House of Commons, Hansard, col. 815, 16 May 2013). This claim to innovation was more than political rhetoric. The government's white paper had asserted that individuals 'need to be', and 'should be', in control of their own care and support (DOH, 2012, pp. 3–9) and such resolute declarations have set the enabling of choice at the centre of adult social care; changing flows of finance and redistributing power accordingly. The report of members of the Joint Committee tasked with scrutinising the Care Bill recognised that new legal rights for 'control of services' by individuals meant direct payments 'are likely to become a much bigger feature of social care in the future' (6 March 2013, para 209).

The disability movement had long sought to establish a legal right to independent living and self-directed care so that disabled people might live lives which are comparable with others in their local communities. The Care Act 2014 exemplifies the fact that these emancipatory objectives have been co-opted by the state in pursuit of increased marketisation (Slasberg and Beresford, 2014). Its statutory words include those of personal dignity, respect, independence and participation; yet the commitments and duties that they create do not secure the right of disabled people to determine their own care needs, nor a right to have those care needs met in full, nor a commitment to adequate levels of state funding (Slasberg and Beresford, 2015). Rather, the Care Act requires that, in exercising a statutory function in the case of an individual, all local authorities have a duty to 'promote that individual's well-being'. The phrase 'well-being' is defined in relation to nine outcomes which are set out at s 1(2) as follows.

> 'Well-being', in relation to an individual, means that individual's well-being so far as relating to any of the following:

(a) personal dignity (including treatment of the individual with respect);

(b) physical and mental health and emotional well-being;

(c) protection from abuse and neglect;

(d) control by the individual over day-to-day life (including over care and support, or support, provided to the individual and the way in which it is provided);

(e) participation in work, education, training or recreation;

(f) social and economic well-being;

(g) domestic, family and personal relationships;

(h) suitability of living accommodation;

(i) the individual's contribution to society.

As a consequence of 1(2)(d) the promotion of control by individuals over their own care is a statutory requirement on grounds of 'well-being'. The control sought is the individual control of caring labour by individuals in need of paid care. To recall a finding set out in my earlier analysis, the objective of individual control subordinates the practical craft of caregiving to the pursuit of relational conditions of informality and volition. However, as a statutory principle, the active promotion of individual control also points to changes in the structural orientation of the state towards individuals in need of paid care; it signals a shift in power. Regard for choice was previously a social policy mechanism relating to the arrangement and delivery of care. However, the conflation of choice with well-being in the Care Act, produces choice as the outcome of the state's commitment to 'care' for older and disabled people. The market logic of service-user-as-consumer has widened to embrace a neo-liberal paradigm of enterprise in which choice serves as a proxy for care. Echoing the place of volition in the Choosy Suzy character narrative, insofar as the responsibilities of the state are concerned, choice is not only a means to care, but it has also become its end. In other words, by promoting individual control over caring labour, local authorities are acting out their statutory duty to promote well-being. One impact is to make a virtue out of measures designed to reduce the cost of care through increased competition, another is to fracture the ability of care workers to access the benefits of employment protection and minimum labour standards by locating the work of paid caregiving at the peripheries of the formal labour market, an issue to which I now turn.

The Care Act and the workforce

The Care Act suggests the cementing of a very different relationship between care workers and the state than that which existed under the prior welfare service model of provision. By redefining care as 'well-being', and by setting in train an enhanced programme of marketisation, the statutory entitlements of individuals in need of paid care have been framed in direct opposition to the interests of the care workforce. The welfare service model of care provision became the subject of critique from within the disability movement at the same time as the concept of care 'has been relegated to a marginal position' in social policy contexts (Barnes, 2012, p. 6). However, having good reason to seek care improvements is not a reason for allowing the craft of care work to play second fiddle to values and practices of choice and control which focus on goals of welfare, well-being and citizenship (Barnes, 2011). As the discussion in this section will illustrate, any devaluing or erasure of care as an explicit value in social policy (especially in statute), ought to raise concerns about its potential capacity to erase or occlude the interests of those who give care.

During the passage of the Care Bill in the 2013/14 parliamentary session, existing problems of low wages, non-compliance with national minimum wage law and job insecurity in the homecare sector were raised in both Houses.[6] However, these concerns failed to gather momentum and the focus of debate turned to assign poor employment to the idea of errant employers rather than to acknowledge that employment conditions in the homecare sector are connected to public policy (for example, Westminster Hall debate, *Home Care Workers,* Hansard, col. 243WH, 6 March 2013). Rebuttals made by the Minister for Social Care suggested that action on employment standards was unnecessary because employment issues would be addressed in forthcoming statutory guidance (House of Commons debate, Hansard, cols. 87–91, 10 March 2014). Consequently, there was little consideration by politicians that specific provisions in the Care Act might serve as a catalyst for further subordinating the interests of care workers or destabilising wages, health and safety or other labour rights. Yet, according to expert commentaries, implementing the Care Act will continue to 'require significant changes to workers' roles and practice to meet new legal expectations' (Centre for Workforce Intelligence, 2015; Kelly, 2013, p. 74).

The Care Act contains a singular explicit reference to the social care workforce. Revealingly, it sits within provisions establishing the market-shaping duties of local authorities, by which local authorities are required to 'promote the efficient and effective operation of a market in services for meeting care and support needs' (s 5(1)(a)–(c)). The overarching purpose of this duty, according to its statutory subsections, is to ensure a variety of providers in each geographic area that will (when taken together) provide people with a variety of high-quality services from which to choose,

---

6 See Lord Warne, House of Lords debate, *Care Bill,* Hansard, col. 1602, 29 July 2013; House of Commons debate, Hansard, cols. 47–91, 10 March 2014; Department of Health, *The Care Bill explained including a response to consultation and pre-legislative scrutiny on the Draft Care and Support Bill* (May 2013), 46.

and sufficient information with which to make an informed choice. Consequently, local authorities are required to have regard to (among other things), 'the importance of fostering a workforce whose members are able to ensure the delivery of high quality services (because, for example, they have relevant skills and appropriate working conditions)' (s 5(2)(f)). Setting aside the weakness of a legal obligation to have mere 'regard' for workforce matters, a statutory reference to regard for 'appropriate working conditions' might be welcome. Yet it is framed within a discourse of choice and s 5 as a whole serves so to construct the roles of local authorities, citizens and care workers as to ensure the exercise of volition. Therefore, weak regard for appropriate working conditions exists within the context of a statutory discourse which undermines structural elements of welfare service provision where doing so is advantageous for the pursuit of stronger and deeper market competition.

The drafting of the duty of local authorities to have regard for the importance of 'fostering a workforce' is indicative of fragmentation, fluidity and a further informalisation of employment. It constructs the workforce as a seemingly nebulous collection of free-floating, and individual 'members', who exist without any reference to employing entities or formal relations of employment. Moreover, this statutory language reveals a previously hidden assumption of a care workforce that is not employed but is, rather, 'fostered'. It is a representation drawn from the entrepreneurial lexicon of a discourse of choice that signals growth, cultivation, advancement, anticipation and binds us to a trajectory in which the risks of care-for-hire are located externally from the state and dissipated between individual (and transacting) parties variously engaged in the performance of social care.

Statutory guidance and *caveat venditor*

In 2014 statutory guidance to the Care Act was issued by the Department of Health to local authorities, and made clear that they are bound by a primary concern for the health of care markets, over and above concern for working conditions. Accordingly, local authorities, '*must* facilitate markets to offer continuously improving, high-quality, appropriate and innovative services, including fostering a workforce which underpins the market' (para 4.18, emphasis added). Here, the workforce is linguistically represented as the market's architectural underpin, a term which emphasises that the workforce is the necessary condition or foundation for the transacting of care. Statutory regard for 'fostering a workforce', discussed above, is expounded in the guidance in relation to pay and reproduced below. It is disappointing that national minimum wage law is identified as the appropriate benchmark for pay. Nevertheless, at a symbolic level, the guidance usefully acknowledges the existence of employers and connects local authority commissioning practice to care worker remuneration.

> When commissioning services, local authorities should assure themselves and have evidence that service providers deliver services through staff remunerated so as to retain an effective workforce. Remuneration should be at least sufficient to comply with the national minimum wage legislation for hourly pay or equivalent salary. This will include appropriate remuneration for any time spent travelling between appointments. (para 4.27)

Yet this guidance is practically meaningless since it does not equate to a recognition that work undertaken between calls is an integral part of the service commissioned by local authorities. An appeal to 'appropriate remuneration' in respect of travelling time merely affirms the existing demands of minimum wage law (see *Whittlestone* v. *BJP Home Support*), with which homecare employers continue to fail to comply (National Audit Office 2016). Minimum wage enforcement problems in homecare are structural and where local authorities are not direct employers they cannot be aware of the prevalence of unpaid working time in any individual homecare worker's work schedule, nor of the quantity of time worked which ought to be included in any minimum wage calculation. At best, the provision amounts to a check of hourly rates and terms of work set out in the job advertisements placed by the companies with which they contract.

Taken as a whole, the statutory guidance is inimical to a goal of improving labour standards in the homecare sector. It throws light on the hierarchy of market over workforce instituted by the Department of Health. While the word 'should' applies in respect of local authority obligations in relation to minimum wage law, the word 'must' is used to instruct them to develop and facilitate markets in adult social care (see paras 4.21, 4.28). This means that local authority concern for the payment of lawful wages is not a legally meaningful requirement, but is rather an indicator of 'best practice' (Department of Health (Feb 2015), *Draft Regulations and Guidance, Care Act 2014*, p. 7). The suggestion made throughout the statutory guidance is that an 'effective workforce' is a cheap workforce and local authorities are repeatedly urged to secure 'value for money' (see paras 4.24–4.95). Prior to the implementation of the Care Act, both governmental and non-governmental bodies identified local authorities as key drivers in the underpayment of homecare workers. The process of care marketisation has afforded low priority to labour standards and job quality and it is concerning that measures set out in the Care Act appear to continue this trajectory rather than to divert from it.

There are illuminating changes in relation to labour standards which occurred between the issuing of draft guidance to the Care Act and the publication of the final version. Draft regulations issued in June 2014 required local authorities to check, within the first six months and annually thereafter, that direct payment recipients who were acting as direct employers were making tax and national insurance payments for their personal assistants and paying wages at rates which were at least equivalent to the rates relevant in national minimum wage law (para 12.47, para 12.61). However, this obligation is erased in subsequent guidance (most recently issued May 9 2016) which instead requires local authorities merely to give direct payment recipients clear advice as to whether they should register with HM Revenue and Customs and notes that many local authorities commission voluntary and charitable organisations to provide direct payment support (paras 12.48–12.49). Evidently, the Department of Health has resolved that it is disproportionate to require local authorities to oversee or intervene with regard to labour standards compliance by individuals who have chosen to directly employ personal assistants with their direct payments.

Consistent with the construction of paid caregiving in a discourse of choice, this approach upholds regard for the independence of disabled people. If individuals are free to choose, they must be free to make 'wrong' choices and hence the erasure of oversight requirements replicates, at an institutional level, interpersonal respect for disabled people as individuals with personal freedom to transgress. However, in the event that a personal assistant is paid at an unlawfully low rate, it is not now possible for her to turn to the local authority in search of a resolution. It seems she would be referred to the national minimum wage enforcement unit at HM Revenue and Customs (HMRC), where pursuing a formal complaint would not only involve a lengthy wait (National Audit Office, 11 May 2016, paras 3.2–3.3) but would also put the person to whom she gives care at risk of being burdened with heavy fines, tax and wage liabilities. If she turned instead to pursue a formal claim through the employment tribunal system she would be required to pay a fee (typically £390 for minimum wage claims at current rates). Such fees have been in place since July 2013 and it is now extremely difficult for low-waged workers to access employment tribunals (Busby et al., 2013). Even if a case of underpayment was upheld by HMRC or a tribunal, the individual employer would be unlikely to have the personal funds available with which to remedy the underpayment. Personal assistants are, consequently, very exposed to the risk of continuing to work for unlawfully low pay or constantly seeking out alternative employment. This intense disjunction between employment as a personal assistant and the realisation of employment rights is a further example of how the Care Act serves to reconstitute the relationship of paid caregivers to the state. Paid caregivers are positioned by the state at the margins of its own interest in regulating the labour market, and the economic risks of social care provision are placed on the shoulders of workers and individuals in need of care.

In a discourse of choice, the construction of personal care workers would seem to represent one of *caveat venditor*, in which the seller of labour must be aware that they are responsible for any problems arising as a consequence of the transactions in which they are engaged. The Choosy Suzy narrative with which this chapter opened included parts of a story told to me by Carrie about her experience of not being paid for work she undertook in order to support her clients' desire to go on holiday. In search of a resolution, Carrie had turned to the independent living organisation which processed her invoices, issued cheques from her clients' direct payments account, and organised for her clients to sign off those cheques. Carrie was shocked when the adviser with whom she spoke initially suggested Carrie had taken the clients on her own holiday rather than having worked to facilitate the clients' choice of a fortnight abroad. The dispute focused on the difference between the amount ordinarily paid to Carrie and the amount due to her for additional hours, which her clients had agreed to fund in recognition of the extra work of providing them with round-the-clock care while abroad. When Carrie vocalised her interests in purely economic terms, the adviser became aware that Carrie was being paid a higher rate of hourly pay than that used as a nominal, but standard, measure by the local authority which had calculated the size of her clients' direct payment. When deciding how to use their budget, Carrie's clients had chosen to buy in fewer hours of care, at a higher hourly rate, because Carrie was very experienced and they valued the fact that she was willing to provide a service to them both. Rather than addressing Carrie's point that her contract had been freely entered into by her clients, the adviser's view was that the contract represented an unreasonable exercise of power by Carrie over her clients and that she had been responsible for establishing contractual terms which could not be honoured. The role played by the independent living organisation in this story was not to resolve the dispute, but to effectively quash it on the basis of *caveat venditor*.

The introduction of the Care Act onto the statute book has been accompanied by other statutory measures that facilitate the informalisation of paid caregiving. For example, while prior regulations prevented the use of direct payments for the employment as paid carers of family members living in the same household, the Care and Support (Direct Payments) Regulations 2014 reg 4(2) now allows the 'paying' of cohabiting family members 'if the local authority considers that it is necessary'. This provision is further relaxed by its interpretation in the statutory guidance of 9 May 2016: 'there should be no unreasonable restriction placed on the use of the payment' (para 12.35). Changes to income tax law introduced in the Finance Act 2015 mean that accommodation provided to live-in paid caregivers is no longer regarded as a taxable benefit. According to the Act, for persons employed to perform homecare duties 'no liability to income tax arises' in respect of board and lodging (s 16). Although the proportion of personal assistants who are directly employed under direct payment arrangements is falling, measures in the Finance Act appear to facilitate live-in care arrangements, and we have considered in the previous chapter statutory provisions of the National Minimum Wage Act 1998 which expedite the potential exemption of live-in care workers from the scope of the UK's minimum wage scheme. Yet as has been explored in this section, live-in care workers are not the only group located at the periphery of the formal labour market for the purposes of employment rights entitlements.

The case for self-employment

Most of the self-employed personal care workers who took part in the research for this book had more than one client and advertised their services online. It is doubtful that they would fall within the definition of 'worker' provided in the National Minimum Wage Act at s 54(3). Despite their potential exposure to low pay outside the protection of law, the existence of the self-employed personal care workforce is under-recognised in social policy and studies of care work in general (Hayes, 2015a). They are not included within Department of Health official estimates of the size of the social care workforce and this omission includes own-account workers; workers who access their clients through organisations offering a recruitment/introduction service; self-employed workers who are placed directly by an employment agency for the duration of an assignment; and workers who are engaged on a self-employed basis by care-users with direct payments (Fenton, 2013, p. 7).

A detailed study in 2014 by the Office of National Statistics sought to uncover the profile of people who worked from home across the labour market. It found that the vast majority of women who regarded their home as the 'base' from which they worked (as opposed to their 'place' of work) were self-employed and the most frequently cited occupation was paid care work. These women were more likely to be engaged as paid caregivers than to be working in any other occupation and their number adds approximately 60,000 to the established population of homecare workers in the UK (Office for National Statistics, 2014). Rising self-employment in the social care sector is taking place in the context of a rapid rise in self-employment across the labour market in general. Self-employed workers now comprise one in seven of the total UK workforce, half of them are low-paid, and there are an estimated 1.7 million self-employed workers paid less than the minimum rate which would apply if they were covered by national minimum wage law (Social Market Foundation, 2016).

The extent to which self-employment is becoming synonymous with poor-quality employment reflects the fact that self-employed workers have few employment rights. In common law, self-employed persons are not classed as employees, but as independent contractors. From the perspective of statutory entitlements, independent contractors who are not operating a business on their own account are likely to qualify for worker status and to fall within the scope of minimum labour standards as well as anti-discrimination provisions. Indicators of operating on an own account basis include having more than one client, advertising one's services, not needing to personally perform the work, using one's own equipment and overseeing the quality of one's own work.

My focus in Chapter 2 was on homecare workers who worked for care providers in the independent sector. I explained that individuals who qualify for basic employment rights as 'workers' might also qualify for employment protection rights and family-friendly entitlements as 'employees'. The deteriorating quality of employment for homecare workers had resulted in a general shift away from the employee status enjoyed by the workforce prior to privatisation and towards the lesser entitlement position of worker status. However, the frequency of self-employment for personal care workers, indicated in data from the Office of National Statistics mentioned above, points to a step-change in the marketisation of paid care, and a further step-down for the legal status of the workforce. Some people who operate as independent contractors will qualify for worker status in relation to statutory employment rights. However, it is unlikely that those who are self-employed, advertise their services and have more than one client will have any employment rights other than to be covered by the anti-discrimination provisions of the Equality Act 2010 on grounds that they have a relation of personal service with their clients (*Allonby* v. *Accrington and Rossendale College*).

It is likely that the number of workers in self-employment will rise sharply as a consequence of the government's introduction of a higher national living wage rate for workers aged 25 and over (Social Market Foundation, 2016). However, in addition, it seems that the number of paid caregivers in self-employment will rise as a consequence of provisions in the Care Act. In the USA, 29 per cent of homecare workers are self-employed, and in that context, wages are reported to have fallen to 'appallingly low' levels (Smith, 2013, pp. 328–9). Health and safety standards have fallen such that homecare workers are frequently exposed to hygiene and infection risks, manual handling accidents, aggression and harassment by disruptive service-users, and injuries from pets, fleas and unsafe home equipment (Taylor and Donnelly, 2006). It is therefore apparent that lack of formal legal access to basic labour standards is not the only problem associated with the routinisation of self-employment within the social care sector.

Nevertheless, the relationship between levels of funding from local authorities in the UK and rates of pay to personal assistants is so close that direct payments represent little more than (re)'routed wages' (Ungerson,

2004). In circumstances of very low pay, personal assistants may feel they have little choice but to trade away employment rights, such as access to maternity pay and statutory minimum holiday, in return for working on a self-employed basis in order to maximise their take-home earnings. The attractions of self-employment to personal care workers include not only the possibility of a better hourly income in lieu of statutory employment benefits, but also the opportunity to provide a personalised service to their clients; the ability to offset vehicle expenses from tax liability; the security of being responsible for their own tax and national insurance payments; and exemption from registration with the Care Quality Commission (CQC).

Homecare providers in the UK must register with the CQC, pay annual registration fees, be subject to inspection and meet registration standards. Failure to do so is a criminal offence which carries the potential of imprisonment and a fine of up to £50,000 (Health and Social Care Act 2008, s 10(4)). However, agencies placing personal care workers with individuals are exempt from registration – so long as they have no ongoing role in the control of services – as are individual care workers who are working under the control of their client (Health and Social Care Act 2008 (Regulated Activities) Regulations 2014, Sch.1, s 1). This means that self-employed workers who are directly engaged by clients lie outside the remit of CQC care standards requirements and they are also exempt from the requirement that registered providers must vet paid caregivers for prior criminal convictions. While local authorities must ensure that people who employ personal assistants via direct payments are made aware of how to access a criminal records check via the Disclosure and Barring Service (DBS) if they so wish, there is no requirement upon them to do so (Department of Health, *Care and Support Statutory Guidance,* May 2016, para 12.50).

The DBS is an arm's-length, semi-independent government body serving the Home Office which seeks to help employers make 'safe' employment decisions and prevent unsuitable people from working with vulnerable adults and children. The organisation processes criminal record checks, is responsible for making decisions about the appropriate inclusion of people on a barring list, and gives employers access to barring list information. Individuals who are cautioned or convicted of a relevant offence in the courts face an automatic bar. However, barring decisions are made by DBS officers on the basis of referrals made by care providers that have dismissed staff on suspicion of risk of harm or abuse, and by local authorities in receipt of complaints which warrant DBS involvement. People included on the barring list do not necessarily have a criminal record and need not ever have been accused of a criminal offence. However, any person who attempts to engage with vulnerable adults or children while their name is on a barring list commits a criminal offence. Regardless of whether they are acting in a voluntary capacity, are employed or self-employed, they face a prison term of up to five years (Safeguarding Vulnerable Groups Act 2007, s 7).

In my conversations with paid caregivers, the UK's system of care standards regulation was cited as a factor which dissuaded self-employed personal care workers from branching out to become small-scale care providers. Sindy was a self-employed personal assistant who had worked in social care all her adult life; she was nearing retirement age and yet was also in the eye of a storm. When I visited her at home, Sindy was considerably distressed and swamped in paperwork that she said she did not understand. A combination of financial naivety and compassion had made Sindy vulnerable to the attention of the authorities after the children of a client who had recently died became embroiled in squabbles about inheritance. She had been accused of running an 'unregistered' homecare service.

For many years, Sindy provided paid care to her client Marie, who regarded Sindy as a long-lost daughter and rarely saw her own children because the relationship was problematic. When Marie became extremely ill, Sindy was unable to cope alone with providing round-the-clock care. Recognising that Marie was in the last few weeks of her life and needed to be well cared for, Sindy arranged for help from two friends, who were also experienced carers. As Marie's personal assistant, it had always been one of Sindy's duties to write bankers' cheques to cover Marie's household bills such as gas, electricity and rent, which Marie would then sign. These cheques also included the payment of Sindy's own invoice. For several months, it had been a real effort for Marie to summon up the energy to even sign her name on these cheques. So when it came to the point where there were three care workers in her home instead of just one, Sindy decided it was best to continue to ask Marie to sign a single cheque and she took it upon herself to distribute the money owed to her friends once the cheque had cleared.

While Sindy may have had the best of intentions, she had handled the financial administration of Marie's care as though she had taken on two subcontractors. This provided grounds for a referral to the local authority by Marie's children after her death. They were irritated to discover that part of the money they regarded as their inheritance had been used to pay for the additional care. While the CQC did not consider the situation to be a significant breach of the rules requiring provider registration, the DBS interpreted the allegation as evidence that Sindy had put a vulnerable older person at risk of harm. She faced the prospect of having her name included on the national barring list. The DBS has neither the legal power nor resource to investigate individual cases, but rather it makes an assessment based on information provided by referring employers or local authority departments (Disclosure and Barring Service, 2012b, para 20). Once a DBS officer has reached a 'minded to bar' position, a care worker is invited to make a written submission as to why she should not be barred and the case is reassessed before a final decision is made (Disclosure and Barring Service, 2012a). Sindy explained to me what it felt like to be accused:

> It is heart-breaking, soul wrenching. I feel like a part of me has died. I don't even think that out of all the English language that I know and love, I can find a word. I feel sick. I've been reported to the barring service. The letter says I have the chance to tell them why I feel I shouldn't be barred. How do you write something like that? I feel sick.

She was clearly very frightened and the extent of her distress suggested that, by placing in question her personal identity as a caring woman, the situation had a negative impact on her mental health. The UK's barring programme has been characterised as a system of 'unprecedented regulation' (Hussein et al., 2009, Ecory, 2012). Although individuals may exercise a right of appeal to a specially convened tribunal (Disclosure and Barring Service, 2012b, para 27), research has found that, like Sindy, many workers are ill-equipped to defend themselves in the event of a referral, they are too poor to be able to afford legal representation and often cannot mount any kind of a defence to allegations (Manthorpe and Stevens, 2006). It would appear that fear of being reported as an unregistered care provider, together with the high costs of annual registration fees with the CQC, prevents personal care workers from seeking to build small businesses from their patchwork portfolios of jobs and clients.

Nevertheless, it was an interesting dimension of the Choosy Suzy character narrative that notions of choice in paid caregiving did not circulate exclusively around the figure of the client. For many paid caregivers, opportunities for self-employment, informal working or direct employment with older and disabled people were regarded as routes promising greater control over their working lives than had been possible when working for care companies. Others, however, portrayed self-employment as the outcome of a lack of choice in the labour market and a shrinking menu of work opportunities in traditionally structured employment. It is perfectly possible, however, that these opposing opinions were mutually reinforcing. Paid caregivers talked about time, money and emotion as the investments that were required of them. When working on zero-hours contracts, they hoped that their trade of available time in return for a proportion of paid time would be adequate to sustain their economic needs. Unpaid time spent during induction training was described by some as a risky investment and, as Hazel expressed it to me, employers didn't pay for induction training because the benefit of training accrued to the worker in person. Mileage expenses were widely understood as an economic risk and the use of their own cars for work was an investment on which paid caregivers made no financial return if employers failed to fully reimburse them. Most women said that work was their only reason for owning a car and several had taken out personal loans which became unmanageable because the basic mileage rate on offer was only half of that approved by HM Revenue and Customs. Workers were expected to wait until after the end of the tax year to 'reclaim' the missing half as a tax rebate. The economic insecurity of zero-hours arrangements had seemingly led many homecare workers to appreciate that their time was bought only on demand and, as a consequence, they had learned to regard paid caregiving in commercial terms.

Prior research has made recommendations about how to ameliorate problems of recruitment and retention in the homecare sector and has stressed that a key attraction of homecare work is the sense of personal responsibility it offers. As homecare worker Lucy said to me, unlike other jobs, homecare was attractive because she could work without 'the boss breathing down your neck'. In return for her intense commitment to the people for whom she cared and her toleration of low wages, Lucy wanted autonomy over how she performed her work. However, local authority budget cuts have hugely reduced employers' capacity to give care workers such autonomy. Intense productivity pressures mean that working in homecare can offer few opportunities to exercise personal discretion since working time is monitored by the minute and schedules are crammed. For working-class women in search of autonomy, working for care providers is an increasingly unappealing option.

Similarly, the prevalence of zero-hours contracts seemed to create a culture in which women were willing to entertain the prospect of self-employment as an alternative to the care-for-hire style of working found with care providers. Jane was a personal assistant who ran an agency which put paid caregivers in touch with potential clients on a self-employed basis. She confirmed that working-class women typically 'panicked' at the idea of being self-employed and those with whom she worked were initially uncertain, cautious and risk-averse. Her approach was to reassure them that they would be no less insecure than when working on a zero-hours contract with a care company. She said, 'I tell them it is exactly the same; if your client was ill and the call was cancelled, you wouldn't get any money.' Indeed, Jane believed that self-employment increased the economic security of the women she supported: 'like I say, you're more guaranteed the way we do it because you work with the same client. The clients are not gonna say "well I don't want them" because they like having the same people.' Indeed, for paid caregivers, one of the key advantages of thinking about paid caregiving as an opportunity for enterprise was to harness the potential to develop personal relationships with clients and to grow that relationship from their knowledge that the client had chosen them personally. As Hazel put it: 'the main reason I get my work is because it will be me and it will be continuity in having the same person.'

In this section of the chapter I have shown how the Care Act provides statutory justification for the fragmentation, individualisation and informalisation of paid care work. I have argued that new statutory objectives of care-user control, market innovation and increased choice are predicated on the further deregulation of paid caregiving. It would seem that a public policy focus on developing systems of personalisation and individual control has attracted considerable political attention without 'getting to the heart' of caregiving (Barnes, 2012, p. 70). That heart, I will suggest in the concluding section which follows, lies with understanding that the Choosy Suzy workforce increasingly works 'from home', works in the homes of other people, and works to create and maintain the gendered meaning of 'home' as a place where women enable others to exercise choice and personal preference without the perceived intrusion of the state.

Gender and the reconstituting of home

The shift from a welfare service provision model of social care to one of personalisation represents the translation of prior statutory duties on local authorities to make arrangements for care into a duty to make cash payments. Since public interest and resistance to privatisation in the UK is much weaker in relation to social care than, for example, in respect of healthcare, adult social care has been ripe for spending cuts (Laing, 2014, p. 10). Budgets have been slashed (ADASS, 2015), and yet the volume of homecare hours purchased with those budgets continues to grow, albeit that growth has slowed, and the tightening of eligibility criteria has cut off access to social care for great swathes of elderly people (Fernandez et al., 2014; IPC Market Analysis Centre, 2012, pp. 7–8). The mathematics insist that services are, and continue to become, cheaper at a time when rising demand for paid care is being driven by the spectre of population ageing, and in conjunction with the neoliberal 're-tasking' of the state (Peck and Tickell, 2007, p. 33). Public policy is designed to contain public spending on older people in the health sector by reducing their reliance on accident and emergency provision, shortening their hospital stays and deterring their admission to residential/nursing homes (Humphries, 2011). Home-care services are the means through which each of these public policy objectives is achieved and care-for-hire is fundamental to the future.

A public policy of personalisation in social care has been set into statute by the Care Act 2014. It rejects the paternalistic remnants of a prior era of welfare service provision, which stereotyped older and disabled people and failed to adequately recognise their distinct claims to personhood. However, personalisation sets in motion its own presumptive stereotypes - one of which is that older and disabled people 'choose' to stay at home because it is the place where the satisfaction of their needs best belongs (Scourfield, 2005, p. 472). This presumption is not based on the active, individual choices of people in need of paid care, but is instead conceptually rooted in a normative (and financially convenient) assumption by the state that care at home is the default choice of people who may be in poor health, with declining opportunities for socialisation and diminishing physical and mental capacities. A presumption of home, the various tenets of which I shall outline below, is a neoliberal foundation of the Choosy Suzy character narrative. Neoliberalism enlarges the social space for private enterprise, competition and individual liberty (Pick and Ticknell, 2007, p. 28). In adult social care, neoliberalism excavates the social space of 'home' in order to reconstitute it as a sphere of enterprise. This transformation is mediated through law and communicated in a discourse of choice. Law is integral to the discursive production of people in need of paid care as market participants with the supposed power of choice. Like neoliberalism, personalisation is as much an ideology as it is a mode of governance. As such, personalisation is a vehicle for introducing market discipline into the entrepreneurial sphere of home. Neoliberalism seeks the 'economization of the informal' in which previously private, domestic, personal aspects of social life are increasingly permeated by principles of individual interest and exchange (Honneth, 2004, p. 49).

Human beings experience social spaces as 'place', and the physical, relational and political dimensions of place reflect the how and where of our coexistence with others. The Choosy Suzy character narrative with which this chapter opened can be best understood as emerging from the 'negotiations of thrown-togetherness' that arise in everyday experiences of paid caregiving (Massey, 2005, p. 81). They include impromptu contracting for care services, attempts to build friendships from business arrangements, the terms of openness and closure that permit care workers to enter personal spaces marked out as private property, those that facilitate their rejection from those same spaces on grounds of client choice, and negotiations about the physical touching and tending of the body as a restricted place which is normatively closed off to others. As the following observation by homecare supervisor Ann alludes, notions of geographic exclusion and inclusion are fundamental to a discourse of choice:

> People in their own homes though, feel they can have their own choice, so they can chuck a person out if needs be, and their choice gets respected. One lady threw a male care worker out of her house, she just didn't want him there. A lot of people that we are dealing with have lost physical abilities and sometimes a bit of mental ability. I think that is the only power in their lives; their care is their only control.

Moreover, Ann's words reveal how the imposition of paid care into private domestic spaces can provide a source of control for people who may otherwise feel powerless. Notions of home carry a symbolic meaning as a place of choice and choosing; the idea of home represents the materiality of choice.

Personalisation is the backdrop for accelerated marketisation. In an earlier phase, iterated through the character narratives of Cheap Nurse and Two-a-Penny in this book, the private homes of older and disabled people were transformed into individual sites of paid work, and paid care was shaped and reshaped to enable it to be traded as a commodity. Hence marketisation shattered the provision of homecare into millions of separate transactions. It fractured relations of employment such that they were thrown outside the conceptual frameworks underpinning legal entitlements to employment protection and minimum labour standards. The subsequent turn to personalisation, however, has required a step change in marketisation. The private homes of older and disabled people are no longer a site of paid labour but rather they constitute thousands upon thousands of individual sites of enterprise.

Indeed, personalisation serves to transform the buildings, living spaces and the personnel we identify with 'home' into novel sites of enterprise. Personalisation co-opts the social practices and informalities which are constitutive of 'home' as a means with which to satisfy (at low cost) that which was recently described in Parliament as 'the rising and remorseless demands' of an ageing population (Rt. Hon. Kenneth Clarke MP, *Junior Doctor's Contract debate*, House of Commons, Hansard, col. 1761, 11 February 2016). Those demands are no longer public but have been (re)privatised in line with the assumption that the needs of older and disabled people 'belong' at home. The promise which lies within the social policy ambition of personalisation is of better care quality, in contracted interpersonal spaces, based on more sharply focused one-to-one contact and longer-term relationships (Needham, 2014). Yet personalisation in practice is much more 'variable' than its proponents may be willing to acknowledge. A review of literature and research to date has found the attentiveness and particularism promised by personalisation fails to materialise for everyone (Needham, 2014). Indeed, reforms designed to promote personalisation appear to create variability and inequality. It would seem that the exercise of choice is not so much a description of caregiving in practice as it is an aspiration which is culturally associated with the home 'space' around which paid caregiving is presumed.

However, the creation of inequalities within personalisation is a key indicator of its alignment with entrepreneurship. Individual citizens, as entrepreneurs of themselves and their own needs, may only enter into relations with others as competitors. Hence, paid caregivers compete with one another for paid work and personal budget holders compete with one another to secure the services of paid caregivers. Most importantly for the argument I have pursued in this chapter, paid caregivers and individuals in need of paid care are cast as competitors with one another (although this competition is not a one-dimensional pursuit of economic interest and must be set more broadly). Under a neoliberal spotlight, paid caregivers are discursively assigned an individual, entrepreneurial identity which papers over alternative, prior potential claims to identity as rights holders in the labour market, as parties to employment relations, or as bearers of occupational standards. Meanwhile, for individuals in need of paid care, new duties of the state set out in the Care Act construct older and disabled people as the subjects of a monetised interest: the interest of well-being. The suggestion is of 'home' reconstituted as an entrepreneurial space in which private interests are maximised, and rights formerly associated with the public sphere are diminished. This competition of interests underpins the social care market. An 'equality of inequality' stimulates competition between people in need of paid care and the women who are paid to craft that care. It feeds off a mode of governance in which the role of the state is to ensure that no one is excluded from 'the game of entrepreneurship' (Donzelot, 2008, p. 130). As a site of enterprise, the home is a cauldron into which the economic rationality of choice, considered to drive efficiency and quality in markets, is combined with the relational practices of choice that give social meaning to domestic spaces of home and family. The one-to-one contact and longer-term relationships which are the presumed outputs of personalisation are qualities which characterise unpaid care and relations of family. It would seem that even under conditions of entrepreneurship, working-class women cannot escape the gendered expectations of unpaid labour, obligation to others and subservience.

From the perspective of paid caregivers, the agenda of personalisation is highly contradictory since it seeks both to change 'home' and to conserve it – to inject commerce into previously uncommodified home spaces, while also stripping those spaces of financial resources and labour regulation. Personalisation is a social policy agenda which depends for its underpinning rationality upon the social and spatial environment of home, because assumptions about the meaning of 'home' enable the state to expand paid caregiving, in order to contract it. On one level, personalisation looks like a rejection of 'the market', in the sense that it is an attempt to disassociate from a sphere of economic activity and site of contracting which is external to the home. However, rather than rejection, personalisation represents a deepening of the market – no longer conceptually separate – but having pierced into and transformed the home into a fluid and dynamic site of competition and enterprise.

Hands-on caregiving, with its low wages and lack of rights, is implicitly 'female'. It is perpetually tethered to the symbolic closure of a 'home space' as a trope of informal labour and a site where human beings purportedly behave in harmony with their supposed 'true nature'. Despite the appearance of state withdrawal from the organisation of care, the market-shaping duties of local authorities set out in the Care Act represent an enduring commitment to gendered state intervention. Homes will be reconstructed as sites of enterprise and personal care workers will be commodified, in person. The character narrative of Choosy Suzy has shed light on the construction of paid caregivers as actors in the care market and has highlighted that the choices they make set that market in motion. However, paid caregivers are also the objects of the processes in which they are engaged; there is no paid caregiving without them. The construction of care-for-hire as enterprise challenges us to think of the paid caregiver herself as both the locus and the object of choice. When personal care workers are produced as tradable objects, the commodification of care and the objectification of women is an inseparable connection; not only are their health, safety and labour rights subordinated to satisfy individual desires for informality, they are portrayed as having no needs of their own. The gendering of the social care market is now exemplified by an entrepreneurial trade in paid caregivers who are assumed to be women with no need of a minimum wage, no need of rest breaks, or of training, or of interaction and solidarity with others. The labour of such women is reductively managed within the home, confined within the domestic sphere and confined without the legitimacy which defines the broader labour market.

Conclusion

This book set out to use the words of homecare workers as a tool with which to illuminate their working lives and understand how labour law intertwines with the materiality of paid caregiving. Each chapter has identified ways in which the labour market participation of paid caregivers is widely judged as inferior. The discussion has located assumptions of sex and class in homecare workers' experience and connected these to inquiries about legal form and function. I have argued that the UK's crisis in social care is co-implicated with the gendered injustice of inadequate labour law. A politics of social care, or indeed the social politics of care, is enmeshed with a politics of class and gender. State provision of social care will continue to be marked by chronic underfunding and antipathy while the craft of paid caregiving is subject to degradations of sexism and class bias. In my concluding comments, I return to consider the institutionalised humiliation of homecare workers as a process which underpins many of the failings of social care and is expressed through law and legal doctrine at work. I believe that transformative change to law at work is urgently required. An appropriate campaign for legal reform would confront the sexist history of labour law, recognise the sexist inclinations of contemporary employment rights and acknowledge that working-class women are still waiting for law at work to extend to them its promise of privilege and protection. To be truly transformative, legal change would signal that paid care work is worthy of full protection in law and enable paid caregivers to be economically valued, legally entitled and afforded the respect of full legal and political recognition for their occupational contribution to the health of our economy, communities and family structures, as well as for their support of individuals with personal care needs.

The stories which homecare workers shared with me are an important and distinctive source of knowledge upon which broader understandings of law and society can be built. Inevitably, generalisable conclusions cannot be drawn from the accounts of 30 individuals working in a single city in the UK. Yet when set and analysed in a wider research context, it is fair to say that the unique data upon which my study is based fits well with what is already known about the working lives of homecare workers.

I have drawn on the studies of researchers working elsewhere in the world, including those operating in different academic disciplines, and examined data drawn from a range of different research methods. The validity of the stories I have gathered is immensely strengthened by this greater pool of empirical, sociological scholarship. I have paid attention to the published opinions of policy-makers, politicians, media commentators, lawyers, experts working within charities, lobbying organisations and trade unions. Significantly, I have also connected homecare workers' experiences to the functioning of legal rights and explored legal knowledge as it is divulged, shared and assimilated through legal processes and procedures. My arguments are open to criticism, they are fallible, will no doubt be honed by their dispute or critique, and represent the sum of my interpretation of the evidence. However, by sandwiching the character narratives of this book between a wider intellectual hinterland of sociology and in-depth legal analysis of statutory and common law provisions, I believe it is possible to draw broad conclusions, to which I now turn.

Humiliation is most commonly regarded as an individual emotional response in which a person feels demeaned, put down or exposed (Klein, 1991; Torres and Bergner, 2010). My claim that homecare workers are institutionally humiliated is distinctive. It draws on a growing body of literature in which humiliation is studied as a collective experience (Leidner et al., 2012; Margalit, 1998). Humiliation is increasingly recognised as having an important role in the structuring of social life, as well as for its political implications, which arise because the experience of humiliation invokes feelings of powerlessness in people who are subject to its harm (Leidner et al., 2012; Mackie DM, 2009).

The phrase 'being humiliated' points to an important dimension of humiliation; it is produced externally by events or actions in which one party imposes or inflicts humiliation on another. Unlike many other human emotional responses, humiliation is anchored to a changing relationship with others and entails a loss of social status or regard. This points to a special quality of humiliation; it is relational. Humiliation cannot be produced in isolation from its social context and it takes effect by undermining social status and offending notions of social justice such as equality, fair treatment, respect and the opportunity of self-expression. Indeed, the ties which bind humiliation to social status, often arise on the basis of 'what one *is*, rather than what one *does*' (Klein, 1991, p. 90). If collective humiliation is understood to be primarily grounded in the experience of belonging to a particular social group, the affective dimensions of humiliation can be seen as those produced in response to violations of respect and social judgments of inferiority that constitute humiliation in action (Margalit, 1998).

The women I spoke with recognised that they were unjustly treated as a group and their testimonies revealed something of the ontology of homecare; by which I mean, what it is to 'be' a homecare worker. Whether viewed as a social, occupational or industrial group, homecare workers hold in common, personal experiences of working life which are worthy of special regard. They partake of, and produce, a collective knowledge which is distinctive within the labour market. Their experiences are unavailable to people who do not work in homecare, and arising from them are distinct ways of knowing the world, 'as homecare workers': of understanding interpersonal relationships, of seeing human vulnerabilities, and of being part of other people's 'privacy'. Homecare workers engage in nomadic forms of emotional attachment: they simultaneously belong in every home and none; they develop relationships based on the intimacies of friendships and family bonds while they remain outsiders; they are accepted and embraced, yet they remain expendable; they are regarded as quasi-wives and daughters by erstwhile strangers, yet they carry and exercise the public duties of the state to support individuals in need of care. This is the collectively understood, background landscape which affirms an individual's belonging to the homecare workforce. The foundations upon which it is built are those of institutionalised humiliation.

Degradations of sex and class in the organisation of homecare work are shaped by a collective history which extends back over the past century and continues to evolve. Contemporary harms inflicted on homecare workers – their underpayment, insecurity, low pay and exposure to risk – are 'felt' collectively through this body of shared experience. The failure of respect afforded by the state exemplifies the institutionalised humiliation of homecare workers as a collective group. With the term 'the state' I am referring to the sum of power and responsibility carried by successive governments and the institutions that are key to the arguments I have advanced, including the judiciary, the legislature, the civil service, the Department of Health and local authorities. Homecare workers are impoverished, disrespected and marginalised through their work and the structural undervaluing of their labour is embedded in the state-led organisation of the UK's homecare industry. The institutionalised humiliation of homecare workers is expressed in the state's denial to them of employment protection and in the imposition of barriers that serve to impede their ability to assert basic legal rights at work. By examining the framing of equal pay law; the judicial doctrine by which employment protection is distributed across the labour market; the operation of the UK's national minimum wage scheme; and the discursive construction of provisions in the Care Act 2014, this book has considered key legal mechanisms through which institutionalised humiliation is created and reproduced in a contemporary context.

The character narratives of Cheap Nurse, Two-a-Penny, Mother Superior and Choosy Suzy have provided a variety of windows through which to observe the dynamics of sexism and class bias that homecare workers are continually battling to overcome. Each has offered a portrayal of institutional humiliation in action and demonstrated that judgments of inferiority (which may be legal, political or managerial) draw legitimacy from legal reasoning and from the structuring of contractual protections and employment rights. The economic contribution and recognisable value of homecare workers have been perpetually eroded by the state. In social policy, and in statute, the economic needs of working-class women who are paid to care for others have been disregarded. Homecare workers are denied a collective voice and their autonomy as a social, occupational and industrial group fails to be recognised in the actions of employers, politicians and judges.

The chapters of this book have discussed long-standing sexist ideas about the inferiority of women and their perceived difference from men, and have shown how these are reinforced and reaffirmed as sexist ideas patterning the construction of homecare workers in law. I have explored how individual legal rights function in relation to experiences of working life, and explained why employment rights are often rendered meaningless in practice for homecare workers. Law and legal thinking is central to the regard afforded to homecare workers in the labour market and shapes the circumstances and situations in which paid care is produced. The book has amply demonstrated how legal thinking and experiential existence are mutually reinforcing. However, institutionalised humiliation is collective not only in its effect, but also in its production. Harms are collectively perpetrated through the institutional (and inimically collective) orientations, language and functioning of the state. Hence, the institutionalised humiliation of homecare workers has both relational and structural dimensions.

At its centre lies the failure of the state to protect homecare workers from sex discrimination in the economic organisation of their work. The structural exclusion of homecare workers from the benefit of equal pay rights is key to their economic deprivation, but it is also a marker of their humiliation at the hands of the state. It represents a deliberate and enforced assault on their social status and has delivered aggressive wage reductions which impoverish homecare workers through their exposure to discrimination. At the next level, their humiliation is supported by the under-protection of homecare employment in law. Employment protection law explicitly declines to value the forms of employment in which homecare workers are typically engaged. The degradation of their conditions of work is part of their humiliation at being defined as inferior through legal doctrine which supports male privilege and seems averse to the adoption of legal standards in pursuit of universal advantage. In a third dimension, the humiliation of homecare workers is exemplified by the operation of minimum wage law which requires homecare workers to work without pay and denies them recognition of their labour as 'work'. They are judged as members of an industrial group which does not qualify in full, according to the most basic proposition that employment entails a rational exchange of labour for economic reward. They are denied the dignity of an equality of recognition in which minimum wage law communicates the worthiness of all paid labour. Finally, in the reorganisation of the responsibilities of the state, the craft of paid caregiving is erased in preference for the regressive (re)presentation of caregiving in domestic spaces as an informal relation, even in its continued and intensified commodification. Homecare workers are humiliated by their inability to be recognised as legitimate workers, at being pushed outside of the boundaries of labour law entitlements, and by legal principles which expose homecare workers to further insecurity, personal risk and wage competition on the grounds of promoting the well-being of the individuals for whom they care.

The material circumstances in which paid caregivers are demeaned and undervalued are made possible by long-standing traditions of underfunding. Yet, it is on account of widespread judgments about inferiority and lack of worth that this scarcity of resources is able to pass as politically possible and socially acceptable. Hence, the persistent and pervasive judging of homecare workers as inferior participants in the labour market is intrinsically interwoven with the stripping away of social care provision. It is to the intimate connection between a politics of social care and the gendering of labour law that I now turn.

The precariousness of social care employment and its sustained dismantling sit alongside the gendered and classed patterns of paid caregivers' labour market experiences, as symptoms of institutionalised humiliation. The state retains, and in several ways has recently hardened, a kernel of normative, sexist, ideology by which the social, economic and political costs of caregiving are borne by women – and by working-class women in particular. It is this deeply ingrained assumption (which is hardening into a matter of normative political insistence) that is causing the responsibility and attendant social costs of care to bear down on individuals.

The determination of the state to continue to offer homecare workers unequal standing in relation to others is exemplified in the recent introduction of criminal sanctions to discipline care workers through fear of prosecution under a new, and care worker-specific, offence of ill-treatment and wilful neglect set out as the Criminal Justice and Courts Act 2015, s 20. The original proposals emerged from a government-commissioned independent inquiry about failures of care in an NHS hospital where denials of dignity and unnecessary suffering had been inflicted on older people at the end of life (Francis, 2013b). Over 80 organisations representing healthcare professionals (such as the Royal College of Midwives, Royal College of Nursing and Royal College of Physicians) submitted opinions to the government's statutory consultation exercise; they argued that new measures were unnecessary, existing law was sufficiently robust and they gave evidence that fear of criminal prosecution would damage care quality. There was no representation of homecare or residential care workers. When the provisions were debated in the House of Lords, Baroness Thornton noted: 'I searched in vain for information from anyone lobbying on behalf of the badly paid social care workers, who are also included in this legislation, because they do not have the lobby that the doctors and nurses have' (Hansard, col. 478, 20 October 2014). It is a powerful illustration of the effectiveness of collective representation in the health professions that, despite its origins in failures of hospital care, the offence which was successfully carried into law is orientated towards hands-on care workers working in a community context and is even entitled 'care worker offence' in the text of the statute. The state's strategic incursion of specific criminal laws into the practice of homecare reflects public awareness of the risks of abuse to which older and disabled people are exposed in an era of marketised care, but also points to an acceleration in the use of law to mark out working-class women engaged in paid care work as less trustworthy, of lower status and of questionable intent.

The collective silencing of homecare workers is especially apparent in comparison with healthcare professionals and their voice in trade unions has been decimated by privatisation, the commodification of care and the fragmentation of their employment. The absence of occupational and industrial recognition for homecare workers is a structural deficiency in the field of health and social care which exacerbates their ongoing, and gendered, subjugation.

It is my intention that this book will have alerted its readers to ways in which stories about care are grounded in labour law yet can be presented in ways which undermine the value of social care. I hope to promote a public intolerance of employment rights which fail to apply in practice as basic labour market standards. In addition, I have sought to advocate for a political restlessness about employment protections which do not protect forms of employment in which working-class women are typically engaged. Where statutory rights or common law principles serve to justify the subordination of working-class women, elected politicians must be held accountable and be expected to advance alterative legal solutions, which are fit for a contemporary economy, in which men and women are both afforded the respect of the state. Securing social and economic equality for women is a demand which must extend far beyond the availability of an equal pay equality clause. Equality for women in the labour market will only be achieved when freedom from sex discrimination can be legally assured in respect of each and every element of the law as it applies to work as well as each and every element of their working lives.

It is also an aspiration that my observations of class and gender oppression might serve to raise awareness of, and break the silencing of, homecare workers in public policy debates. Homecare workers are routinely excluded from public policy consultations, from research about social care and from discussions about the future of homecare services. Their degraded construction, as people who are without meaningful knowledge, insight or observation, damages the interests of older people who rely upon their care. As a consequence, neither social policy documents nor industry commentators give adequate regard to the question as to whether the organisation and design of the homecare industry enables paid caregivers to achieve their economic objectives or even to satisfy their basic economic needs. Bringing the experiences of homecare workers into an ongoing conversation about the adequacy of homecare services for older people would increase the possibility of service improvement.

However, the central message of this book is an appeal for labour standards to be more widely understood as fundamental to the future of social care. Wide-ranging, transformative, legal change is required which can embrace a reversal of the state's strategic criminalisation of care workers, a fundamental reform of equal pay law, a new suite of legal rights which deliver universal protections, and the establishment of collective bargaining between trade unions, the state and employer representative bodies across the adult social-care industry. Anyone who is concerned about care of the elderly and disabled ought to put centre stage a concern for poor-quality jobs and the disrespect of homecare workers. The provision of high-quality social care in private homes demands a revolution in the regard in which care workers are held. It is one which must recognise the rights of older and disabled people to exercise choice in the delivery and arrangement of their care. However, the interests of people in need of social care must be protected in ways which promote, rather than undermine, the security of paid caregivers. This demands a rebalancing of power between homecare workers and the state, which could usefully begin with the establishment by the state of sector-wide systems of collective bargaining between workers' and employers' organisations. As has been noted in work by Jonathan Fineman (2013), an important insight to be gained from the study of public service employment is that the state acts to define itself when it acts to define the responsibilities and privileges of public service industry employers. It is in redefining the relation of paid caregivers to the state, and in remedying the harms of institutionalised humiliation via the state, that transformative change becomes possible. Homecare workers' long-standing and historic experience of sex discrimination makes it clear that in critiquing present-day arrangements, there is no 'glorious past' to which to return. However, history shows us that employment law has the capacity to deliver advantages to working people and collective bargaining has a track record of achieving better terms and conditions which, in the past, considerably improved the working lives of homecare workers. There is no reason why the contemporary plurality of the care at home industry could not be embraced through sector-wide recognition of trade union-negotiated agreements which respected and recognised the interests of people in need of social care as well as those of workers employed directly as personal assistants, homecare workers engaged by independent sector providers, the employees of local authorities, and paid caregivers operating on a self-employed basis to provide a personal service. The introduction of collective bargaining across the sector would affirm the link between labour standards and care standards and secure the dignity of socially valuable caring relationships.

The UK's twenty-first-century crisis of social care is a product of the gendered crisis in the regulation of work. The deterioration of labour market conditions which has accompanied the marketisation of homecare has resulted from reforms which have emulated notions of economic and social privacy. Yet social care lacks all meaning save a presumption of socialisation because the essence of 'social' care lies in its juxtaposition with 'private' care. For care to be 'social', it must be conceptually elevated out of the private realm of home and family, recognised as a public good and founded upon the socialisation of caring labour. Accordingly, it is a goal which cannot be fully realised without significant changes to law at work. It is essential that terms and conditions of employment are not permitted to rest as private matters, in private houses, but are recreated as a topic of urgent public interest. Political demands for change must take account of social care as a socialised and multidimensional concern. It is only with such an approach that the gendered crisis in the regulation of work which is being played out in the homecare industry can be brought to the fore. Hence, the future strength of social care provision in the UK depends upon public conversations in which questions about the value of women's contribution to the economy in general, and the value which is placed on their labour, can be connected to concern for the chronic underfunding of homecare. There are overwhelmingly pragmatic reasons why discussions about social care must not be 'constrained' by regard for private, individualised needs. Changes to the world of work, to the economy, to the role of the state and to the structure of families exemplify that social care is a public and political issue and its erosion demands a vocal response from the public at large. The creation of state-led private markets in caregiving has highlighted that without adequate attention to the realisation of universal labour standards and the importance of collective bargaining, sexism and class bias are (re)constituted in the labour market and justified in law.

The aversion of some politicians to the social provision of care is occasionally laid bare in their contributions to House of Commons debates. For example, the antipathy towards state-funded social care of Sir Alan Duncan MP was inherent in his observation that people who were concerned about the non-payment of tax by the wealthy were merely 'low achievers' who 'hate people who look after their own families' (Hansard, col. 34, 11 April 2016). He appeared to conveniently overlook the fact that it is the labour of working-class women which enables people with greater economic resources to carry such delusions of independence. While wealthy people 'look after their own' by buying in the domestic labour of others, women without wealth are destined to look after the families of others, either through their employment as modern-day domestic servants or through their deployment in the service of the state. On a separate occasion, Dr Phillip Lee MP intervened in a House of Commons debate about the abuse of older people in residential care homes to ponder, 'Why our society outsources the care of elderly loved ones to the state?' He proposed that the abuse of older people in residential care would be remedied if elderly relatives were looked after by their own families, rather than the state (Hansard, col. 955, 1 May 2014). Setting aside his failure to take into account the frequency with which older people are exposed to abuse by family members, his political perspective rests on gendered assumptions about family responsibility and a class-based rejection of universal state support.

The basic tenets of the post-war social care settlement between the state and the British people, in which the state carries responsibility for meeting care needs, are under systematic political attack. A major speech by Jeremy Hunt MP as Secretary of State for Health, illustrates how conceptions of excessive dependency are deployed as political justifications for the erosion of homecare services (Local Government Association Conference, Speech: *Personal Responsibility,* 1 July 2015). He characterised Britain's ageing population as a 'burning platform' upon which public services stood and warned, 'if we are to rise to the challenges we face, taking care of older relatives and friends will need to become part of everyone's life'. He chastised his audience in relation to 'our national shame', in which one in ten older people have contact with their family less than once a month, and he sounded a warning bell that this 'national picture is far from kind and far from decent'. His underpinning message, that dependence on the state is repugnant, shifted from depicting the care needs of older people as being so excessive as to warrant fear and panic, to the apparent laziness and irresponsibility of families who fail to meet an imagined normative threshold of monthly familial oversight. Set within a framework of 'national shame', the implication is of a threat to the social fabric of the nation. It is presumed that when women fall short of their family obligations (because care within families is gendered) they also err in their duty as responsible citizens. Meanwhile, the Health Secretary praised the 'magnificent' work of the nation's 6 million unpaid carers and did not mention paid caregivers; not even once. This points to the gendering of class and the ease with which moral distinctions are drawn between paid and unpaid care. It is hard to imagine that a major political speech by a government minister could be made about the NHS without mention of the doctors and nurses who populate it. However, such is the humiliation of homecare workers that they not only pass without acknowledgment, but their work is represented by the government as an excess of state dependency, a symbol of social weakness and an indicator of national shame.

It is also the case that judges in the UK's highest courts do not shy away from asserting that care of the elderly is not a fitting responsibility of the state. In *YL* v. *Birmingham City Council*, Lord Mance expressed, 'I do not regard the actual provision [...] of care and accommodation for those unable to arrange it themselves as an inherently governmental function' ([2007] UKHL 27 [115]). In support, Lord Neuberger asserted that the provision of care is not a function which is 'intrinsically, of a public nature' [138]. When tasked with shaping the responsibilities of the state in relation to the future of social care, it is evident that people in positions of considerable decision-making power may be predisposed to regard care as a private matter and believe it ought to be provided by families (presumably as the unpaid labour of women). According to this view, intervention by the state feeds social dependencies and disrupts patterns and rhythms of class and gender which are assumed to represent a pre-existing, natural and morally robust social order. It is the site of a titanic ideological clash, within which the working lives of homecare workers are situated. People who regard care as a private matter are responsible for the distribution of public standards and entitlements which are explicated in labour law. Labour standards, whether derived from common law or from statutory rights, are public standards. They are publicly deliberated, publicly available and represent the publicly settled terms upon which parliament has decided employment relationships should rest.

Meanwhile, social care is the antithesis of political conceptions in which care is regarded as a private matter into which the state should not ordinarily intrude. Social care is a consequence of care which has been *socialised* and is a political achievement that has changed the life opportunities of millions of women in the UK (and beyond). It has been essential to the twentieth-century liberation of women. The socialisation of care has enabled both women and men to have greater choice about whether or not, and how, to take up paid work. Adult children are no longer necessarily tethered to the communities where their parents live and the availability of social care to people of ordinary means has relieved the pressure to have children in order that someone might care for them in old age. Yet the political project of social care cannot be fully realised while the provision of paid care upon which it is based is subjected to derision, devaluation and discrimination. The promise of social care has floundered because it has depended upon a framework of labour law which continues to uphold sexist ideology and privileges notions of male interests. The structures, substance and application of labour law must now begin to reflect the economic and political imperative of paid care work to the contemporary organisation of families, to the economy and to the health of relations between men and women across society. For the socialisation of care to be a viable political project in the twenty-first century, the gendered inadequacies of labour law must be rectified through transformative legal change which respects the needs, voices and labour of working-class women.

References

ACAS 2013. *Disabled and elderly people and their personal assistants: the challenges of a unique employment relationship*. Policy Discussion Paper.
ACAS 2014. Changes to TUPE. http://www.acas.org.uk/media/pdf/t/r/9908-2901767-TSO-ACAS-TUPE_is_changing-ACCESSIBLE.pdf, date accessed 19 November 2016.
ACKER, J. 2006. *Class questions: feminist answers*. Rowman & Littlefield Publishers.
ADASS 2015. Budget Survey 2015 Report.
AGE CONCERN AND HELP THE AGED 2009. *One voice: shaping our ageing society*.
AGE UK 2013. *Direct payments for social care: options for managing the cash*.
AGE UK 2015. *Later life in the United Kingdom*.
ALKESON, V. & D'ARCY, C. 2014. *Zeroing in: balancing protection and flexibility*.
ANDERSON, B. 1983. *Imagined communities*. Verso.
ANDERSON, B. 2000. *Doing the dirty work? The global politics of domestic labour*. Zed Books.
ANDERSON, B. 2003. Just another job? The commodification of domestic labor. In: B. EHRENREICH & A. R. HOCHSCHILD (eds), *Global Woman: Nannies, Maids and Sex Workers in the New Economy*. Granta Books.
APEL, S. B. 1997. Gender and invisible work: musings of a woman law professor. *University of San Fransisco Law Review*, 31(4), 993–1016.
ARMSTRONG, D. 2002. *A new history of identity: A sociology of medical knowledge*. Palgrave.
ARONSON, J. & NEYSMITH, S. 1996. 'You're not just in there to do the work': Depersonalizing Policies and the Exploitation of Home Care Workers' Labor. *Gender & Society*, 10(1), 59–77.
ATKINSON, C., CROZIER, S. & LEWIS, L. 2016. *Factors that affect the recruitment and retention of domiciliary care workers and the extent to which these factors impact upon the quality of domiciliary care: Interim findings summary*, Welsh Government. http://gov.wales/docs/caecd/research/2016/160317-factors-affect-recruitment-retention-domiciliary-care-workers-final-en.pdf, date accessed 19 November 2016.
BARMES, L. 2015a. Common law confusion and empirical research in labour law. In: A. BOGG, C. COSTELLO, A. DAVIES & J. PRASSL (eds), *The Autonomy of Labour Law*. Hart/Bloomsbury.
BARMES, L. 2015b. Individual rights at work, methodological experimentation and the nature of law. In: A. LUDLOW & A. BLACKHAM (eds), *New Frontiers in Empirical Labour Law*. Hart.
BARNES, M. 2011. Abandoning care? A critical perspective on personalisation from an ethic of care. *Ethics and Social Welfare*, 5(2), 153–167.
BARNES, M. 2012. *Care in everyday life*. Policy Press.
BARRETT, M. 2014 [1980]. *Women's oppression today: The Marxist / Feminist encounter*. Verso.
BARRON, K. 2010. *House of Commons Health Committee, Social care: third report of session 2009–10, Vol. 2: Oral and written evidence*. Stationery Office.

BAUM, B. 2004. Feminist politics of recognition. *Signs*, 29, 1073–1102.
BEECROFT, A. 2011. Report on Employment Law, HM Gov.
BENETTO, J. 2009. *Staying on*. Equality and Human Rights Commision.
BENNETT, S. & STOCKTON, S. 2010. *Think local, Act personal. Best practice in direct payment support*, London Joint Improvement Partnership. http://www.thinklocalactpersonal.org.uk/_assets/BPDPS.pdf, date accessed 19 November 2016.
BERNSTEIN, S. 2006. The regulation of paid care work in the home in Quebec. In: J. FUDGE & R. OWENS (eds), *Precarious work, women and the new economy: The challenges to legal norms*. Hart.
BESSA, I., FORDE, C., MOORE, S. & STUART, M. 2013. *The National Minimum Wage, earnings and hours in the domiciliary care sector*. University of Leeds and Low Pay Commission.
BLACKETT, A. 2011. Emancipation in the idea of Labour Law: Commoditization, Resistance and Distributive Justice beyond borders. In: B. LANGUILLE & G. DAVIDOV (eds), *The Idea of Labour Law*. Oxford University Press.
BOFFEY, D. 2015. Cash-starved, demoralised, and sometimes cruel: How England's social care system fails the most vulnerable. *The Observer*, 8 August.
BOLTON, S. 2005. Women's work, dirty work: The gynaecology nurse as 'Other'. *Gender Work and Organisation*, 12(2), 169–86.
BOLTON, S. C. 2000. Who cares? Offering emotion work as a 'gift' in the nursing labour process. *Journal of Advanced Nursing*, 32(3), 580–586.
BOLTON, S. C. & WIBBERLEY, G. 2014. Domiciliary care: The formal and informal labour process. *Sociology*, 48 (4), 682–97 .
BORIS, E. & KLEIN, J. 2007. We were the invisible workforce: Unionizing homecare. In: D. COBBLE (ed.), *The sex of class*. Industrial Labor Relations (ILR) Press Cornell University.
BORIS, E. & KLEIN, J. 2014. The fate of care worker unionism and the promise of domestic worker organizing: An update. *Feminist Studies*, 40(2), 473–9.
BOWDEN, P. 1997. *Caring: Gender-sensitive ethics*. Routledge.
BOWDEN, P. 2000. An 'ethic of care' in clinical settings: encompassing 'feminine' and 'feminist' perspectives. *Nursing Philosophy*, 1(1), 36–49.
BOYDSTON, J. 1990. *Home & Work: Housework, wages, and the ideology of labor in the early republic*. Oxford University Press.
BRIGGS, C., MEAGHER, G. & HEALY, K. 2007. Becoming an industry: The struggle of social and community workers for award coverage, 1976–2001. *Journal of Industrial Relations*, 49, 497–521.
BROWN, W., DEAKIN, S., NASH, D. & OXENBRIDGE, S. 2000. The employment contract: From collective procedures to individual rights. *British Journal of Industrial Relations*, 38(4), 611–29.
BRUEGEL, I. & PERRONS, D. 1998. Deregulation and women's employment: The diverse experiences of women in Britain. *Feminist Economics*, 4(1), 103–125.
BUSBY, N. 2011. *A right to care?: Unpaid work in European Employment Law*. Oxford University Press.
BUSBY, N., MCDERMONT, M., ROSE, E., SALES, A. 2013. *Access to Justice in Employment Disputes: Surveying the terrain*. Institute of Employment Rights.

CANCIAN, F. M. & OLIKER, S. J. 2000. *Caring and gender.* Pine Forge Press.
CANGIANO, A., SHUTES, I., SPENCER, S. & LEESON, G. 2009. *Migrant Care Workers in Ageing Societies: Research findings in the UK.* COMPAS (ESRC Centre on Migration, Policy and Society), University of Oxford.
CARE QUALITY COMMISSION 2015. *The state of health care and adult social care in England.*
CARR, S. 2010. *Personalisation, productivity and efficiency.* Social Care Institute for Excellence.
CAVENDISH, C. 2013. *The Cavendish Review: Review of Healthcare assistants and support workers in the NHS and social care.* HM Government, https://www.gov.uk/government/uploads/system/uploads/attachment_data/file/236212/Cavendish_Review.pdf, date accessed 19 November 2016.
CENTRE FOR WORKFORCE INTELLIGENCE 2013. *How can we recruit and retain enough domiciliary care workers to meet future demand?* Horizon Scanning Workforce Briefing.
CENTRE FOR WORKFORCE INTELLIGENCE 2015. *Horizon 2035. Future demand for skills: Initial results.*
CHARLEBOIS, J. 2010. *Gender and the construction of hegemonic and oppositional femininities*, Lexington Books.
CHORLEY, M. 2014. Poor English of home help 'is putting the elderly at risk': Government adviser says care agencies must ensure staff have decent language skills. *Daily Mail*, 7 May.
CHRIS SKIDMORE MP 2012. *The social care market: Fixing a broken system.* Free Enterprise Group.
CLARK, H., GOUGH, H. & MACFARLANE, A. 2004. *'It pays dividends' Direct Payments and Older People*, Policy Press.
CLARKE, L. 1984. *Domiciliary services for the elderly*, Croom Helm.
CLISBY, S. & HOLDSWORTH, J. 2014. *Gendering women: Identity and mental wellbeing through the lifecourse.* Policy Press.
CLOUGH, P. & BARTON, L. 1998. *Articulating with difficulty: Research voices in inclusive education*, SAGE Publications.
CONAGHAN, J. 1999. Feminism and Labour Law: Contesting the terrain. In: A. MORRIS & T. O'DONNELL (eds), *Feminist perspectives on Employment Law.* Cavendish.
CONAGHAN, J. 2000. Reassessing the Feminist Theoretical Project in Law. *Journal of Law and Society*, 27(3), 351–385.
CONAGHAN, J. 2013. *Law and gender*, Oxford University Press.
CONNELLY, F. M. & CLANDININ, D. J. 1990. Stories of experience and narrative inquiry. *Educational Researcher*, 19(5), 2–14.
DAVIDOV, G. 2008. A purposive interpretation of the National Minimum Wage Act. *Modern Law Review*, 72(4), 581–606.
DAVIES, M. 2013. Law's truths and the truth about Law: Interdisciplinary refractions. In: M. DAVIES & V. E. MUNRO (eds), *The Ashgate Research Companion to feminist legal theory.* Ashgate.
DAVIS, P. & FREEDLAND, M. 1997. The impact of public law on labour law. *Industrial Law Journal*, 26(4), 311–35.

DEAKIN, S. 2001. The contract of employment: A study in legal evolution. *Historical Studies in Industrial Relations,* 11(Spring), 1–36.

DEAKIN, S. 2007. Does the 'personal employment contract' provide a basis for the reunification of Employment Law? *Industrial Law Journal,* 36(1), 68–83.

DEAKIN, S. 2010. Labour and Employment Laws. In: P. CANE & H. KRITZER, H. (eds), *The Oxford Handbook of Empirical Legal Research.* Oxford University Press.

DEAKIN, S. & MORRIS, G. 2009. *Labour Law.* Hart.

DEPARTMENT OF HEALTH 2006. Our Health, Our Care, Our Say – A new direction for Community Services (White paper). *Cm 6737.*

DEPARTMENT OF HEALTH 2007. *Putting people first: A shared vision and commitment to the transformation of adult social care.* http://webarchive.nationalarchives.gov.uk/20130107105354/http:/www.dh.gov.uk/prod_consum_dh/groups/dh_digitalassets/@dh/@en/documents/digitalasset/dh_081119.pdf, date accessed 19 November 2016.

DEPARTMENT OF HEALTH 2012. *Caring for our future: Reforming care and support.* Presented to Parliament by the Secretary of State for Health by Command of Her Majesty.

DEPARTMENT OF HEALTH 2012. *Reforming the law for adult care and support.* The Government's response to Law Commission report 326 on adult social care.

DEPARTMENT FOR BUSINESS, 2013. *Revision of the Transfer of Undertakings (Protection of Employment) Regulations 2006: Impact Assessment.*

DEPARTMENT FOR BUSINESS, 2014. *The Impact of the Working Time Regulations.*

DEPARTMENT FOR BUSINESS, 2016. *Tackling exploitation in the labour market: UK Government Response.* January.

DEXTER, M. & HARBERT, W. B. 1983. *The Home Help Service,* Tavistock.

DHSS 1976. *A lifestyle for the elderly.* HMSO.

DIAPER, A. & YEOMANS, P. 2016. Contribution to society: A footnote for the Care Act? *Practice: Social work in action,* 28(5), 331–9.

DISCLOSURE AND BARRING SERVICE 2012a. *DBS referrals guide: referral and decision making process. Version 3.*

DISCLOSURE AND BARRING SERVICE 2012b. *Referral Guidance: Frequently asked questions.*

DONZELOT, J. 2008. Michel Foucault and Liberal Intelligence. *Economy and Society,* 37(1), 115–134.

DORLING, D. 2014. Older people in Britain are dying before their time. *New Republic,* 15 February.

DU BOIS, W. E. B. 1903. *The Souls of Black Folk.* AC McClurg.

DUFFY, M. 2005. Reproducing Labor Inequalities. *Gender & Society,* 19(1), 66–82.

DUFFY, M. 2007. Doing the dirty work. *Gender & Society,* 21(3), 313–36.

DUFFY, M. 2011. *Making care count: A century of gender, race, and paid care work,* Rutgers University Press.

DUFFY, M., RANDY, A. & HAMMONDS, C. 2013. Counting care work: The empirical and policy applications of care theory. *Social Problems,* 60(2), 145–67.

EBORALL, C., FENTON, W. & WOODROW, S. 2010. *The state of the adult social care workforce in England.* Skills for Care.

ECORY 2012. *Safeguarding in the Workplace: What are the lessons to be learned from cases referred to the Independent Safeguarding Authority?* Independent Safeguarding

Authority http://ineqe.com/chscb/wp-content/uploads/2015/02/ISA-Safeguarding-in-the-Workplace-Research-Report-May-2012.pdf, date accessed 19 November 2016.

EHRC 2011. *Close to home: An inquiry into older people and human rights in home care.* Equality and Human Rights Commission.

EHRC 2015. *Is Britain fairer? The state of equality and human rights.* Equality and Human Rights Commission.

ENGLAND, K. & DYCK, I. 2011. Managing the body work of home care. *Sociology of Health and Illness*, 33(2), 206–19.

ENGLAND, P. 2005. Emerging theories of care work. *Annual Review of Sociology*, 31(1), 381–99.

ESTÉVEZ-ABE, M. & HOBSON, B. 2015. Outsourcing domestic (care) work: The politics, policies, and political economy. *Social Politics: International Studies in Gender, State and Society*, 22(2), 133–46.

EWICK, P. & SILBEY, S. 1998. *The common place of law: Stories from everyday life*, University of Chicago Press.

EWING, K. 1988. The state and industrial relations: Collective laissez-faire revisited. *Historical Studies in Industrial Relations*, 5(Spring), 1–31.

EWING, K. 2005. The function of trade unions. *Industrial Law Journal*, 34(1), 1–22.

FENTON, W. 2013. *Size and structure of the adult social care sector and workforce in England*. Skills for Care.

FERGUSON, I. 2012. Personalisation, social justice and social work: A reply to Simon Duffy. *Journal of Social Work Practice*, 26(1), 55–73.

FERNANDEZ, J.-L., SNELL, T. & WISTOW, G. 2014. *Changes in the patterns of social care provision in England 2005/6 to 2012/13.* Personal Social Services Research Unit Discussion Paper 2867.

FINEMAN, J 2013, Cronyism, corruption and political intrigue: A new approach for old problems in public sector employment, *Charleston Law Review*, 8(1), 51–112.

FINEMAN, M. A 2008, The vulnerable subject: Anchoring equality in the human condition, *Yale Journal of Law and Feminism*, 20(1), 1–23.

FLOOD, J. 2005. Socio-legal ethnography. In: R. BANAKAR, R. & M. TRAVERS, M. (eds), *Theory and method in socio-legal research.*

FOLBRE, N. 1994. Children as public goods. *American Economic Review*, 84(2), 86–90.

FOLBRE, N. 2001. *The invisible heart: Economics and family values.* New Press.

FORDER, J., KNAPP, M. & WISTOW, G. 1996. Competition in the Mixed Economy of Care. *Journal of Social Policy*, 25(2), 201–221.

FORREST, A. 1996. Women and Industrial Relations Theory: No room in the discourse. *Industrial Relations*, 48(3), 409–40.

FRANCIS, J. 2013a. An Overview of the UK domiciliary care sector. UK Homecare Association, Version 33.

FRANCIS, R. C. 2013b. *The Mid Staffordshire NHS Foundation Trust Public Inquiry.*

FRASER, N. 2013. *Fortunes of Feminism.* Verso.

FREDMAN, S. 2004. Women at work: The broken promise of flexicurity. *Industrial Law Journal*, 33(4), 299–319

FREDMAN, S. 2006. Precarious norms for precarious workers. In: J. FUDGE & R. OWENS (eds), *Precarious Work, Women and the New Economy. The Challenges to Legal Norms.* Hart.

FREDMAN, S. 2008. Reforming Equal Pay Laws. *Industrial Law Journal,* 37(3), 193–218.

FRIEDMAN, H. & MEREDEEN, S. 1980. *The dynamics of industrial conflict: Lessons from Ford,* Croom Held.

FUDGE, J. 1996. Rungs on the Labour Law ladder: Using gender to challenge heirarchy. *Saskatchewan Law Review,* 60(2), 237–64.

FUDGE, J. 2011. Global care chains, employment agencies, and the conundrum of jurisdiction: Decent work for Domestic Workers in Canada. *Canadian Journal of Women and the Law,* 23(1), 235–64.

FUDGE, J. 2012. Blurring Legal Boundaries: Regulating for Decent Work. In: J. FUDGE, S. MCCRYSTAL & K. SANKARAN (eds), *Challenging the legal boundaries of work regulation.* Hart.

FUDGE, J. 2013. From women and Labour Law to putting gender and law to work. In: M. DAVIES, & V. MUNRO, V. (eds) *A research companion to Feminist Legal Theory.* Ashgate.

FUDGE, J., MCCRYSTAL, S. & SANKARAN, K. 2012. *Challenging the legal boundaries of work regulation.* Hart Publishing.

FUDGE, J. & MCDERMOTT, P. 1991. *Just wages: A feminist assessment of pay equity,* University of Toronto Press.

FUDGE, J. & VOSKO, L. 2001. By whose standards? Regulating the Canadian Labour Market. *Economic and Industrial Democracy* 22(3), 327–56.

GARDINER, L. 2016. *Rising to the Challenge: Early evidence on the introduction of the National Living Wage in the social care sector.* Resolution Foundation.

GARDINER, L. 2015. *The rise and rise(?) of zero-hours contracts.* Resolution Foundation.

GARDINER, L. & HUSSEIN, S. 2015. *As if we cared? The costs and benefits of a living wage for social care workers.* Resolution Foundation.

GAUTIE, J. & SCHMITT, J. 2010. *Low-wage work in the wealthy world.* Russell Sage Foundation.

GHEERA, M. 2012. *Direct payments and personal budgets for social care.* SN/SP/3735 House of Commons Library.

GLASBY, J. & LITTLECHILD, R. 2009. *Direct payments and personal budgets: Putting personalisation into practice.* Policy Press.

GLENDINNING, C. 2000. New kinds of care, new kinds of relationships: How purchasing affects relationships of giving and recieving personal assistance. *Health and Social Care in the Community,* 8(3), 201–211.

GLUCKSMANN, M. A. 2005. Shifting boundaries and interconnections: Extending the total social organisation of labour. *Sociological Review,* 53(2), 19–36.

GRAHAM, H. 1991. The concept of caring in feminist research: The case of domestic service. *Sociology,* 25(1), 61–78.

GRANT, L., YEANDLE, S. & BUCKNER, L. 2006. *Gender and employment in local labour markets: Working below potential, women and part-time work.* Sheffield Hallam University.

GREGG, P. & GARDINER, L. 2015. *A steady job? The UK's record on labour market security and stability since the millenium.* Resolution Foundation.

HALL, L. & WREFORD, S. 2007. *National Survey of Care Workers FINAL Report.* JN142079, Skills for Care.

HALL, P. & LAMONT, M. 2013. Why social relations matter for politics and successful societies. *Annual Review of Political Science,* 16(May), 49–71.

HAMMERSLEY, M. & ATKINSON, P. 2007. *Ethnography: Principles in practice*. Routledge.

HASLER, F. & MARSHALL, S. 2013. *Trust is the key: Increasing the take-up of direct payments*. Think Local Act Personal and Disability Rights UK.

HASTINGS, S. 2003. *Pay Inequalities in Local Government*. Submission to Local Government Pay Commission on behalf of the Trade Union side.

HAYES, L. J. B. 2015a. Care and Control: Are the national minimum wage entitlements of homecare workers at risk under the Care Act 2014? *Industrial Law Journal*, 44(4), 492–521.

HAYES, L. J. B. 2015b. Sex, class and CCTV: The covert surveillance of paid homecare workers. In: L. ADKINS & M. DEVER (eds), *The Post-Fordist sexual contract: Living and working in contingency*. Palgrave Macmillan.

HAYES, L. J. B. & MOORE, S. 2017. Care in a time of austerity: The electronic monitoring of working time in homecare. *Gender, Work & Organization*. In press.

HAYES, L. & NOVITZ, T. 2014. *Trade unions and economic inequality*, Institute of Employment Rights. http://www.ier.org.uk/publications/trade-unions-and-economic-inequality date accessed 19 November 2016.

HSCI 2012. *Community Care Statistics, Social Services Activity, England, 2011–2012, Final Release*.

HSCI 2016. *Personal Social Services: Staff of Social Services Departments, England, as at Sept 2015*.

HEBSON, G. 2009. Renewing class analysis in studies of the workplace: A comparison of working-class and middle-class women's aspirations and identities. *Sociology*, 43(1), 27–44.

HELD, V. 2002. Care and the extension of markets. *Hypatia*, 17(2), 19–33.

HILLS, J. 2010. *An anatomy of economic inequality in the UK: Report of the National Equality Panel*. Government Equalities Office and London School of Economics.

HIMMELWEIT, S. 2008. Policy on care: A help or hindrence to gender equality? In: J. L. SCOTT, S. DEX & H. JOSHI (eds), *Women and employment: Changing lives and new challenges*. Edward Elgar.

HIRSCH, B. T. 2005. Why do part-time workers earn less? The role of worker and job skills. *Industrial and Labor Relations Review*, 58(4), 525–51.

HM REVENUE AND CUSTOMS 2013. *National Minimum Wage compliance in the social care sector*. Evaluation Report published November 2013.

HOCHSCHILD, A. 2000. Global care chains and emotional surplus value. In: A. GIDDENS & W. HUTTON (eds), *On the edge: Living with global capitalism*. Jonathon Cape.

HOCHSCHILD, A. R. 1983. *The managed heart: Commercialization of human feeling*, University of California Press.

HOLMES, J. 2015. An overview of the UK domiciliary care sector. UK Home Care Association.

HOLSTEIN, J. & GUBRIUM, J. 2005. Interpretive practices and social action. In: N. K. DENZIN & Y. S. LINCOLN (eds), *Sage Handbook of Qualitative Research*. 3rd edition. Sage.

HONNETH, A. 2004. Organising self-realisation: Some paradoxes of Individualization. *European Journal of Social Theory*, 7(4), 463–78.

HONNETH, A. & HARTMANN, M. 2006. Paradoxes of Capitalism. *Constellations*, 13(1), 41–58.

HOWARD, C. & KENWAY, P. 2004. *Why worry any more about the low paid?* New Policy Institute.
HOWARD, R. 2012. The Care Professionals Benevolent Fund. *carehome.co.uk*, 19 June.
HOWELL, C. 2005. *Trade Unions and the State: The construction of industrial relations institutions in Britain, 1890–2000*. Princeton University Press.
HUMPHRIES, R. 2011. *Social care funding and the NHS – An impending crisis?* The King's Fund.
HUNTER, R. 2013. Contesting the dominant paradigm: Feminist critiques of Liberal Legalism. In: M. DAVIES & V. E. MUNRO (eds), *The Ashgate Research Companion to Feminist Legal Theory*. Ashgate.
HUPPATZ, K. 2009. Reworking Bourdieu's 'Capital': Feminine and female capitals in the field of paid caring work. *Sociology,* 43(1), 45–66.
HUSSEIN, S. 2011. Men in the English care sector. *Social Care Workforce Periodical*, Issue 14, Social Care Workforce Research Unit, Kings College London.
HUSSEIN, S. & MANTHORPE, J. 2014. Structural marginalisation among the long-term care workforce in England: Evidence from mixed-effect models of national pay data. *Ageing & Society,* 34(1), 21–41.
HUSSEIN, S., STEVENS, M., MANTHORPE, J., RAPAPORT, J., MARTINEAU, S., & HARRIS, J. 2009. Banned from working in social care: A secondary analysis of staff characteristics and reasons for their referrals to the POVA list in England and Wales. *Health & Social Care in the Community,* 17(5), 423–33.
INSTITUTE OF HOME-HELP ORGANISERS 1958. *The training of home-helps: Correspondence course.*
INSTITUTE OF PUBLIC CARE 2013. *Evidence review – Adult safeguarding.* https://ipc.brookes.ac.uk/publications/pdf/Evidence_Review_-_Adult_Safeguarding.pdf, date accessed 19 November 2016.
IPC MARKET ANALYSIS CENTRE 2012. *Where the heart is ... A review of the older people's homecare market in England.* Oxford Brookes University.
JAFFE, M., MCKENNA, B. & VENNER, L. 2008. *Equal Pay, privatisation and procurement,* Institute of Employment Rights.
JAMES, N. 1992. Care = organisation + physical labour + emotional labour. *Sociology of Health & Illness,* 14(4), 488–509.
JENSON, J. 1989. The talents of women, the skills of men: Flexible specialisation and women. In: S. HYMAN (ed.), *The Transformation of Work?*. Unwin Hyman.
JOHNSON, E. K. 2015. The business of care: The moral labour of care workers. *Sociology of Health & Illness,* 37(1), 112–26.
JULIUS, D. 2008. *Public Services Industry Review: Understanding the Public Services Industry.* HM Gov., BERR Dept. http://webarchive.nationalarchives.gov.uk/20121212135622/http:/www.bis.gov.uk/files/file46965.pdf, date accessed 19 November 2016.
KAPLAN DANIELS, A. 1987. Invisible work. *Social Problems,* 34(5), 403–15.
KELLY, D. 2013. Reflecting on the implications of the Care Act 2014 for providers. *Journal of Care Services Management,* 7(3), 74–5.
KETER, V. & JARRETT, T. 2011. Transfer of Undertakings (TUPE), SN/BT/1064, House of Commons Library.
KILPATRICK, C. & FREEDLAND, M. 2004. United Kingdom. In: S. SCIARRA, P. DAVIES & M. FREEDLAND (eds), *Employment policy and the regulation of part-time work in the European Union: A comparative analysis*. Cambridge University Press.

KINGSMILL, D. 2014. *The Kingsmill Review: Taking Care*. An Independent Report into working conditions in the care sector.
KLEIN, D.C. 1991 The humiliation dynamic: An overview. Journal of Primary Prevention, 12(2),93– 121.
KNAPP, M., FERNÁNDEZ, J.-L., KENDALL, J., BEECHAM, J., NORTHEY, J., & RICHARDSON, A. 2005. *Developing social care: The current position. Executive Summary*. Personal Social Services Research Unit.
KOEHLER, I. 2014. Key to Care. *Report of the Burstow Commission on the future of the home care workforce*, Local Government Information Unit, http://www.lgiu.org.uk/wp-content/uploads/2014/12/KeyToCare.pdf, date accessed 19 November 2016.
KOSNY, A. & MACEACHEN, E. 2010. Gendered, invisible work in non-profit social service organizations: Implications for worker health and safety. *Gender, Work & Organization*, 17(4), 359–380.
KOTISWARAN, P. 2011. *Dangerous sex, invisible labor: Sex work and the law in India*, Princeton University Press.
LACEY, N. 1987. Legislation against sex discrimination: Questions from a feminist perspective. *Journal of Law and Society*, 14(4), 411–21.
LACEY, N. 1998. *Unspeakable subjects: Feminist essays in Legal and Social Theory*, Hart.
LAING, W. 2014. *Strategic commissioning of long term care for older people*. Laing Buisson.
LAKEY, J. 1994. *Caring about independence: Disabled people and the Independent Living Fund*, Policy Studies Institute.
LAND, H. & HIMMELWEIT, S. 2010. *Who cares: Who pays?* Unison.
LAQUEUR, T. W. 1990. *Making sex: Body and gender from the Greeks to Freud*, Harvard University Press.
LAW COMMISSION 2011. Adult social care. *LAW COM No 326*, House of Commons Stationary Office https://www.gov.uk/government/uploads/system/uploads/attachment_data/file/247900/0941.pdf, date accessed 19 November 2016.
LAWSON, A. 2007. Geographies of Ccare and responsibility. *Annals of the Association of American Geographers*, 97(1), 1–11.
LEECE, J. 2006. Working with direct payments: 'It's not like being at work': A study to investigate stress and job satisfaction in employees of direct payments users. In: J. LEECE & J. BORNAT (eds.), *Developments in direct payments*. Policy Press.
LEECE, J. 2010. Paying the piper and calling the tune: Power and the direct payment relationship. *British Journal of Social Work*, 40(1), 188–206.
LEECE, J. & LEECE, D. 2011. Personalisation: perceptions of the role of social work in a world of brokers and budgets. *British Journal of Social Work*, 40, 1847–1865.
LEIDNER, B., SHEIKH, H. & GINGES, J. 2012. Affective dimensions of intergroup humiliation. *PLoS One*, 7(9): e46375. doi:10.1371/journal.pone.0046375.
LESSA, I. 2006. Discursive struggles within social welfare: Restaging teen motherhood. *British Journal of Social Work*, 36(2), 283–98.
LEWIS, J. & GLENNERSTER, H. 1996. *Implementing the New Community Care*, Open University Press.
LEWIS, J. & WEST, A. 2014. Re-shaping social care services for older people in England: Policy development and the problem of achieving 'good care'. *Journal of Social Policy*, 43(1), 1–18.
LIEBLING, A. 2015. Description at the edge? I-it I-thou relations and action in Prisons Research. *International Journal for Crime, Justice and Democracy*, 4(1), 18–32.

LIVINGSTONE, D. & SAWCHUK, P. 2005. Hidden knowledge: Working-class capacity in the knowledge-based economy. *Studies in the Education of Adults,* 37(2), 110–22.

LOCAL GOVERNMENT ASSOCIATION. 2014. *Local Government Earnings Survey 2013/2014.* http://www.local.gov.uk/research-pay-and-workforce/-/journal_content/56/10180/4094123/ARTICLE, date accessed 19 November 2016.

LOCAL GOVERNMENT EMPLOYERS ASSOCIATION 2006. *Unblocking the Route to Equal Pay.*

LOPEZ, S. 2004. *Reorganizing the Rust Belt: An inside study of the American labor movement,* University of California Press.

LOURIE, J. 1998. Working Time Regulations Research Paper 98/82. London: House of Commons Library Research Paper.

LOURIE, J. 1999. National Minimum Wage Research Paper 99/18. London: House of Commons Library Research Paper.

LOW PAY COMMISSION 2011. National Minimum Wage Report. UK Government.

LUCAS, R., ATKINSON, C. & GODDEN, J. 2009. *Reward and incentives research: Nursing homes, residential homes and domiciliary care establishments. Phase 2: case studies.* Skills for Care.

LUDLOW, A. 2015. *Privatising public prisons,* Hart.

LUDLOW, A. & BLACKHAM, A. (eds.) 2015. *New frontiers in Labour Law research.* Hart.

MCCALL, L. 1992. Does Gender fit? Bourdieu, Feminism and conceptions of social order. *Theory and Society,* 21(6), 837–61.

MCCANN, D. & MURRAY, J. 2014. Prompting formalisation through labour market regulation: A 'Framed Flexibility' Model for domestic work. *Industrial Law Journal,* 43(3), 319–48.

MACDONALD, C. L. & MERRILL, D. A. 2002. 'It shouldn't have to be a trade': Recognition and redistribution in care work advocacy. *Hypatia,* 17(2), 67–83.

MCGRATH, S. & DEFILIPPIS, J. 2009. Social reproduction as unregulated work. *Work, employment and society,* 23(1), 66–83.

MCINNES, T., ALDRIDGE, H., BUSHE, S., KENWAY, P. & TINSON, A. 2013. *Monitoring poverty and social exclusion.* Joseph Rowntree Foundation and New Policy Institute.

MCKAY, S. 2013. Migrant workers in hard times. In: B. RYAN (ed.), *Labour migration in hard times: Reforming labour market regulation?.* Institute of Employment Rights.

MCKIE, L., GREGORY, S. & BOWLBY, S. 2002. Shadow times: The temporal and spatial frameworks and experiences of caring and working. *Sociology,* 36(4), 897–924.

MACKIE DM, M. A., SMITH ER 2009. Intergroup Emotions Theory. *Handbook of prejudice, stereotyping, and discrimination,* T. D. Nelson.

MACKINNON, C. A. 2007. *Women's lives, Men's laws,* Belknap Press of Harvard University Press.

MCMULLEN, J. 2006. An analysis of the Transfer of Undertakings (Protection of Employment) Regulations. *Industrial Law Journal,* 35(2), 113–39.

MCMULLEN, J. 2012. Re-structuring and TUPE. *Industrial Law Journal,* 41(3), 358–62.

MCNAY, L. 2009. Self as enterprise: Dilemmas of control and resistance in Foucault's *The Birth of Biopolitics. Theory, Culture and Society,* 26(6), 55–77.

MANNING, A. & PETRONGOLO, B. 2005. *The part-time pay penalty.* Centre for Economic Performance, LSE Discussion Paper No 679.

MANTHORPE, J. & STEVENS, M. 2006. Decision and debate: Addressing the implications of the POVA banning list. *Journal of Adult Protection,* 8(2), 3–14.

MARGALIT, A. 1998. *The Decent Society,* Harvard University Press.

MARX-FERREE, M. 1976. Working-class jobs: Housework and paid work as sources of satisfaction. *Social Problems,* 23(4), 431–41.

MASSEY, D. 2005. *For Space,* Sage.

MASSEY, D. 2013. Vocabularies of the economy. In: S. HALL, D. MASSEY & M. RUSTIN (eds), *After Neoliberalism? The Kilburn Manifesto.* Soundings.

MEAGHER, G. 2006. What can we expect from paid carers? *Politics and Society,* 34(1), 33–54.

MEAGHER, G. & KING, D. (eds.) 2009. *Paid care in Australia: Politics, profits, practices.* Sydney University Press.

MEANS, R. & SMITH, R. 1985. *The development of welfare services for elderly people,* Croom Helm.

MILLIGAN, C. & WILES, J. 2010. Landscapes of care. *Progress in Human Geography,* 34(6), 736–54.

MOORE, F. 2013. 'Go and see Nell; She'll put you right': The wisewoman and working-class health care in early twentieth-century Lancashire. *Social History of Medicine,* 26(4), 695–714.

MORRIS, A. & O'DONNELL, T. 1999. *Feminist perspectives on employment law,* Cavendish.

MORRIS, J. 2004. Independent living and community care: A disempowering framework. *Disability & Society,* 19(5), 427–42.

MORTIMER, J. & GREEN, M. 2015. Briefing: The health and care of older people in England.

MOUSTAKAS, C. E. 1994. *Phenomenological research methods.* Sage.

MULLAN, P. 2000. *The imaginary time bomb.* I.B.Tauris.

MURRAY, P. R. 2013. Behind the panel: Examining invisible labour in the comics publishing industry. *Publishing research quarterly,* 29(4), 336–43.

NATIONAL AUDIT OFFICE 11 May 2016. *Ensuring employers comply with National Minimum Wage Regulations.* Department for Business, Innovation and Skills; HM Revenue and Customs.

NATIONAL AUDIT OFFICE 2014. *Adult social care in England: Overview.* Report by the Comptroller and Auditor General; Department of Health; Department for Communities and Local Government.

NATIONAL CARE FORUM 2015. *Personnel Statistics Survey Report.*

NATIONAL JOINT COUNCIL FOR LOCAL GOVERNMENT 1998. Report of the Bonus Technical Working Group.

NEEDHAM, C. 2014. The spaces of personalisation: Place and distance in caring labour. *Social Policy and Society,* 14(3), 357–69.

NÄRE, L. 2011. The moral economy of domestic and care labour: Migrant workers in Naples, Italy. *Sociology,* 45(3), 396–412.

OECD 2010. *How good is part-time work?* Employment Outlook: Moving Beyond the Jobs Crisis, Organisation for Economic Co-operation and Development.

OFFICE FOR NATIONAL STATISTICS 2013a. *Full Report:Women in the labour market.*

OFFICE FOR NATIONAL STATISTICS 2013b. *General Lifestyle Survey 2011.*

OFFICE FOR NATIONAL STATISTICS 2013c. *Hourly Pay for All Employee Jobs*
OFFICE FOR NATIONAL STATISTICS 2014a. *Characteristics of Home Workers*. June.
OFFICE FOR NATIONAL STATISTICS 2014b. *Health Expectancies at Birth and at Age 65 in the United Kingdom, 2009–11.*
OFFICE FOR NATIONAL STATISTICS 2015a. *Estimate of employee jobs paid less than the living wage.*
OFFICE FOR NATIONAL STATISTICS 2015b. *Contracts with no guaranteed hours, Labour Force Statistics.*
OFFICE FOR NATIONAL STATISTICS 2016. *All Employees: Annual Survey of Hours and Earnings*, October.
PAHL, R. 2005. Are all communities communities in the mind? *Sociological Review*, 53(4), 621–40.
PALMER, E. & EVELINE, J. 2012. Sustaining Low Pay in Aged Care Work. *Gender, Work and Organization*, 19(3), 254–75.
PAVOLINI, E. & RANCI, C. 2008. Restructuring the Welfare State: Reforms in long-term care in Western European countries. *Journal of European Social Policy*, 18(3), 246–59.
PAZ-FUCHS, A. 2008. *Welfare to work: Conditional rights in social policy*, Oxford University Press on Demand.
PEACOCK, M., BISSELL, P. & OWEN, J. 2014. Shaming encounters: Reflections on contemporary understandings of sociali and health. *Sociology*, 48(2), 387–402.
PECK, J. & TICKELL, A. 2007. Conceptualising Neoliberalism, Thinking Thatcherism. In: H. LEITNER, J. PECK & E. S. SHEPPARD (eds) *Contesting Neoliberalism: Urban frontiers*. Guildford Press.
POLLERT, A. & CHARLWOOD, A. 2009. The vulnerable worker in Britain and problems at work. *Work, Employment and Society*, 23(2), 343–62.
POLLIO, H. R., HENLEY, T. B. & THOMPSON, C. J. 1997. *The phenomenology of everyday life*, Cambridge University Press.
POOLE, T. 2000. Commentary. Judicial review and public employment: decision-making on the public–private divide. *Industrial Law Journal*, 29(1), 61–7.
POTTER, J. 2004. Discourse analysis as a way of analysing naturally occurring talk. In: D. SILVERMAN (ed.), *Qualitative Research: Theory, method and practice*. Sage.
PRATT, G. 1997. Stereotypes and ambivalence: The construction of domestic workers in Vancouver, British Columbia. *Gender, Place and Culture*, 4(2), 159–78.
PUBLIC ACCOUNTS COMMITTEE 2014. *Sixth Report – Adult Social Care in England.* 2 July. QUIGLEY, C. 2005. *The corpse: A history*, McFarland.
REAY, D. 1998. Rethinking social class: Qualitative perspectives on class and gender. *Sociology*, 32(2), 259–75.
REAY, D. 2001. Finding or losing yourself?: Working-class relationships to education. *Journal of Education Policy*, 16(4), 333–46.
REAY, D. 2003. A risky business? Mature working-class women wtudents and access to higher education. *Gender and Education*, 15(3), 301–17.
REAY, D. 2004. Gendering Bourdieu's Concept of Capitals? Emotional capital, women and social class. In: L. ADKINS & B. SKEGGS (eds), *Feminism after Bourdieu*. Blackwell.
RHODES, R. 2005. The hollowing out of the State: The changing nature of the public service in Britain. *The Political Quarterly*, 65(2), 138–51.
RINGROSE, J. & WALKERDINE, V. 2008. Regulating the Abject. *Feminist Media Studies*, 8(3), 227–46.

RODGERS, L. 2009. The notion of working time. *Industrial Law Journal*, 38(1), 80–8.
RUBERY, J. & GRIMSHAW, D. 2007. *Undervaluing women's work*. Equal Opportunities Commission.
RUBERY, J., GRIMSHAW, D., HEBSON, G. & UGARTE, S. 2015. 'It's All About Time': Time as Contested Terrain in the Management and Experience of Domiciliary Care Work in England. *Human Resource Management*. 54(5), 753–72.
RUBERY, J., HEBSON, G., GRIMSHAW, D., CARROLL, M., SMITH, L., MARCHINGTON, L. & UGARTE, S. 2011. *The recruitment and retention of a care workforce for older people*, Department of Health.
RUBERY, J. & UNWIN, P. 2011. Bringing the employer back in: Why social care needs a standard employment relationship. *Human Resource Management Journal*, 21(2), 122–37.
RUHS, M. & ANDERSON, B. 2010. *Who needs migrant workers?: Labour shortages, immigration, and public policy*. Oxford University Press.
SANDERS, P. 1982. Phenomenology: A new way of viewing organizational research. *Academy of Management Review*, 7(3), 353–60.
SAYER, A. 2000. Moral economy and political economy. *Studies in Political Economy*, 61(1), 79–104.
SAYER, A. 2005. Class, moral worth and recognition. *Sociology*, 39(5), 947–963.
SCOTT, H. 2004. Reconceptualising the nature and health consequences of work related insecurity for the new economy. *International Journal of Health Services*, 34(1), 143–53.
SCOTT, J. W. 1986. Gender: A useful category of historical analysis. *American Historical Review*, 91(5), 1053–1075.
SCOURFIELD, P. 2005. Implementing the Community Care (Direct Payments) Act: Will the supply of personal assistants meet the demand and at what price? *Journal of Social Policy*, 34(3), 469–488.
SEVENHUIJSEN, S. 2005. A third way? Moralities, ethics and families. In: A. CARLING, S. DUNCAN & R. EDWARDS (eds), *Analysing families: Morality and rationality in policy and practice*. Taylor & Francis.
SHUTES, I. 2011. *The role of migrant workers in the social care sector*. All-Party Parliamentary Group on Migration Briefing.
SHUTES, I. & CHIATTI, C. 2012. Migrant labour and the marketisation of care for older people: The employment of migrant care workers. *Journal of European Social Policy*, 22(40), 392–405.
SIMPSON, B. 2009. The Employment Act 2008's Amendments to the National Minimum Wage Legislation. *Industrial Law Journal*, 38(1), 57–64.
SKEGGS, B. 1997. *Formations of class and gender: Becoming respectable*. Sage.
SKEGGS, B. 2005. The making of class and gender through visualizing moral subject formation. *Sociology*, 39(5), 965–982.
SKILLS FOR CARE 2010. *Issue 14 – Migrant Workers*. nmds-sc briefing. https://www.nmds-sc-online.org.uk/Get.aspx?id=648745 date accessed 23 December 2016.
SKILLS FOR CARE 2013. *Issue 20 – Meeting the future workforce challenges of adult social care*. nmds-sc briefing. https://www.nmds-sc-online.org.uk/Get.aspx?id=/Research/Briefings/NMDS-SC%20briefing%20issue%2020%20vfweb.pdf date accessed 23 December 2016.

SKILLS FOR CARE 2015a. *The size and structure of the adult social care sector and workforce.*
SKILLS FOR CARE 2015b. *The state of the adult social care sector and workforce in England.*
SKILLS FOR CARE. 2016. *Workforce Ethnicity Profile Calculator* [Online]. Available at: https://www.nmds-sc-online.org.uk/reportengine/GuestDashboard.aspx?type=Ethnicity [Accessed 22 February 2016].
SLASBERG, C. & BERESFORD, P. 2014. Government guidance to the Care Act – Undermining Ambitions of Change. *Disability and Society,* 29(10), 1677–82.
SLASBERG, C. & BERESFORD, P. 2015. Building on the original strength of direct payments to create a better future for social care. *Disability & Society,* 30(3), 479–83.
SMITH, H. 1981. The problem of equal pay for equal work in Great Britain during World War II. *The Journal of Modern History,* 53(4), 652–72.
SMITH, H. 1990. *War and social change: British society in the Second World War,* Manchester University Press.
SMITH, P. R. 2013. Who will care for the elderly?: The future of home care. *Buffalo Law Review,* 61(2), 323–343.
SOCIAL MARKET FOUNDATION 2016. *Tough gig: Low-paid self-employment in London and the UK.*
SOLARI, C. 2006. Professionals and Saints: How immigrant careworkers negotiate gender identities at work. *Gender and Society,* 20(3), 301–331.
STACEY, C. L. 2011. *The caring self: The work experiences of home care aides.* Industrial Labor Relations (ILR) Press, Cornell University.
STEWART, A. 2011. *Gender, work and justice in a global market,* Cambridge University Press.
STONE, D. 2000. Caring by the book. In: M. H. MEYER (ed.), *Care work: Gender, labor and the welfare state.* Routledge.
STUDDERT, D. 2006. *Conceptualising community: Beyond the state and the individual.* Palgrave Macmillan.
SUMMERFIELD, P. 1998. *Reconstructing women's wartime lives,* Manchester University Press.
TAYLOR, B. J. & DONNELLY, M. 2006. Risks to home care workers: Professional perspectives. *Health Risk and Society,* 8(3), 239–256.
TAYLOR, C. 2004. *Modern social imaginaries,* Duke University Press.
THINK LOCAL ACT PERSONAL 2010a. *Next steps for transforming adult social care: A proposed sector-wide commitment to moving forward with personalisation and community-based support.*
THINK LOCAL ACT PERSONAL 2010b. *Personal budgets – checking the results.* http://www.thinklocalactpersonal.org.uk/_assets/PPF/NCAS/personal_budgets_checking_the_results_final_29_October_2010.pdf, date accessed 19 November 2016.
THOMSON, P., ELLISON, L., BYROM,T., BULMAN, D. 2007. Invisible labour: home–school relations and the front office. *Gender and education,* 19(2), 141–58.
THORNLEY, C. 2006. Unequal and low pay in the public sector. *Industrial Relations Journal,* 37(4), 344–58.
THORNLEY, C. 2007. Working part-time for the State: Gender, class and the public sector pay gap. *Gender, Work & Organization,* 14(5), 454–475.
TNS February 2015. *Tracker Survey for Age UK (adults aged 50+ in Great Britain).*

TOD, A. & KENNEDY, F. 2016. Good quality social care for people with Parkinson's Disease: A qualitative study. *BMJ Open,* British Medical Journal, 6(2) BMJ Open 2016;6:e006813 doi:10.1136/bmjopen-2014-006813.

TOMLINSON, C. & LIVESLEY, M. 2013. *Individual Service Funds for Homecare.* In Control. http://www.in-control.org.uk/media/128547/inc14877%20-%20sf%20 report%20single%20pages-web.pdf, date accessed 19 November 2016.

TRIGGLE, N. 2015. One million people in need 'struggle alone'. *BBC News,* 21 October.

TRONTO, J. 1993. *Moral boundaries: A political argument for an ethic of care.* Routledge.

TRONTO, J. 2013. *Caring democracy,* New York University Press.

TUC 2013. CEDAW Shadow Report. *Section 11. Supplementary information on Equal Pay.*

TUC 2015. *The Decent Jobs Deficit.* Trade Union Congress (TUC), 21 October.

TUC COMMISSION ON VULNERABLE EMPLOYMENT 2008. *Hard work, Hidden lives.*

TWIGG, J. 2000. *Bathing – The body and community care,* Routledge.

TYLER, I. 2008. Chav Mum Chav Scum. *Feminist Media Studies,* 8(2), 17–34.

UKHCA 2012. *Care is not a commodity.* United Kingdom Homecare Association.

UKHCA 2014. *A Minimum Price for Homecare. Version 2.1.* United Kingdom Homecare Association.

UKHCA 2016. *The impact of the National Living Wage on the care sector in Wales.* United Kingdom Homecare Association.

UNGERSON, C. 1999. Personal assistants and disabled people: An examination of a hybrid form of work and care. *Work Employment and Society,* 13(4), 583–600.

UNGERSON, C. 2004. Whose empowerment and independence? A cross-national perspective on 'cash for care' schemes. *Ageing & Society,* 24(2), 189–212.

UNISON 2005. *Single status, job evaluation and pay and grading reviews. Guidance on Negotiating and Settlements.* as quoted in Hayes, LJB, 2014, Women's Voice and Equal Pay (pp35–45), in *Voices at Work: Continuity and Change in the Common Law World* (Eds: Bogg, A; Novitz, T) p42, Oxford University Press.

UNISON 2014. *Ethical Care Charter.* https://www.unison.org.uk/content/uploads/ 2013/11/On-line-Catalogue220142.pdf (accessed 1st Feb 2017).

UNISON 2016. *Suffering alone at home: A report on the lack of time in our homecare system.*

WACQUANT, L. J. D. 1989. Towards a Reflexive Sociology: A Workshop with Pierre Bourdieu. *Sociological Theory,* 7(1), 26–63.

WALKERDINE, V. 2010. Communal beingness and affect: An exploration of trauma in an ex-industrial Community. *Body & Society,* 16(1), 91–116.

WALKERDINE, V. & JIMENEZ, L. 2012. *Gender, work and community after de-industrialisation: A psychosocial approach to affect,* Palgrave Macmillan.

WEILER, P. 1993. *Ernest Bevin,* Manchester University Press.

WELSH ASSEMBLY GOVERNMENT 2011. *Sustainable Social Services for Wales: A framework for action.* WAG10-11086.

WHEELAHAN, L. 2007. How competency based training locks the working-class out of powerful knowledge: A Bernsteinian analysis. *British Journal of Sociology of Education,* 28(5), 637–51.

WOOD, C. 2010. *Personal Best,* Demos.

WYNN-EVANS, C. 2008. Service provision fragmentation and the limits of TUPE protection. *Industrial Law Journal,* 37(4), 371–6.

ZARB, G. & NADASH, P. 1994. *Cashing in on Independence.* British Council of Organisations of Disabled People and Joseph Rowntree Foundation.

Index

ACAS (Advisory, Conciliation & Arbitration Service)   105–106, 160, 166–167
Abdulla v. *Birmingham City Council* [2012] UKSC 47   43 fn 2, 59
Abellio v. *Musse* [2012] IRLR 360   107
Aguebor v. *PCL Whitehall Security Group* unreported UKEAT/0078/14/JOJ   101, 107
Airfix Footware v. *Cope* [1978] ICR 1210 EAT   89
Al-Malki v. *Reyes* [2015] EWCA Civ 32   144, 146
Allen v. *Flood* [1898] AC 1 HL   42
Allonby v. *Accrington and Rossendale College* [2004] ECR I-873   62, 184
Autoclenz v. *Belcher* [2011] UKSC 41   88–89
Autonomy   92–96, 160, 162, 165, 188, 197
Austerity (*see* financial crisis)

Barker v. *Birmingham City Council* [2010] unreported 3921 23/04/2010 ET   58
Benvenista v. *University of Southampton* [1989] ICR 617 CA   43
Bilka-Kaufhaus v. *Weber Von Hartz* [1986] 2 CMLR 701   45 fn 3
Bowling v. *Secretary of State for Justice* [2012] IRLR 382 EAT   43–44
Breadwinner / main wage earner   9, 33, 35, 42, 92, 131, 142
British Coal v. *Smith and North Yorkshire County Council* v. *Ratcliffe* [1994] IRLR 342 CA   56
British Nursing Association v. *Inland Revenue* [2002] EWCA Civ 494   138, 141–142, 146, 148
Botzen v. *Rotterdamsche Droogdok Maatschappij* [1985] ECR 519   103

Burrow Down Support Services v. *Rossiter* [2008] ICR 1172 EAT   149
Byrne Brothers (Farmwork) v. *Baird* [2002] IRLR 96 EAT   88

CCTV covert filming   21
Care Act 2014   25–26, 108, 157, 159, 166, 168–169, 173, 175–184, 189, 192–193, 196
s 1(2).   176–177
s 5.   108, 178
s 10.   166
s 24(1).   166
s 26.   169
s 31–33.   166
and choice / control   173–176
and the workforce   177–179
and well-being (*see also* well-being)   176–177
statutory guidance   179–182
Care (*see also* commodification; home-care; family; neoliberalism; unpaid labour)
and choice   159–165
and gender   7, 26, 28, 38, 66, 120, 125, 134–135, 143, 151, 203
and social class   7, 26, 120, 124–131, 134–135
as a gift   123–124, 130, 133
as enterprise   26–27, 158–159, 171–173, 177, 188, 191–193
as democratising / politicising   27–29, 194, 198
as individualised relations   64–67, 70–71
as socialised / collective   28, 65–69, 70–71, 196
caregiving relationships   65,68
quality of care   3, 28–29, 37, 53, 55, 66, 97, 119–120, 125, 151, 161–162, 178–179, 191–192, 199–200

Index

Care and Support (Direct Payments) Regulations 2014
  regulation 4. 142–143, 182
Care Standards Act 2000 53
Care Professionals Benevolent Fund 13
Care Quality Commission (CQC) 29, 185–187
Carers (Equal Opportunities) Act 2004 166
Carmichael v. *National Power* [2000] IRLR 43 HL 88–89, 92–93, 112
Carter v. *Prestige Nursing Care* [2012] unreported UKEAT/0014/12/ZT 161
Character narratives 1, 23–28, 191, 195, 197
  Cheap Nurse 30–33
  Choosy Suzy 153–157
  Mother Superior 114–118
  Two-a-Penny 72–76
Class (*see* social class)
Clay Cross (Quarry Services) v. *Fletcher* [1978] 1 WLR 1429 CA 44
Clearsprings Management v. *Ankers* [2008] Unreported UKEAT/0054/08/LA 106–107
Cleaning 22, 32–33, 38, 41, 52, 81, 107 fn 6, 126, 130
Collective bargaining 9, 29, 46, 49, 54, 56, 59, 70, 95, 98, 200–202
Collective imaginary 119–121, 150–151
Collective Redundancies and Transfer of Undertakings (Protection of Employment) (Amendment) Regulations 2014 100
Cornwall County Council v. *Prater* [2006] EWCA Civ 102 90
Coventry City Council v. *Nicholls* [2009] IRLR 345 EAT 54
Coventry City Council v. *Nicholls* [2009] EWCA Civ 1449 54
Commission of the European Communities v. *United Kingdom* [1982] ECR 601 42

Commodification
  of care 37, 54–55, 69, 127, 162, 171, 191–193, 198–199
  of care workers 132, 162, 193
Community Care (Direct Payments) Act 1996 165
Community Care (Direct Payments) Regulations 1997 165
Community Care (Direct Payments) Amendment Regulations 2000 166
Contracts of Employment Act 1963 40–41
Contractual status (*see also* employee status; worker status; self-employment) 86–89
  mutuality of obligation 89–91
Cotswold Developments Construction Ltd v. *Williams* [2006] IRLR 181 EAT 87–88
Criminal Justice and Courts Act 2015 s 20. 148 fn 5, 198
Crisis of Care 27–29, 194, 201
Cumbria County Council v. *Dow* [2008] IRLR 91 EAT 66

Death and dying 31, 116, 130, 186
Defence Regulations 1944 39 fn 1
Defrenne v. *Belgium* [1974] 1 CMLR 494 42
Defrenne v. *Sabena* [1976] 2 CMLR 98 42
Dines v. *Initial Healthcare Services* [1995] ICR 11 CA 102
Direct payments 142, 153–155,160, 165–170, 173, 176, 181–185
Discrimination / discriminatory pay (*see also* sexism) 25, 33–35, 38–39, 41–48, 54–64, 70–71, 77–78, 95, 98, 124, 145, 157, 184, 197, 200–201, 204
Dismissal from employment
  fear of 25, 85, 95, 110
  length of service criterion 93–94
  unfair dismissal 10, 25, 47, 79, 82, 85–89, 90, 93–94, 96

Duncan Web Offset (Maidstone)
  v. *Cooper* [1995] IRLR 633   103–104

EOC v. *Secretary of State for Employment*
  [1994] 1 All ER 910 HL   81
Eddie Stobart v. *Moreman* [2012] IRLR
  365 EAT   106, 108
Edinburgh City Council v. *Lauder* [2012]
  Unreported UKEATS/0048/11/B1
  EAT   148
Edmunds v. *Lawson* [2000] QB 501   140
Emotion (*see* social class and fear, hope,
  love, shame)
Emotional labour   118, 121–123, 125,
  147
Employee status (*see also* contractual
  status; worker status)   87, 89–91,
  93, 109
Employment Protection Act 1975   95
Employment rights   5, 10–11, 29, 78,
  142–143, 159, 167, 181, 183–185,
  197, 199
  gendering of   27, 40–41, 78, 194
Employment Rights Act 1996
  (ERA)   87–88, 93, 96, 138
Employment Rights (increase of limits)
  Order 2011   93
Enderby v. *Frenchay Health Authority*
  [1993] ECR 1–5535   56
Enterprise / entrepreneurship (*see* care
  as enterprise; self-employment)
Enterprise Management Services v.
  Connect-Up [2012] IRLR 190
  EAT   106
Equality and Human Rights Commission (EHRC)   6, 170
Equality / inequality   2, 10, 29, 35, 57, 81,
  126, 129, 175, 191–192, 195, 198–199
  equality clause (*see* equal pay)
  and economic entitlement   28, 44–45,
  47, 57, 62–63, 69, 98, 107, 127
  and emotion   127
Equal pay (*see also* discrimination)
  24–25, 33–35, 39, 41–48, 54, 56–64,
  66, 70–71, 77–78, 95, 196–197,
  199–200

Invisibility of pay inequality   44–46, 63
Invisibility of right to equal pay
  60–63, 70
Equal Pay Act 1970   25, 35, 41–42,
  45–47, 54, 59, 70, 95
Equal Pay Act (Amendment)
  Regulations 1983   42
Equal Pay Act 1970 (Amendment)
  Regulations 2003   58 fn 4
Equal Pay Directive 75/117/EEC   42
Equality Act 2010   25, 35, 41, 45, 47,
  59, 70, 184
Ethnography (*see* research methods)

Feminism   7
  and labour law   9, 42, 63
  feminist scholarship   7, 37
Finance Act 2015
  s 16.   182–183
Financial crisis   1, 5, 28, 82, 93, 136, 168
Fitzpatrick v. *Evans & Co* [1901] 1 QB
  756   104
Family   14, 35–36, 72, 81, 84, 87, 92,
  96, 114, 116–117, 124, 129–130,
  144–145, 152, 177, 184, 192, 194,
  196, 201–203
  and direct payments   143, 163–166,
  182
  economic dependence   94, 136, 202
  exemption from minimum
  wage   119, 142–145, 152
  familial care work (unpaid care)   2,
  5, 7, 13, 26–28, 36, 39–40, 49, 52,
  55, 60, 68, 70, 92–93, 112, 148, 152,
  159, 172–173, 192, 202–203
  family as a moral landscape   119,
  132–135, 151, 202–203
  family wage (*see* breadwinner)
  relationships / treatment 'like family'
  118, 144, 152, 166, 192

Gale v. *Northern General Hospital Trust*
  [1994] ICT 426   103
Gender (*see also* identity; labour market,
  gendering of; mothering; sexism;
  skill; stereotyping)

and care work   7, 8, 66, 118–120, 128, 131,151
and 'home' (*see also* home, meaning of)   159, 189–193
and knowledge (*see also* homecare and knowledge)   12, 123–124, 126, 130–132, 134, 150, 161, 196, 200
and labour law   2, 8–16, 24, 27, 66, 78–82, 92–96, 98, 101, 106, 108–113, 150–152, 159, 193–194, 198–204
and marketisation   56, 68
and national service   129
and religion   129
and research / researching gender   11–12, 22–24, 27, 118–119, 125–126, 129–131
and social class   7–16, 27, 37–38, 46, 78, 118, 123–131, 159, 192, 194, 200
and unpaid care (*see also* family and familial care work; unpaid labour)   2, 7, 131, 135, 143, 151–152, 192, 203
feminine / femininity   8, 121, 123–126, 131, 134, 150
gendered experience   9, 11–12, 50–52, 65, 77, 79–81, 94, 112, 124, 126, 128, 135, 158, 194, 198
production of gender   27, 80–81, 95–97, 121, 130–131
stereotypes (*see also* stereotyping)   24, 79
Glasgow City Council v. *Marshall* [2000] IRLR 272 HL   43
Government of Wales Act 2006   174

Handley v. *H Mono* [1978] IRLR 534 EAT   44
Halawi v. *WDFG UK* [2014] EWCA Civ 1387 [2015] 1 CMLR 31   88
Haq v. *Audit Commission* [2012] EWCA Civ 1621   45
Hayward v. *Cammell Laird Shipbuilders* [1988] ICR 464 HL   43

Health and Social Care Act 2001   166
Health and Social Care Act 2008   185
Health and Social Care Act 2008 (Regulated Activities) Regulations 2014   185
HM Revenue and Customs (HMRC)   97, 119, 135, 146, 181, 188
Home
as a site of enterprise   190–193
meaning of home   26, 30, 33, 36–37, 50, 67, 71, 93–94, 138–143, 146, 149–150, 159, 164, 183, 189–193, 201
Homecare (*see also* labour market position of homecare workers; labour turnover; marketisation; privatisation)
and austerity   5, 28
and employment rights   78, 108–109, 142, 184, 151
and knowledge   3, 12, 15–17, 27, 34, 51–52, 67, 69, 120, 122–124, 131–133, 188, 194, 196, 200
and religion   129
as paid labour   22, 35–38, 48–52, 129, 134, 145, 148, 171, 197
as socialised   28–29, 122, 201–204
cost of   20, 98
definition of   2, 5–6, 66, 196
demographics   2 fn 1, 5–6, 7–8, 18, 20
health and safety   159, 167, 181, 183–184, 197
history of   39–40, 44, 48, 52
impact of inequality   126–127
invisibility of   15, 35, 37, 79
media representation   13–14, 120
quality of employment   3–8, 15, 38, 56, 77–78, 96, 110–112, 180, 183–184, 200
Home help service (*see* homecare, *history of*)
Hughes v. *Jones* [2008] Unreported UKEAT/0159/08MAA   149–150

Human Rights Act 1998
    article 8. 134

Identity 8–9, 11, 21, 23, 49, 71, 85, 100, 118, 121, 129–131, 150, 166, 187, 192
Inex Home Improvements v. *Hodgkinson* [2016] ICR 71   106
Inferiority 4–5, 10, 24, 26, 41, 79–82, 93–94, 96, 98, 101, 109–112, 172, 194–195, 197–198
Insecure employment 25, 66, 77–79, 82–84, 86, 92, 94, 96, 109–110, 121, 142, 178, 188, 196–198
Institutionalised humiliation 4–5, 11, 23, 27–29, 194, 196–198, 200
Invisible labour 25, 34–41, 46, 49–50, 54, 70, 167
Interviews (*see* research methods interviews)

James v. *Redcats* [2007] IRLR 296 EAT   140
Jenkins v. *Kingsgate* [1981] ICR 715   44
Judging of homecare workers 4–5, 12, 24, 54, 94, 112, 125–126, 134, 142, 145–148, 150, 157, 194–195, 197–198
Judicial interpretation / reasoning 4, 24, 26, 42, 44, 54, 61–63, 66, 70, 79, 82, 87, 89–92, 94, 96, 100, 102–107, 111–113, 140–151, 203

Kimberley v. *Hambley* ([2008] IRLR 682 EAT   102–105
Knowledge (*see also* homecare and knowledge)
    class and gendering of 12, 28, 130–132, 196

Labour law (*see also* employment rights; equal pay; national minimum wage; transfer of undertakings) 8–10, 12, 26–29, 40–41, 194, 198–199, 203–204
    and gender 2, 8–16, 24, 27, 66, 78–82, 92–96, 98, 101, 106, 108–113, 145, 150–152, 159, 193–194, 198–204

and social class 8–12, 25, 27–29, 40–41, 78, 143, 194, 199, 201–204
    as a moral landscape 132–135
    empirical research 10, 78
    employment protection law 79–81, 86–89, 97–100, 110–113
Labour turnover 6, 15, 85, 94, 97, 121, 127
Labour market
    and social class 9–10, 29, 49, 97, 113, 124, 159, 202
    feminisation of 78, 161
    gendering of 2, 9, 25, 29, 35–37, 40–41, 47, 49, 63, 71, 78–82, 89, 91–96, 106–113, 129, 144, 148, 159, 193, 199
    position of homecare workers 3, 4, 8, 10, 17–18, 25–26, 29, 34–35, 40, 48, 68, 78, 82, 85, 93–94, 97–98, 108–109, 111–113, 124, 129, 148, 161, 173, 183, 187, 192–198, 201
Landeshauptstadt Keil v. *Jaeger* [2003] IRLR 804   145
Law and gender (*see also* labour law; social class and labour law; social class and working-class women) 8–13, 24, 26–27, 39–41, 78, 80–82, 92, 101, 108–109, 143, 145, 194–195, 152
Law and social class (*see also* labour law; social class and labour law; social class and working-class women) 8–11, 78, 159, 194, 197
Law Commission 166, 174
Lawrence v. *Regent Office Cleaning* [2002] ECR I-7325   62
Leverton v. *Clywd County Council* ([1989] AC 706 HL   46, 56
Levez v. *TH Jennings* [1999] IRLR 36   58 fn 4
Living Wage (*see also* National Minimum Wage, national living wage) 97–98, 136
Live-in care workers 142–143, 182–183
Local Government Act 1988 61

Low pay / low wages 2, 6, 7, 9, 13, 15, 25, 28, 34–35, 37–38, 40–41, 44, 47–48, 58–59, 63, 70, 76–77, 79, 82, 84, 96, 97–98, 110, 113, 118, 120–121, 131, 133, 135, 143, 151, 168, 178, 181, 183, 185, 192, 196
Lynch v. *Bromley Arts Council* [2007] Unreported UKEAT/0390/06DA 139

Macarthy's v. *Smith* [1980] IRLR 210 47
MacCartney v. *Oversley House Management* [2006] IRLR 514 EAT 149–150
Marketisation (*see also* privatisation) 3, 26, 34–35, 48, 52–56, 64, 67–68, 70, 108, 112, 158–159, 172–173, 175–180, 184, 191, 199, 201
Market-shaping duties 178–180, 190–193
Media 4–5, 11–14, 120
Melhuish v. *Redbridge CAB* [2005] IRLR 419 EAT 89
Metropolitan Resources v. *Churchill Dulwich* [2009] IRLR 700 EAT 106
Methodology (*see* research methods)
Migration 7–8, 18, 129
Minimum wage (*see* national minimum wage)
Mothering / mothers' work 118–119, 121–123, 126, 131
Mutuality of obligation (*see* employment status)

Nambalat v. *Taher* and *Udin* v. *Chamsi-Pasha* [2012] EWCA Civ 1249 142–143
National Assistance Act 1948 40, 175
National Health and Community Care Act 1990 52, 55
National Health Service Act 1946 39
National Minimum Wage 25, 88, 96–98, 118–119, 133–152, 179–181, 183, 193, 196, 198
  enforcement 93 fn 3, 150, 180–181
  exemption 142–145, 166, 183

  gendered assumptions 150–152
  home as a place of work 138–140
  national living wage 97 fn 4, 136–137, 184
  non-compliance / unlawful pay 5, 83, 119, 137, 150–152, 178
  recognising services of value 140
  understandings of 'work' 138, 140–150
National Minimum Wage Act 1998 (*see also* national minimum wage) 26, 119, 136–142, 152, 183
National Minimum Wage Regulations 1999 (*see also* national minimum wage) 26, 119, 137, 139, 141–150
  regulation 2. 142
  regulation 3–6. 137
  regulation 15. 141, 148, 150
  regulation 16. 141, 149–150
  regulation 27. 145
  regulation 28. 145–146
National Minimum Wage (Amendment) Regulations 2016 137, 151
National Living Wage (*see* National Minimum Wage national living wage)
National Service (Armed Forces) Act 1939 39
Narrative (*see* research methods narrative method; character narratives)
Neoliberalism (*see also* care as enterprise; commodification; self-employment and entrepreneurship) 26, 158–159, 162, 170, 172, 175, 177, 189–192
Nelson v. *Carillion Service* [2003] EWCA 544 44
Nethermere (St Neots) v. *Gardiner* [1984] ICR 612 89–90
Nokes v. *Doncaster Amalgamated Collieries* [1940] AC 1014 HL 100
North v. *Dumfries and Galloway Council* ([2013] UKSC 45 46
Nottinghamshire Healthcare NHS Trust v. *Hamshaw* [2011] Unreported UKEAT/0037/11/JOJ 106

O'Kelly v. *Trusthouse Forte* [1984] QB 90 CA   88, 90, 112
Ojutiku v. *Manpower* [1983] ICR 661 CA   43
Ottimo Property Services v. *Duncan* [2015] ICR 895   107

Participants (*see also* research methods)   18, 19
Personalisation / personal budgets   160, 165, 168–171, 173–175, 185, 187–191
Personal assistants / personal care workers (*see also* homecare)   19, 97 fn 3, 118, 132, 153–154, 157, 160–169, 173, 175, 181–188, 193
 as an employment model   165–168
Phenomenology (*see also* research methods)   20
Poor quality employment (*see* homecare, quality of employment)
Privatisation (*see also* marketisation)   3, 6, 25, 35–39, 53, 55, 57–65, 68–71, 77, 88, 98, 100, 108, 132, 184, 189, 199
Public Interest Disclosure Act 1998   95

Quashie v. *Stringfellow Restaurants* [2012] EWCA Civ 1735   88–89

R v. *Sec. of State for Employment* v. *ex p. Seymour Smith* [2000] 1 All ER 857 HL   82
Race / racism   7–8, 18, 20, 22
Race Relations Act 1976   46
Rainey v. *Greater Glasgow Health Board* [1987] IRLR 26 HL   43, 61
Ratcliffe v. *North Yorkshire County Council* [1995] IRLR 439 HL   61–64
Ready Mixed Concrete (SE) v. *Minister of Pensions and National Insurance* [1968] 2 QB 497   87–89
Redcar and Cleveland Borough Council v. *Bainbridge* [2007] EWCA Civ 929   57
Redcar and Cleveland Borough Council v. *Degnan* [2005] EWCA Civ 726   58

Regulation and Inspection of Social Care (Wales) Bill 2016   173 fn 5
Research design (*see also* research methods)   12, 16–20
Research methods (*see also* research design; gender and research; social class and research)   17, 28
 data collection & analysis   20–23
 discourse analysis   158
 consent   17–18
 empirical methods in labour law   10, 78
 experience   3, 5, 21, 23–25, 194
 ethnography   1, 16–17, 21–22
 interviews   12, 16–18, 20–21
 methodology   1, 16, 20, 23–24, 28
 narrative method (*see also* character narratives)   20–27
 narrative silence   11–15
 participants   18–19
 socio-legal method   1, 3, 24, 27–28
Revenue and Customs v. *Rinaldi-Tranter* [2006] Unreported UKEAT/0486/06/DM   140
Roberts v. *Hopwood* [1925] AC 587 HL   63–64
Rockfon A/S v. *Specialarbejderforbundet I Danmark* [1995] ECR 1–4291   45
Rynda (UK) v. *Rhijnsburger* [2015] EWCA 75   107

SIMAP v. *Conselleria de Sanidad y Consumo de la Generalidad Valenciana* [2000] IRLR 845   145
Safeguarding Vulnerable Groups Act 2007 s 7.   185
Saha v. *Viewpoint Field Services* [2014] Unreported UKEAT /0116/13/ DM   89–91
Scattolon v. *Ministero dell'Istruzione, dell'Universita e della Ricerca* [2012] 1 CMLR 17   100
Scottbridge Construction v. *Wright* [2003] IRLR 21 CoS   141–142, 146, 149
Secretary of State for Justice v. *Windle* [2016] EWCA Civ 495   88, 91

Self-employment 7, 18–20, 87, 89, 153–157, 160–161, 165, 169, 173, 183–189, 201
  and entrepreneurship 162, 173, 179, 188, 190–193
Sex Discrimination Act 1975 47
Sexism 5, 23–26, 34–35, 38–41, 47–48, 51–56, 63, 66–71,78–80, 93, 98, 108, 111–112, 119, 131–132, 144, 149, 151, 159, 194, 197–198, 202, 204
Shields v. *E. Coomes Holdings* [1978] IRLR 263 CA 43
Simmons v. *Heath Laundry Co.* [1910] 1 KB 543 91–92
Single Status Agreement in local government (*see also* collective bargaining) 57–58
Skills and training 25, 34–37, 40, 48–55, 57, 60, 63–64, 69, 77, 79, 118–119, 121–125, 128, 130, 132, 161–165, 168, 179
  and equal pay 43, 44, 57
  invisibility of skill 48–52
  nursing skill 8, 48–50, 130, 162–164
  training 31, 36, 40, 47–54, 65, 72, 74, 76–77, 79, 83–84, 98, 110, 115, 123, 133, 168, 187, 193
  unskilled work 9, 40, 48, 81, 112, 126, 165, 168
Skills Development Scotland v. *Buchanan* [2011] Eq LR 955 EAT 43
Social Care (Self-directed Support) (Scotland) Act 2013 173
Social class 7–16, 25, 27, 29, 49, 56, 79, 97, 113, 124–131, 159, 202
  agency / motivation of working-class women 4, 11–13, 15, 17, 26, 28, 124, 129, 160, 175, 193
  and fear 25, 68–69, 85–86, 110, 127, 187, 198–199
  and hope 18, 38, 49, 132, 187
  and labour law 8–12, 25, 27–29, 40–41, 78, 143, 194, 199, 201–204
  and love 26, 32, 114, 121, 127–128, 133–134, 159

  and research / researching social class, 11–16, 27, 109–110, 118–119
  and respectability / social respect / disrespect 32, 37–38, 110, 118, 120, 124–125, 127, 129, 130–131, 135, 151, 194–196, 199, 200, 204
  and self-employment 188, 193
  and shame 22, 118, 127, 135, 151, 202–203
  middle-class 7, 26, 118, 124–126, 131, 135
  working-class women 4, 5, 7, 8, 11–12, 14–16, 25–28, 49, 78–80, 111–113, 119, 124–131, 134–135, 151, 159, 188, 192, 194, 197, 198, 199, 202–204
  silencing of working-class women 11–16, 27, 145–147, 152, 199, 200
Social Services and Well-being (Wales) Act 2014 173
Socio-legal research (*see* research methods)
Social policy 4, 5, 11–12, 15, 27, 66, 70, 97, 127, 160, 165, 168–169, 177–178, 183, 191–192, 197, 200
South Holland v. *Stamp* [2003] All ER (D)19 EAT 147
South Manchester Abbeyfield v. *Hopkins* ([2011] IRLR 300 EAT 149–150
South Tyneside Metropolitan Council v. *Anderson* [2007] EWCA 654 58
Stack v. *Ajar Tee* [2015] EWCA Civ 46 134, 140
Stereotyping (*see also* gender stereotypes)
  in law 24, 27, 66, 79, 111, 119
  of older and disabled people 189–190
  of working-class women 25, 56, 118–119, 151
Stevedoring and Haulage Services v. *Fuller* [2001] EWCA Civ 651 89
Suzen v. *Zehnacker Gebaudereinigung* [1997] CMLR 768 102

Thomas-James v. *Cornwall County Council* [2007] Unreported ET 1701021-22/07   105
Transgender   85
Trade union (*see also* collective bargaining)   7, 9, 16–17, 39, 46, 53, 56, 59, 77, 84, 93 fn 3, 95, 97, 98, 99, 108, 195, 199, 200–201
Training (*see* skills and training)
Transfer of Undertakings Directive 77/187/EEC   99
Transfer of Undertakings (Protection of Employment) Regulations 1981   99
Transfer of Undertakings (Protection of Employment) Regulations 2006 (TUPE)   25–26, 99–109
  regulation 2.   100
  regulation 3.   101
  regulation 4.   100
  doctrine of displacement (fragmented TUPE)   79, 105–109
  service provision change   100–105
Treaty of Rome 1957
  article 119.   41–42
Truslove v. *Scottish Ambulance Service* [2014] ICR 1232 EAT   138–139

Unpaid labour / unpaid working time (*see also* family familial care work)   7, 26, 37, 68, 83, 92, 110, 118, 124, 126–127, 133–135, 142–145, 147–152, 164, 180, 187, 192, 203
Unskilled work (*see* skills and training)

Villalba v. *Merrill Lynch* [2006] IRLR 437 EAT   43

Walton Centre for Neurology v. *Bewley* [2008] IRLR 588 EAT   47
Walton v. *Independent Living Organisation* [2003] EWCA Civ 199   145–147
Whittlestone v. *BJP Home support* [2014] IRLR 176   142, 180
Welfare   1, 36, 67–70, 74, 123, 175
  welfare state   1, 3, 39, 57
  welfare support   82, 112, 126, 136
  welfare policy   2, 3, 127
  service provision model   163, 165, 171–172, 177–179, 189
Well-being   67, 78, 124, 134, 143, 166, 169, 177–178, 192, 198
  as a statutory principle   173–178, 192, 198
Westwood v. *Hospital Medical Group* [2012] EWCA Civ 1005   88
Wilson v. *Health and Safety Executive* [2009] EWCA Civ 1074   43
Woods v. *Somerset CC* [2014] unreported UKEAT/0121/14/DA   89
Worker status (*see also* employee status; contractual status)   87–88, 90, 92–97, 109, 161
Working-class women (*see* social class)
Working Time Directive 2003/88/EC   138
Working Time Regulations 1998   95, 136, 139–140, 145
Wren v. *Eastbourne Borough Council* [1993] 3 CMLR 955   102

YL v. *Birmingham City Council* [2007] UKHL 27   103

Zero-hours contracts   13, 19, 25, 72, 82–92, 138 fn 3, 171, 187–188

CPI Antony Rowe
Chippenham, UK
2018-09-19 22:53